Old Testament
Men of Faith

Old Testament
Men of Faith

F. B. MEYER

26

Good News Publishers
Westchester, Illinois

A NOTE ABOUT THE SCRIPTURE REFERENCES:
F. B. Meyer was so thoroughly familiar
with the Scriptures that he was accustomed
to draw on them from memory in his sermons
and books. The publishers have retained
Dr. Meyer's informal approach to quoting
Scripture so that none of the flavor and
immediacy of his unique writings will be
lost. For those who wish to read the
Scriptures he quotes from in context, or
to see what the exact wording of the texts
is, we have provided references.

Contents

BOOK III: MOSES

BOOK IV: DAVID

BOOK V: ELIJAH

BOOK I: ABRAHAM

1

The Hole of the Pit

Genesis 12

In the grey dawn of history the first great character that arrests our attention at any length is that of Abraham, the
"Friend of God." Surely it must be well worthy of our devout
consideration to study the inner life, and outward carriage,
of such a man that we too, in our smaller measure, may
become the favored confidants of God—from whom He will
not hide His secrets, to whom He will make known His will.

Many rays of interest focus in the story of Abraham. His
portrait is drawn with such detail, that it lives before us.
Then, also, his life is so constantly referred to in the Old
Testament, and in the New, that it would seem as if the right
understanding of it is necessary to understand many a difficult passage, and many a sacred doctrine. The wild Bedouin
of the desert and the modern Englishman—the conservative
East, and the progressive West; the Mohammedan and the
Christian—find in the tent of the first Hebrew a common
meeting ground, and in himself a common origin.

Our story takes us back 2,000 years before the birth of
Christ, and to the ancient city of Ur, in the near vicinity of
the Persian Gulf. Forty centuries, slowly silting up the shore,
have driven the sea back about 100 miles. But at the time of
which we speak it is probable that Abraham's natal city
stood upon the coast near the spot where the Euphrates
poured the volume of its waters into the ocean waves.

It would be foreign to our purpose to attempt a description

of the luxuriance of that Chaldaean land. Suffice it to say, that it was a long green strip of garden land sufficient to attract and maintain vast populations of men, and specially suitable for the settlement of those shepherd tribes which required extensive pasture lands.

These sons of Ham were grossly *idolatrous*. The race seemed verging again on the brink of those horrible and unnatural crimes which had already necessitated its almost total destruction; and it was evident that some expedient must be speedily adopted to arrest the progress of moral defilement, and to save mankind. And God accomplished His purpose then, as so often since, by *separating* to Himself one man.

Four centuries had passed since the Flood; and they must have been centuries abounding in emigrations. Leaving the first seats of life, swarm after swarm must have hived off in every direction. The sons of Japheth pushed northwards, to colonize Europe and Asia. The sons of Ham pushed southwards, over the fertile plains of Chaldaea. They are said to have been proficient in mathematics and astronomy; in weaving, metal-working, and gem-engraving; and to have preserved their thoughts by writing on clay tablets.

Into the midst of this Hamite colonization came a family of Shem. This clan, under Terah, settled in the rich pasture lands outside Ur. The walled cities, and civilized arts, and merchant traffic, had little attraction for them. They were rather a race of shepherds, living in tents, or in villages. And if Noah's prediction were verified (Gen. 9:26), we may believe that their religious life was sweeter and purer than that of the people among whom we find them.

But, alas! The close association of this Shemite family with the idolatrous children of Ham, tainted the purity and simplicity of its early faith. Joshua (Joshua 24:15) says distinctly that the fathers of the children of Israel, who dwelt beyond the flood of the Euphrates, served other gods. And there are traces of the evil in the home of Laban, from which Rachel stole the images *(teraphim)*, the loss of which so kindled her father's wrath (Gen. 31:19-35). It is a heavy responsibility for godly people to live amid godlessness and sin. If they escape the snare, their children may be caught in it.

Amid such scenes Abraham was born; and grew from youth to manhood. But, if we may credit the traditions which have lingered in the common talk of the unchanging East, as a young man Abraham offered an uncompromising opposition to the evil practices not only in the land, but in his father's house. Thus early was he being detached from the quarry of heathendom, dug from "the hole of the pit," preparatory to being shaped as a pillar in the house of the Lord.

There is nothing of all this in Scripture, but there is nothing inconsistent with it. The mature character, faith, and ready obedience of this man, when he first comes under our notice, convince us that there must have been a long previous period of severe trial and testing.

At last, the God of glory appeared unto him. In what form of glory Jehovah revealed Himself we cannot guess; but we must believe that there was some outward manifestation which dated an epoch in Abraham's life, and gave him unmistakable basis of belief for all his future. In any case, the celestial vision was accompanied by a call: "Get thee out of thy country, and from thy kindred, and from thy father's house, unto the land that I will show thee" (Gen. 12:1). If we live up to our light, we shall have more light. God's choice is never arbitrary; but is based on some previous traits in those whom He summons from among their fellows to His aid. "Whom He foreknew, He also did predestinate" (Rom. 8:29).

Lonely confessors of Christ in worldly and vicious societies; where there is everything to weaken, and nothing to reinforce the resistance of the brave but faltering spirit, take heart! You are treading a well-worn path, which was much more difficult in days when few were found in it, and specially in that day, when a solitary man, the "father of many nations," trod it.

One symptom of being on that path is *loneliness*. "I called him alone" (Isa. 51:2). It was a loneliness that pressed hard on the heart of Jesus. But it is a loneliness which assured of the Divine companionship (see John 8:16, 29; 16:32). And though no eye seems to notice the struggles, and protests, and endeavors of the solitary spirit, they are watched with the sympathy of all heaven; and presently there will be heard a call, like that which started Abraham as a pilgrim, and opened before him the way into marvelous blessedness.

2
The Divine Summons
Genesis 12

While Abraham was living quietly in Ur, protesting against the idolatry of his times, and according to tradition, suffering bitter persecution for conscience sake, "The God of glory appeared unto him, and said, Get thee out of thy country, and from thy kindred, and come into the land which I shall show thee" (Acts 7:2, 3).

When this Divine appearance came we do not know. But suddenly there shone from heaven a great light round about him, and a visible form appeared in the heart of the glory, and a voice spake the message of heaven in his ear. Not thus does God now appear to us; and yet it is certain that He still speaks in the silence of the waiting spirit.

Hardship
It was no small matter for Abraham to break up his camp, to tear himself from his nearest and dearest, and to start for a land which, as yet, he did not know. The summons of God will ever involve a wrench from much that nature holds dear. Each step of real advance in the Divine life will involve an altar on which some dear fragment of the self-life has been offered.

God's Wisdom
It was wise for *Abraham himself*. Nothing strengthens us so much as isolation and transplantation. So long as we are

quietly at rest amid favorable and undisturbed surroundings, faith sleeps as an undeveloped sinew within us. But when we are pushed out from all these surroundings, with nothing but God to look to, then faith grows suddenly into a cable, a monarch oak, a master principle of the life.

It may not be necessary for us to withdraw from home and friends; but we shall have to withdraw our hearts' deepest dependence from all earthly props and supports, if ever we are to learn what it is to trust simply and absolutely on the eternal God. It may be that He is breaking away just now the shores on which we have been leaning, that the ship may glide down upon the ocean wave.

God's Promise

God's commands are not always accompanied by reasons, but always by promises, expressed or understood. We can understand the promise, though the reason might baffle and confuse us. The reason is intellectual, metaphysical, spiritual; but a promise is practical, positive, literal. As a shell encloses a kernel, so do the Divine commands hide promises in their heart. So in this case: Though thou art childless, I will make of thee a great nation: though thou art the youngest son, I will bless thee, and make thy name great: though thou art to be torn from thine own family, in thee shall all the families of the earth be blessed. And each of those promises has been literally fulfilled.

It may seem that the hardships involved in the summons to exile are too great to be borne; yet study well the promise which is attached. And as the "City which hath foundations" looms on the view, it will dwarf the proportions of the Ur in which you have been content to spend your days; and you will rise to be gone. Sometimes, therefore, it seems easier not to dwell on the sacrifice involved, but on the contents of the Divine and gracious promise.

The Meaning of Election

Everywhere we find beings and things more loftily endowed than others of the same kind. This is markedly evident in the religious sphere. And there is at first a jarring wonder at the apparent inequality of the Divine arrangements; until we understand that the superior endowment of the few is intended to enable them the better to help and bless the rest. "I will bless thee, and thou shalt be a blessing" (v. 2).

Thus the intention of God, in selecting Abraham, and in him the whole family of Israel, was not so much with a view to their personal salvation, though that was included; but that they might pass on the holy teachings and oracles with which they were entrusted. It would have been worse than useless to have given such jewels directly to mankind. To say the least, there was no language ready in which to enshrine the sacred thoughts of God.

The deep question is, whether election has not much more to do with our ministry than with our personal salvation. It brings less of rest, and peace, and joy, than it does of anguish, bitterness, and sorrow of heart. There is no need to envy God's elect ones. They are the exiles, the cross bearers, the martyrs among men; but careless of themselves, they are all the while learning God's deepest lessons, away from the ordinary haunts of men; and they return to them presently with discoveries that pass all human thought, and are invaluable for human life.

The Key to Abraham's Life

It rang a clarion note at the very outset, which continued to vibrate through all his after-history. He was from first to last a *separated man*. Separated from his fatherland and kinsfolk, from Lot, as a pilgrim and stranger, from the people of the land, from his own methods of securing a fulfillment of the promises of God, from the rest of mankind by special sorrows, which brought him into closer fellowship with God than has ever been reached by man, and separated to high and lofty fellowship in thoughts and plans, which God could not hide from him.

The Separation of Faith

There is a form of separation known among men, in which

the lonely soul goes apart, to secure uninterrupted leisure for devotion. This is not the separation to which God called Abraham, or to which we are summoned. Because the heart has seen the Vision of God, and cannot now content itself with the things that once fascinated and entranced it, it reaches out its hands in eager longing for eternal realities, and thus is led gradually and insensibly out and away from the seen to the unseen, and from temporal to the eternal.

May such separation be ours!

3

He Obeyed

Hebrews 11:8

Ah, how much there is in those two words! Blessedness in heart, and home, and life; fulfilled promises; mighty opportunities of good—lie along the narrow, thorn-set path of obedience to the word and will of God. If Abraham had permanently refused obedience, he would have sunk back into the obscurity of an unknown grave in the land of Ur. But, thank God, Abraham obeyed, and in that act laid the foundation-stone of the noble structure of his life.

It may be that some will read these words whose lives have been a disappointment, and a sad surprise. You have failed to realize the early promise of your life. And may not the reason lie in this, that away back in your life, there rang out a command which summoned you to an act of self-sacrifice from which you shrank?

Would it not be well to ascertain if this be not so, and to hasten back to fulfil even now the long-delayed obedience. "He is merciful and gracious, slow to anger, and plenteous in goodness and truth" (Neh. 9:17). Do not use your long delay as an argument for longer delay, but as a reason for immediate action. "Why tarriest thou?"

Abraham, as the story shows, at first met the call of God with a mingled and partial obedience; and then for long years neglected it entirely. But the door stood still open for him to enter, and that gracious Hand still beckoned him. It was a partial failure, which is pregnant with invaluable lessons for ourselves.

Partial Obedience

He took Terah with him. How Terah was induced to leave the land of his choice we cannot tell. Was Abraham his favorite son, from whom he could not part? Had he been brought to desire an opportunity of renouncing his idols? We do not know. This, at least, is clear, that he was not wholehearted; and his presence in the march had the disastrous effect of slackening Abraham's pace, and of interposing a parenthesis of years in an obedience which, at first, promised so well. Probably for as many as fifteen years, Abraham's obedience was stayed; and for that period there were no further commands, no additional promises, no hallowed communings between God and His child.

It becomes us to be very careful as to whom we take with us in our pilgrimage. Take care, young pilgrim to eternity, to whom you mate yourself in the marriage bond. Beware, man of business, lest you find your Terah in the man with whom you are entering into partnership. Let us all beware of that fatal spirit of compromise, which tempts us to tarry where beloved ones bid us to stay.

"When his father was dead, He removed him into this land" (Acts 7:4). Here we may get a solution for mysteries in God's dealings with us, and understand why our hopes have withered, our schemes have miscarried, our income has dwindled, our children have turned against us. All these things were hindering our true development; and, out of mercy to our best interests, God has been compelled to take the knife in hand, and set us at liberty.

And he took Sarai his wife, and Lot, his brother's son, and all their substance that they had gathered, and the souls that they had gotten in Haran, and they went forth" (Gen. 12:5). Whither he went, he knew not; it was enough for him to know that he went with God. He leant not so much upon the promise as upon the Promiser: he looked not on the difficulties of his lot—but on the King eternal, immortal, invisible, the only wise God; who had deigned to appoint his course, and would certainly vindicate Himself.

Ah, glorious faith! this is thy work, these are thy

possibilities!—contentment to sail with sealed orders, because of unwavering confidence in the love and wisdom of the Lord High Admiral: willingness to arise up, leave all, and follow Christ, because of the glad assurance that earth's best cannot bear comparison with heaven's least.

Complete Obedience

"They went forth to go into the land of Canaan, and into the land of Canaan they came" (Gen. 12:5). For many days after leaving Haran, the eye would sweep a vast monotonous waste, broken by the scantiest vegetation; the camels treading the soft sand beneath their spreading, spongy feet; and the flocks finding but scanty nutriment on the coarse, sparse grass.

At one point only would the travelers arrest their course. In the oasis, where Damascus stands today, it stood then, furnishing a welcome resting place to weary travelers over the waste. And there is surely a trace of his slight sojourn there in the name of his favorite and most trusted servant, Eliezer of Damascus.

But Abraham would not stay here. The luxuriance and beauty of the place were very attractive; but he could not feel that it was God's choice for him. And, therefore, ere long he was again on the southern track, to reach Canaan as soon as he could. Our one aim in life must ever be to follow the will of God, and to walk in those ways in which He has preordained us to walk. And it is well when the pilgrim of eternity refuses to stay short, in any particular, of perfect consecration and obedience to the extreme demands of God. Anything short of complete obedience nullifies all that has been done. The Lord Jesus must have all or none; and His demands must be fulfilled up to the hilt. But they are not grievous.

What a glorious testimony was that which our Master uttered when He said, "The Father hath not left Me alone; for I do always those things that please Him" (John 8:29). Would that it might be true of each of us!

4

The First of the Pilgrim Fathers

Genesis 12:4-9

All through the history of mankind there has been a little band of men, in a sacred and unbroken succession, who have confessed that they were pilgrims and strangers upon earth. Certain indications, not difficult to note, betray the pilgrims of the Unseen and Eternal. Sometimes they are found afar from the haunts of men. But very often they are to be found in the marketplaces and homes of men, distinguished only by their simpler dress; their girded loins; their restrained and abstemious appetite; their loose hold on gold; their independence on the maxims and opinions and applause of the world around; and the far-away look which now and again gleams in their eyes, the certain evidence of affections centered, not on the transitory things of time and earth, but on those eternal realities which are only revealed to faith.

We left the patriarch moving leisurely southward; and thus he continued to journey forward through the land of promise, making no permanent halt, till he reached the place of Sichem, or Shechem, in the very heart of the land, where our Lord in after years sat weary by the well. There was no city or settlement there then. The country was sparsely populated. The only thing that marked the site was a venerable oak, whose spreading arms in later ages were to shadow the excesses of a shameful idolatry. Beneath this oak on the plain of Sichem, the camp was pitched; and there, at last, the long silence was broken, which had lasted since the first summons was spoken in Chaldaea, "And the Lord appeared unto Abram, and said, Unto thy seed will I give this land: and there builded he an altar unto the Lord, who appeared unto him" (Gen. 12:7).

He did not, however, stay there permanently, but moved a little to the south, to a place between Bethel and Ai; where, according to Dr. Robinson, there is now a high and beautiful plain, presenting one of the finest tracts of pasturage in the whole country.

Three things then engage our thought: the Tent, the Altar, and the Promise.

The Tent

When Abraham left Haran his age was seventy-five. When he died he was one hundred and seventy-five years old. And he spent that intervening century moving to and fro, dwelling in a frail and flimsy tent, probably of dark camel's hair, like that of the Bedouin of the present day. And that tent was only a befitting symbol of the spirit of his life.

He held himself aloof from the people of the land. He was among them, but not of them. He did not attend their tribal gatherings. He carefully guarded against inter-marriage with their children, sending to his own country to obtain a bride for his son. He would not take from the Canaanites a thread or a sandal thong. He insisted on paying full market value for all he received. He did not stay in any permanent location, but was ever on the move. The tent which had no foundations; which could be erected and struck in half-an-hour—this was the apt symbol of his life.

And why? The question is fully answered in that majestic chapter which recounts the triumphs of faith. "Abraham dwelt in tents, because he looked for the City which hath the foundations" (Heb. 11:9). Precisely so: and the tent-life is the natural one for those who feel that their fatherland lies beyond the stars.

It is of the utmost importance that the children of God should live this detached life as a testimony to the world.

How will people believe us, when we talk about our hope, if it does not wean us from excessive devotion to the things around us? If we are quite as eager, or careworn; quite as covetous or grasping; quite as dependent on the pleasures and fascinations of this passing world—as themselves: may they not begin to question whether our profession be true on the one hand; or whether after all there be a real city yonder on the other.

Let us rather paint with glowing colors that City which John saw. Let us unfold the glories of that world to which we are bound. And surely there will come into many a life a separateness of heart and walk which shall impress men with the reality of the unseen, as no sermon could do, however learned or eloquent.

The Altar

Wherever Abraham pitched his tent, he built an altar. And long after the tent was shifted, the altar stood to show where the man of God had been.

Ah, it would be a blessed token of our religious fervor if we could set up altars in every house where we pass the night, and in every locality where it might be our hap to live, setting the example of private and family prayer, which would live long after we had passed away.

Let us also remember that the altar means sacrifice, whole burnt offering, self-denial, and self-surrender. In this sense the altar and the tent must ever go together. We cannot live the detached tent life without some amount of pain and suffering, such as the altar bespeaks. But it is out of such a life that there spring the most intense devotion, the deepest fellowship, the happiest communion.

If your private prayer has been lately hindered, it may be that you have not been living enough in the tent. The tent-life of separation is sure to produce the altar of self-denial and of heavenly fellowship. Confess that you are a stranger and a pilgrim on the earth; and you will find it pleasant and natural to call on the name of the Lord.

But Abraham's altar was not for himself alone. At certain periods the whole clan gathered there for common worship. A motley group that, in which slaves bought in Egypt or Ur mingled with those born in the camp; in which children and parents, young and old, stood in silent awe around the altar, where the patriarch stood to offer their common sacrifice and worship. "I know Abraham," said God, "that he will command his children and his household after him" (Gen. 18:19). He, in whom all families of the earth were to be blessed, practiced family religion; and in this he sets a striking example to many Christians whose homes are altarless. Would that Christians might be stirred by the example of the patriarch to erect the family altar, and to gather around it the daily circle of their children and dependents, for the sweetening and ennobling of their family life!

The Promise
"Unto thy seed will I give this land" (Gen. 12:7). As soon as Abraham had fully obeyed, this new promise broke upon his ear. And it is ever thus. Disobey—and you tread a path unlit by a single star. Obey, live up to the claims of God—and successive promises beam out from heaven to light your steps, each one richer and fuller than the one before. Hitherto God had pledged Himself only to show the land: now He bound Himself to give it. The separated pilgrim-life always obtains promises.

There was no natural probability of that promise being fulfilled. "The Canaanite was then in the land." They had settled and taken root. They built towns, and tilled the land. They knew the use of money and writing; and administered justice in the gate. Every day built up their power, and made it more unlikely that they could ever be dispossessed by the descendants of a childless shepherd.

But God had said it; and so it came to pass. "The counsel of the Lord standeth fast for ever; the thoughts of His heart to all generations" (Ps. 33:11). I know not what promise may be over-arching your life, my reader, with its bow of hope; but this is certain, that if you fulfill its conditions, and live up to its demands, it will be literally and gloriously fulfilled. Look not at the difficulties and improbabilities that block the path, but at the might and faithfulness of the Promiser.

5
Gone Down Into Egypt

Genesis 12:10

The path of the separated man can never be an easy one. He must be willing to stand alone. When Faith is strong, we dare cut ourselves adrift from the moorings which coupled us to the shore; and launch out into the deep, depending only on the character and word of Him at whose command we go. But when Faith is weak, we dare not do it; and, leaving the upland path, we herd with the men of the world, who have their portion in this life, and who are content with that alone. Ah, how can we say enough of His tender mercy, who, at such times, bends over us, with infinite compassion, waiting to lift us back into the old heroic life!

Famine in the Land
A famine in the Land of Promise? Yes, as afterwards, so then; the rains that usually fall in the latter part of the year had failed; the crops burned up before the harvest; and pasture for the flocks was scanty, or altogether absent. If a similar calamity were to befall us now, we could still draw sufficient supplies for our support from abroad. But Abraham had no such resource. A stranger in a strange land; weighted with the responsibility of vast flocks and herds—it was no trivial matter to stand face to face with the sudden devastation of famine.

Did it prove that he had made a mistake in coming to Canaan? Happily the promise which had lately come to him forbade his entertaining the thought. And this may have been one principal reason why it was given. It came, not only as a reward for the past, but as a preparation for the future. And thus it often happens that a time of special trial is ushered in by the shining forth of the Divine presence, and the declaration of some unprecedented promise.

How often do professing Christians adopt a hurt and injured tone in speaking of God's dealings with them! They look back upon a sunny past, and complain that it was better with them before they entered the wicket gate and commenced to tread the narrow way. And they complain that the service of God has brought them misfortune rather than a blessing.

But is not this the point to be borne in mind on the other side? These misfortunes would probably have come in any case; and how much less tolerable would they have been had there not been the new sweet consciousness that God had now become the refuge of the soul! Do not be surprised if a famine meets you. It is no proof of your Father's anger, but is permitted to come to test you—or to root you deeper, as the whirlwind makes the tree grapple its roots deeper into the soil.

In the figurative language of Scripture, Egypt stands for alliance with the world, and dependence on an arm of flesh. "Woe to them that go down to Egypt for help; and stay on horses; and trust in chariots because they are many; and in horsemen because they are very strong; but they look not unto the Holy One of Israel, neither seek the Lord!" (Isa. 31:1).

There were occasions in Jewish history when God Himself bade His servants seek a temporary asylum in Egypt. There may be times in all our lives when God may clearly indicate that it is His will for us to go out into the world, with a view of accomplishing some Divine purpose with respect to it. And when God sends us, by the undoubted call of His providence, He will be as sure to keep and deliver us as He did Jacob and his seed, or the Holy Child.

But it does not appear that Abraham received any such Divine direction. He acted simply on his own judgment. He looked at his difficulties. He became paralyzed with fear. He grasped at the first means of deliverance which suggested itself, much as a drowning man will catcn at a straw. And thus, without taking counsel of his heavenly Protector, he went down into Egypt.

Ah, fatal mistake! But how many make it still. They may be true children of God: and yet, in a moment of panic, they will adopt methods of delivering themselves which, to say the least, are questionable; and sow the seeds of sorrow and disaster in after life, to save themselves from some minor embarrassment.

How much better would it have been for Abraham to have thrown the responsibility back on God, and to have said, "Thou hast brought me here; and Thou must now bear the whole weight of providing for me and mine: here will I stay till I clearly know what Thou wilt have me to do." If any should read these lines who have come into positions of extreme difficulty, through following the simple path of obedience, let them not look at God through difficulties, but let them look at difficulties through God. Has He not thus brought you into difficulties, that He may have an opportunity of strengthening your faith, by giving some unexampled proof of His power? Wait only on the Lord, trust also in Him: His name is Jehovah-jireh; He will provide.

One Sin Leads to Another
When Abraham lost his faith, and went down into Egypt, he also lost his courage, and persuaded his wife to call herself his sister. He had heard of the licentiousness of the Egyptians, and feared that they might take his life, to get possession of Sarah. It was a mean and cowardly act on Abraham's part, which was utterly indefensible. It was a cruel wrong to one who had faithfully followed his fortunes for so long. And it endangered the promised seed. Yet so it happens; when we lose our faith, and are filled with panic for ourselves, we

become regardless of all and every tie, and are prepared to sacrifice our nearest and dearest, if only we may escape.

How thankful should we be that the Bible does not shrink from recording the story of the sins of its noblest saints! What a proof of its veracity is here, and what encouragement there is for us!—for if God was able to make His friend out of such material as this, may we not aspire to a like privilege, though we, too, have grievously violated the high calling of faith? The one thing that God requires of His saints is implicit obedience—entire surrender. Where these are present, He can still make Abrahams out of us, though, by nature, the soil of our being is prone to barrenness and weeds.

6

Separated From Lot

Genesis 13

By nature Abraham was not superior to some Orientals, who do not hesitate to lie, in order to gain a point or to avert a disaster. It is hard to imagine that such a man would ever arrive at a stature of moral greatness so commanding as to overtop all his contemporaries, and look across the ages to see the day of Christ. Yet so it was. And from that thought we may take courage.

Our God does not need noble characters, as the groundwork of His masterpieces. He can raise up stones as children. We are not much by nature—but God will be the more magnified, if from such stones He can raise up children unto Abraham.

"Abraham went up out of Egypt, he, and his wife, and all that he had, and Lot with him, into the south" (v.1).

Contrary to all human anticipation, Jehovah appears on the behalf of His most unworthy servant. In after-years the Psalmist gives us the very words, which He uttered in the heart of the king: "Touch not Mine anointed, and do My prophets no harm" (Psalm 105:15). What a marvel of tenderness! Notwithstanding repeated falls and shortcomings, He lovingly pursues His Divine purpose with the soul in which the "root of the matter" is found, until He sets it free from its clinging evils, and lifts it into the life of faith, and power, and familiar friendship with Himself.

So complete was the delivering power of God, that the

Egyptian monarch did not even take back the gifts which he
had bestowed as a dowry for Sarah. And we are, therefore,
prepared to learn, that "Abram was very rich, in cattle, in
silver, and in gold" (v. 2). That visit to Egypt beyond doubt
laid the foundation of the immense wealth of the family in
after-time; and it was out of this that the next trouble sprang.

Who was Lot?

The son of Abraham's dead brother, Haran. He seems to
have been one of those men who take right steps, not because they are prompted by obedience to God, but because
their friends are taking them. Around him was the inspiration of an heroic faith, the fascination of the untried and
unknown; the stir of a great religious movement: and Lot
was swept into the current, and resolved to go too. He was
simply an echo; a dim afterglow; a chip on the bosom of a
mighty current.

Nothing but supreme principle can carry any one through
the real, separated, and surrendered life of the child of God.
If you are prompted by anything less, such as excitement,
enthusiasm, fashion, contagious example—you will first be a
hindrance, and end by being a failure. If you are consciously
acting from a low and selfish motive, ask God to breathe into
you His own pure love.

The Necessity of Separation

Failure in Egypt may have been due, to a larger extent than
we know, to the baneful influence of Lot. Had Abraham been
left to himself, he might never have thought of going down
to Egypt: and, in that case, there would have been another
paragraph or passage in the Bible describing the exploits of a
faith which dared to stand to God's promise, though
threatened by disaster, and hemmed in by famine; waiting
until God should bid it move, or make it possible to stay.
There is something about that visit to Egypt which savors of
the spirit of Lot's afterlife. In any case, the time had come, in
the providence of God, when this lower and more worldly

spirit must go its way; leaving Abraham to stand alone, without prop, or adviser, or ally; thrown back on the counsel and help of God alone.

The outward separation of the body from the world of the ungodly is incomplete, unless accompanied and supplemented by the inner separation of the spirit. It is not enough to leave Ur, Haran, and Egypt. We must be rid of Lot also. So long as there is an alien principle in our breast, a Lot in our heart-life, there cannot be that separation to God which is the condition of the growth of faith.

It may be that Abraham had already felt for himself the ill effect of association with Lot, and may have longed to be free from him, without knowing how the emancipation could be effected. In any case, somewhat akin to this may be the condition of some who shall read these words. Declare to God continually your eager desire to be emancipated. Wait patiently till God's hour strikes, and His hand opens the fast-locked door, and bids you be free. That time will come at length; for God has a destiny in store for you, so great that neither He nor you can allow it to be forfeited for any light or trivial obstacle.

How the Separation was Brought About

The valleys around Bethel, which had been quite adequate for their needs when first they came to Canaan, were now altogether insufficient. The herdsmen were always wrangling for the first use of the wells, and the first crop of the pastures. The cattle were continually getting mixed. "The land was not able to bear them, that they might dwell together" (v. 6).

Abraham saw at once that such a state of things must not be allowed to go on: especially as "the Canaanite and the Perizzite dwelt then in the land" (v. 7). For if those warlike neighbors heard of the dissensions in the camp, they would take an early opportunity of falling upon it. Besides, there was the scandal of the thing, which might work prejudicially on the name and worship of that God to whom Abraham was

known to bow the knee. Would that the near presence of the
world might have the same wholesome effect of checking
dissension and dispute among the children of the same
Father!

And so Abraham called Lot to him, and said, "Let there be
no strife between me and thee, and between my herdsmen
and thy herdsmen: for we be brethren. Is not the whole land
before thee? Separate thyself, I pray thee, from me. If thou
wilt take the left hand, then I will go to the right; or if thou
depart to the right hand, then I will go to the left" (vv. 8, 9).

His line of action was very magnanimous. As the elder and
the leader of the expedition, he had undoubted right to the
first choice. But he waived his right in the interests of reconciliation.

But, above all, it was based on faith. His faith was beginning to realize its true position; and, like a fledgling, to
spread its wings for further and still further flights. Had not
God pledged Himself to take care of him, and to give him an
inheritance? There was no fear, therefore, that Lot could ever
rob him of that which was guaranteed to him by the faithfulness of God.

The man who is sure of God can afford to hold very lightly
the things of this world. God Himself is his inalienable heritage; and, in having God, he has all.

7

The Two Paths

Genesis 13

Abraham and Lot stood together on the heights of Bethel, the Land of Promise spread out before them as a map. Even from the distance they could discern to the southeast the rich luxuriance, which may have recalled to them traditions of the garden once planted by the Lord God in Eden. This specially struck the eye of Lot; eager to do the best for himself, and determined to make the fullest use of the opportunity which the unexpected magnanimity of his uncle had thrown in his way. Did he count his relative a fool for surrendering the right of choice? Perhaps so. For he had little sympathy with the pilgrim spirit. He did not ask what God had chosen for him. He did not consider the effect which the morals of the place might exert upon his children and himself. His choice was entirely determined by the lust of the flesh, the lust of the eyes, and the pride of life.

Let us not condemn Lot too much because he chose without reference to the moral and religious conditions of the case; lest, in judging him, we pronounce sentence on ourselves. Lot did nothing more than is done by scores of professing Christians every day.

If Abraham had remonstrated with Lot, do you not suppose that he would have answered petulantly: "Do you not think that we are as eager as you are to serve the Lord? Sodom needs just that witness which we shall be able to give. Is it not befitting that the light should shine in the darkness; and that the salt should be scattered where there is putrefaction?" Abraham might not be able to contest these assertions, and yet he would have an inner conviction that these were not the considerations which were determining his nephew's choice. Of course, if God sends a man to Sodom, He will keep him there; as Daniel was kept in Babylon: and nothing shall by any means hurt him. But if God does not clearly send you to Sodom, it is a blunder, a crime, a peril to go.

Mark how Lot was swiftly swept into the vortex; he saw; he chose; he separated himself from Abraham; he journeyed east; he pitched his tent toward Sodom; he dwelt there; he became an alderman of the place, and sat in the gate. His daughters married two of the men of Sodom; and they probably ranked among the most genteel and influential families of the neighborhood. But his power of witness bearing was gone. His righteous soul might vex itself; but it met with no sympathy. He was carried captive by Chedorlaomer. His property was destroyed in the overthrow of the cities. His wife was turned into a pillar of salt. And the blight of Sodom left but too evident a brand upon his daughters. Wretched, indeed, must have been the last days of that hapless man, cowering in a cave, stripped of everything, face to face with the results of his own shameful sin.

It is, indeed, a terrible picture; and yet some such retribution is in store for every one whose choice of home, and friends, and surroundings, is dictated by the lust of worldly gain, or fashion, or pleasure, rather than by the will of God.

Now, let us turn to a more inviting theme, and further consider the dealings of the Almighty God with Abraham, the one man who was being educated to hold fellowship with Jehovah as a friend.

God's Nearness
"And the Lord said unto Abraham, after that Lot was separated from him" (v. 14). It may be that Abraham was feeling very lonely. We all dread to be separated from companions

and friends. It is hard to see them stand aloof, and drop away one by one; and to be compelled to take a course by oneself. And yet, if we really wish to be only for God, it is inevitable that there should be many a link snapped; many a companionship forsaken; many a habit and conventionalism dropped.

But let this be understood, that, when once the spirit has dared to take up that life of consecration to the will of God to which we are called, there break upon it visions, voices, comfortable words, of which the heart could have formed no previous idea.

God's Faithfulness
Twice here in the context we meet the phrase—"lifting up the eyes." But how great the contrast! Lot lifted up his eyes, at the dictate of worldly prudence, to spy out his own advantage. Abraham lifted up his eyes, not to discern what would best make for his material interests, but to behold what God had prepared for him. How much better it is to keep the eye steadfastly fastened on God till He says to us!—"Lift up now thine eyes, and look from the place where thou art—northward, and southward, and eastward, and westward: for all the land which thou seest, to thee will I give it, and to thy seed for ever" (vv. 14, 15).

It is difficult to read these glowing words, *northward, and southward, and eastward, and westward*, without being reminded of "the length, and breadth, and depth, and height, of the love of Christ, that passeth knowledge." Much of the land of Canaan was hidden behind the ramparts of the hills; but enough was seen to ravish that faithful spirit. Similarly, we may not be able to comprehend the love of God in Christ, but the higher we climb the more we behold. The upper cliffs of the separated life command the fullest view of that measureless expanse.

God's promises are ever on the ascending scale. One leads up to another, fuller and more blessed than itself. In Mesopotamia, God said, "I will show thee the land." At Bethel, "This is the land." Here, "I will give thee all the land, and children innumerable as the grains of sand." And we shall find even these eclipsed. It is thus that God allures us to saintliness. Not giving anything till we have dared to act—that He may test us. Not giving everything at first—that He may not overwhelm us. And always keeping in hand an infinite reserve of blessing. Oh, the unexplored remainders of God! Who ever saw His last star?

Appropriating God's Gifts

"Arise, walk through the land in the length of it and in the breadth of it" (v. 17). This surely means that God wished Abraham to feel as free in the land as if the title-deeds were actually in his hands. He was to enjoy it; to travel through it; to look upon it as his. By faith he was to act towards it as if he were already in absolute possession.

The difference between Christians consists in this. For us all there are equal stores of spiritual blessing laid up in our Lord; but some of us have learnt more constantly and fully to appropriate them. We walk through the land in its lengths and breadths. We avail ourselves of the fulness of Jesus. Not content with what He is for us in the counsel of God, our constant appeal is to Him in every moment of need.

8
Refreshment Between the Battles

Genesis 14

The strife recorded in Genesis 14 was no mere border foray. Chedorlaomer was the Attila, the Napoleon of his age. Years before Abraham had entered Canaan as a peaceful emigrant, this dreaded conqueror had swept southwards, subduing the towns which lay in the Jordan Valley, and thus possessing himself of the master-key to the road between Damascus and Memphis. When Lot took up his residence towards Sodom, the cities of the plain were paying tribute to this mighty monarch.

At last the men of Sodom and Gomorrah, of Admah and Zeboiim, became weary of the Elamite yoke and rebelled, and Chedorlaomer was compelled to undertake a second expedition. Combining his own forces with those of three vassal and friendly rulers in the Euphrates Valley, which lay in his way, he swept across the desert, and fell upon the wild tribes that harbored in the mountains of Bashan and Moab. His plan was evidently to ravage the whole country contiguous to those Jordan towns before actually investing them.

At last the allied forces concentrated in the neighborhood of Sodom, where they encountered fierce resistance. However, the day went against the effeminate and dissolute men of the plain. The defeat of the troops was followed by the capture and sack of those wealthy towns; and all who could not escape were manacled as slaves, and carried off in the train of the victorious army.

Sated at length with their success, the foreign host began slowly to return along the Jordan Valley on its homeward march. "And they took Lot, Abram's brother's son, who dwelt in Sodom, and his goods, and departed" (v. 12). Then one of the survivors of that fatal day climbed the hills, and made for Abraham's encampment, which he may have known in earlier days, when, as one of Lot's many servants, he lived there. "And when Abram heard that his brother was taken captive, he armed his trained servants . . . and divided himself against them" (vv. 14, 15).

Abraham's Success
Hidden in the configuration of the country, and confederate with his friends, Abraham had watched the movements of the devastators from afar. Common prudence would have urged him not to embroil himself. But true separation never argues thus. The separated one is set apart for God, yet he is set apart that he may react more efficiently on the great world over which God yearns. Genuine separation—an unattachedness to the things of time and sense, because of an ardent devotion to the unseen and eternal—is the result of faith, which always works by love; and this love tenderly yearns for those who are entangled in the meshes of worldliness and sin. Faith makes us independent, but not indifferent.

But Abraham's interposition was as *successful* as it was unselfish and prompt. The force with which he set out was a very slender one; but his raw recruits moved quickly, and thus in four or five days they overtook the self-reliant and encumbered host amid the hills where the Jordan takes its rise. Adopting the tactics of a night attack, he fell suddenly on the unsuspecting host, and chased them in headlong panic, as far as the ancient city of Damascus. "And he brought back all the goods, and also brought again his brother Lot, and his goods, and the women also, and the people" (v. 16).

Is it not always so? The men who live the life of separation and devotion towards God, are they who act with most promptness and success when the time for action comes. Lot being in Sodom, could neither elevate its morals nor save it from attack. Abraham living among the hills is alone able to cope successfully with the might of the tyrant king. Oh, do not listen to those who say you must live on the level, and in the midst of worldly men, in order to elevate and save them. If you would lift me, you must stand above me. If Archimedes is to move the world, he must rest his lever on a point far enough outside the earth itself.

Temptation Following Success

The King of Sodom had not been among the prisoners. When therefore he received tidings of the patriarch's gallant and successful expedition, he set out to meet and welcome him. The two met at the King's Dale, situated near the city of Salem—Jerusalem. Grateful for Abraham's succor and deliverance, the King of Sodom proposed to him to surrender only the persons of the captives, while he kept all the spoils to himself and his allies.

It must have been a very tempting offer, the chance of appropriating all the spoils of settled townships, so large and opulent; especially when he seemed to have some claim on them.

But he would not hear of it for a moment. Indeed, he seems to have already undergone some exercise of soul on the matter, for speaking as of a past transaction, he said, "I have lift up mine hand unto the Lord, the Most High God, the Possessor of heaven and earth, that I will not take from a thread even to a shoelatchet; and that I will not take anything that is thine, lest thou shouldst say, 'I have made Abraham rich' " (vv. 22, 23). What a magnificent contempt of specious offer! What a glorious outburst of the independence of a living faith!

There is a close parallel between this suggestion of the King of Sodom and the temptation of our Lord in the wilderness, when Satan offered Him all the kingdoms of the world for one act of obeisance. And does not this temptation assail us all?

In theory it may be argued that we can turn to good account the wealth which has been ill gotten. But practically, we shall not find it so. The wealth of Sodom will scorch the hand that handles it, and will blight every godly enterprise to which it may be put. Besides, what right have we to depend on the revenues of the world, we, who are heirs to the Possessor of heaven and earth, the children of the Great King: to whom, in giving us His Son, He has also pledged to give us all things? Happy they who prefer to be pensioners on the daily providence of God to being dependent on the gold of Sodom—the wages of iniquity.

We may not stay to speak now of all the interest that gathers around this sacred figure, sacred as the type of our blessed Lord. He brought bread and wine, and blessed the weary conqueror, and coined in his hearing a new name for God. For the first time God received the title, "Possessor of heaven and earth"—one which seems to have made a deep impression upon Abraham; for we find him using it in his encounter with the King of Sodom—and it was the talisman of victory. Why should he need to take aught from man, when this new revelation of God had just fallen upon his ear, and enriched his heart for ever?

Is not this the work of the Lord Jesus still? He comes to us when wearily returning from the fight. He comes to us when He knows we are on the eve of a great temptation. He not only prays for us, as for Peter; but He prepares us for the conflict. Some new revelation; some fresh glimpse into His character; some holy thought—these are given to fill the memory and heart against the advent of the foe. Oh, matchless mercy! He forewarns and forearms us. He prevents us with the blessings of His goodness.

O King of loyal hearts, may we meet Thee more often on life's highway, especially when some tempter is preparing to weave around us the meshes of evil; and bending beneath Thy blessing, may we be prepared by the communications of Thy grace for all that may await us in the unknown future!

9
Melchizedec
Hebrews 7

There is a sense in which Christ was made *after the order of Melchizedec;* but there is a deeper sense in which Melchizedec was made *after the order of the Son of God.* The writer to the Hebrews tells us that Melchizedec was "made like unto the Son of God" (v. 3). Christ is the Archetype of all; and from all eternity has had those qualities which have made Him so much to us. It would seem as if they could not stay to be manifested in the fulness of the ages; they chafed for expression. And so this mysterious royal priest was constituted that there might be given among men some premonition, some anticipation, of that glorious life which was already being lived in Heaven on man's behalf, and which, in due course, would be manifested on our world, and at that very spot where Melchizedec lived his Christ-like life. Oh that we, too, might be priests after the order of Melchizedec in this respect, if in no other, that we are made as like as possible to the Son of God!

The Priesthood of Melchizedec
There was one heart at least which was true in its allegiance to the Most High God: and which bore up before Him the sins and sorrows of the clans that clustered near. He seems to have had that quick sympathy with the needs of his times which is the true mark of the priestly heart (Heb. 4:15). Man must have a priest. His nature shrinks from contact with the All Holy. And in all ages, men have selected from among

their fellows one who should represent them to God, and God to them. It is a natural instinct. And it has been met in our glorious Lord, who, while He stands for us in the presence of God, face to face with uncreated Light, ever making intercessions, at the same time is touched with the feeling of our infirmities, succors us in our temptations, and has compassion on our ignorance.

Priesthood From God
The priests of the house of Levi exercised their office because they had sprung from the special sacerdotal tribe. The Priesthood of Christ, on the other hand, is God's best gift to men. Without it our souls would wander ever in a Sahara desert. "Christ glorified not Himself to be made a High Priest" (Heb. 5:5), but He was called of God to be a High Priest after the order of Melchizedec (v. 10). And such was the solemnity of His appointment, that it was ratified by "the word of the oath." "The Lord sware and will not repent, Thou art a Priest for ever after the order of Melchizedec" (Heb. 7:21-28). Here is "strong consolation" indeed. No unfaithfulness or ingratitude can change this priesthood. The eternal God will never run back from that word and oath. The heart may well sing, when, amid the fluctuation of earth's change, it touches at length the primeval rock of God's eternal purpose. He is "consecrated" Priest "for evermore."

A Universal Priesthood
Abraham was not yet circumcised. He was not a Jew, but a Gentile still. It was as the father of many nations that he stood and worshipped and received the benediction from Melchizedec's saintly hands. Not thus was it with the priesthood of Aaron's line. To share its benefit a man must needs become a Jew, submitting to the initial rite of Judaism. None but Jewish names shone in that breastplate. Only Jewish wants or sins were borne upon those consecrated lips. *But Christ is the Priest of man.* He draws *all men* unto Himself. The one sufficient claim upon Him is that thou bear the nature which He has taken into irreversible union with His own—

that thou art a sinner and a penitent pressed by conscious need. Then hast thou a right to Him, which cannot be disallowed. He is thy Priest—thine own; as if none other had claim on Him than thou.

A Superior Priesthood

If ever there were a priesthood which held undisputed supremacy among the priesthoods of the world, it was that of Aaron's line. It might not be as ancient as that of Nineveh, or so learned as that of Memphis and Thebes; but it had about it this unapproachable dignity—in that it had emanated, as a whole, from the Word of God. Yet even the Aaronic must yield obeisance to the Melchizedec Priesthood. For Levi was yet in the loins of Abraham when Melchizedec met him; and he paid tithes in Abraham, and knelt in token of submission, in the person of the patriarch, beneath the blessing of this greater than himself (Heb. 7:4-10). What have we to do with any other than with this mighty Mediator, this Daysman, who towers aloft above all rivals; Himself sacrifice and Priest who has offered a solitary sacrifice, and fulfils a unique ministry!

An Eternal Priesthood

We need not suppose that this mystic being had literally no father, or mother, beginning of days, or end of life. The fact on which the inspired writer fixes is—that no information is afforded us on any of these points. There is an intention in the golden silence, as well as in the golden speech of Scripture. And these details were doubtless shrouded in obscurity, that there might be a still clearer approximation of the type to the glory of the Antitype, who abides continually. He is the Ancient of Days; the King of the Ages; the I AM. "He is made after the power of an endless life." "He ever liveth to make intercession." "He continueth ever, and hath an unchangeable priesthood." "He is the same yesterday, today, and for ever." He does for us now what He did for the world's grey fathers, and what He will do for the last sinner who shall claim His aid.

A Royal Priesthood

"Melchizedec, King of Salem, priest." Here again there is no analogy in the Levitical priesthood.

The royal and priestly offices were carefully kept apart. Uzziah was struck with the white brand of leprosy when he tried to unite them. But how marvelously they blended in the earthly life of Jesus! As Priest, He pitied, and helped, and fed men: as King, He ruled the waves. As Priest, He uttered His sublime intercessory prayer: as King, He spoke the "I will" of royal prerogative. As Priest, He pleaded for His murderers, and spake of Paradise to the dying thief: while His Kingship was attested by the proclamation affixed to His cross. As Priest, He breathed peace on His disciples: as King, He ascended to sit down upon His throne.

He was *first* "King of Righteousness," and after that also King of Salem, which is King of Peace (v. 2). Mark the order. Righteousness first—the righteousness of His personal character; the righteous meeting, on our behalf, of the just demands of a Divine and holy law. And then founded on, and arising from, this solid and indestructible basis, there sprang the Temple of Peace, in which the souls of men may shelter from the shocks of time.

A Tithe-Receiving Priesthood

"The patriarch Abraham gave the tenth of the spoils" (v. 4). This ancient custom shames us Christians. The patriarch gave more to the representative of Christ than many of us give to Christ Himself. Come, if you have never done so before, resolve to give your Lord a tithe of your time, your income, your all. Nay, thou glorious One, we will not rest content with this; take all, for all is Thine. "Thine is the greatness, and the power, and the glory, and the victory, and the majesty: for all that is in heaven and in the earth is Thine; Thine is the Kingdom, O Lord, and Thou art exalted as King above all. Now, therefore, we thank Thee and praise Thy glorious name" (I Chron. 29:11, 13).

10
The Firmness of Abraham's Faith

Genesis 15

In this chapter, for the first time in Scripture, four striking phrases occur; but each of them is destined to be frequently repeated with many charming variations. Now, first, we meet the phrase, "the word of the Lord came." Here, first, we are told that "the Lord God is a shield." For the first time rings out the silver chime of that Divine assurance, "Fear not!" And now we first meet in human history that great, that mighty word, "believed." What higher glory is there for man than that he should reckon on the faithfulness of God? For this is the meaning of all true belief.

The "word of the Lord" came to Abraham about two distinct matters.

Abraham's Fear

Abraham had just returned from the rout of Chedorlaomer and the confederate kings in the far north of Canaan; and there was a natural reaction from the long and unwonted strain as he settled down again into the placid and uneventful course of a shepherd's life. In this state of mind he was most susceptible to fear; as the enfeebled constitution is most susceptible to disease.

And there was good reason for fear. He had defeated Chedorlaomer, it is true; but in doing so he had made him his bitter foe. There was every reason, therefore, to expect him back again to inflict condign punishment. And, besides all this, as a night wind in a desert land, there swept now and again over the heart of Abraham a feeling of lonely desolation, of disappointment, or hope deferred. More than ten years had passed since he had entered Canaan. Three successive promises had kindled his hopes, but they seemed as far from realization as ever. Not one inch of territory! Not a sign of a child! Nothing of all that God had foretold!

It was under such circumstances that the word of the Lord came unto him, saying, "Fear not, Abram: I am thy Shield, and thy exceeding great Reward" (v. 1). Ah, our God does not always wait for us to come to Him; He often comes to us, and on our souls break His tender assurances of comfort, "Be of good cheer; it is I; be not afraid."

But God does not content Himself with vague assurances. He gives us solid ground for comfort in some fresh revelation of Himself. And oftentimes the very circumstances of our need are chosen as a foil to set forth some special side of the Divine character which is peculiarly appropriate. What could have been more reassuring at this moment to the defenseless pilgrim, with no stockade or walled city in which to shelter, but whose flocks were scattered far and wide, than to hear that God Himself was around him and his, as a vast, impenetrable, though invisible shield. "I am thy Shield."

Mankind, when once that thought was given, eagerly caught at it; and it has never been allowed to die. Again and again it rings out in prophecy and psalms, in temple anthem and from retired musings. "The Lord God is a sun and shield." We go every day into the midst of danger; men and devils strike at us; now it is the overt attack, and now the stab of the assassin; unkind insinuations, evil suggestions, taunts, gibes, threats; all these things are against us. But if we are doing God's will and trusting in God's care, ours is a charmed life. Happy are they who have learned the art of abiding within the inviolable protection of the eternal God.

Nor does God only defend us from without, He is the *reward* and satisfaction of the lonely heart. It was as if He asked Abraham to consider how much he had in having

Himself. Our God, who is love, and love in its purest, divinest essence, has given us much, and promised us more; but still His best and greatest gift is His own dear self; our reward, our great reward, our exceeding great reward. All lovely things sleep in Him, as all colors hide in the sunbeam's ray, waiting to be unraveled. To have God is to have all, though bereft of everything. To be destitute of God is to be bereft of everything, though having all.

Abraham's Childlessness

It was night, or perhaps the night was turning towards the morning, but as yet myriads of stars were sparkling in the heavens. The patriarch was sleeping in his tent, when God came near him in a vision; and it was under the shadow of that vision that Abraham was able to tell God all that was in his heart. We can often say things in the dark which we dare not utter beneath the eye of day. And in that quiet watch of the night, Abraham poured out into the ear of God the bitter, bitter agony of his heart's life. "Behold, to me Thou hast given no seed: and, lo, one born in my house is mine heir" (v. 3). It was as if he said, "I promised for myself something more than this; I have conned Thy promises, and felt that they surely prognosticated a child of my own flesh and blood; but the slowly moving years have brought me no fulfilment of my hopes; and I suppose that I mistook Thee. Thou never intendest more than that my steward should inherit my name and goods. Ah, me! It is a bitter disappointment; but Thou has done it, and it is well."

So we often mistake God, and interpret His delays as denials. What a chapter might be written of God's delays! It is the mystery of the art of educating human spirits to the finest temper of which they are capable. What searchings of heart; what analyzing of motives; what testings of the Word of God; what upliftings of soul—searching what, or what manner of time, the Spirit of God signifies! All these are associated with those weary days of waiting, which are, nevertheless, big with spiritual destiny. But such delays are not God's final answer to the soul that trusts Him. They are but the winter before the burst of spring. "And, behold, the word of the Lord came unto him, saying, This shall not be thine heir; but thine own son shall be thine heir. Look now toward heaven, and tell the stars, if thou be able to number them. So shall thy seed be" (vv. 4, 5). And from that moment the stars shone with new meaning for him, as the sacraments of Divine promise.

Abraham's Belief

"And he believed in the Lord" (v. 6). What wonder that those words are so often quoted by inspired men in after ages; or that they lie as the foundation stone of some of the greatest arguments that have ever engaged the mind of man! (See Rom. 4:3; Gal. 3:6; Jas. 2:23.)

He believed in the face of strong natural improbablities. Appearances were dead against such a thing as the birth of a child to that aged pair. The experience of many years said, "It cannot be." The nature and reason of the case said, "It cannot be." Any council of human friends and advisers would have instantly said, "It cannot be!" And Abraham quietly considered and weighed them all "without being weakened in faith" (Rom. 4:19). Then he as carefully looked unto the promise of God. And, rising from his consideration of the comparative weight of the one and the other, he elected to venture everything on the word of the Eternal.

His faith was destined to be severely tried. Some men pass through life without much trial, because their natures are light and trivial, and incapable of bearing much, or of profiting by the severe discipline which, in the case of others, is all needed, and will yield a rich recompense, after it has had its perfect work. God will not let any one of us be tried beyond what we are able to bear. But when He has in hand a nature like Abraham's, which is capable of the loftiest results, we must not be surprised if the trial is long continued, almost to the last limit of endurance. The patriarch had to wait fifteen years more, making five-and-twenty years in all, between the first promise and its fulfilment in the birth of Isaac.

His faith was counted to him for righteousness. Faith is the seed germ of righteousness; and, when God sees us possessed of the seed, He counts us as also being in possession of the harvest which lies hidden in its heart.

But there is a deeper meaning still than this—in the possession through faith of a judicial righteousness in the sight of God. The righteousness of Abraham resulted not from his works, but from his faith. "He believed God; and it was reckoned unto him for righteousness." "Now it was not written for his sake alone, that it was reckoned unto him; but for our sake also, unto whom it shall be reckoned, who believe on Him that raised Jesus our Lord from the dead" (Gal. 3:6; Rom. 4:23, 24). We cannot realize all that is included in those marvelous words. This only is evident, that faith unites us so absolutely to the Son of God that we are one with Him for evermore; and all the glory of His character—not only what He was when He became obedient unto death, but what He is in the majesty of His risen nature—is reckoned unto us.

11
Watching with God
Genesis 15

It is not easy to watch with God, or to wait for Him. The orbit of His providence is so vast. The stages of His progress are so wide apart. He holds on His way through the ages; we tire in a few short hours. And when His dealings with us are perplexing and mysterious, the heart that had boasted its unwavering loyalty begins to grow faint with misgivings, and to question—When shall we be able to trust absolutely, and not be afraid?

At this stage, at least, of his education, Abraham had not learned this lesson. But in that grey dawn, as the stars which symbolized his posterity were beginning to fade in the sky, he answered the Divine assurance that he should inherit the land of which he as yet did not own a foot, by the sad complaint: "Lord God, whereby shall I know that I shall inherit it?" (v. 8).

How human this is! It was not that he was absolutely incredulous: but he yearned for some tangible evident token that it was to be as God had said. Do not wonder at him; but rather adore the love which bears with these human frailties, and stoops to give them stepping stones by which to cross the sands to the firm rock of an assured faith.

Watching by the Sacrifice
In those early days, when a written agreement was very rare, the contracting party was required to bring certain animals, which were slaughtered and divided into pieces. These were

laid on the ground in such a manner as to leave a narrow lane between; up and down which the covenanting party passed to ratify and confirm his solemn pledge.

It was to this ancient and solemn rite that Jehovah referred, when he said, "Take Me an heifer of three years old, and a she-goat of three years old, and a ram of three years old, and a turtledove, and a young pigeon. And he took unto him all these, and divided them in the midst, and laid each piece one against another" (vv. 8, 10).

It was still the early morning. Abraham sat down to watch. Hour after hour passed by; but God did not give a sign or utter a single word. Higher and higher the sun drove his chariot up the sky, but still no voice or vision came. Did Abraham ever permit himself to imagine that he was sitting there on a fool's mission? Did he shrink from the curious gaze of his servants, and of Sarah his wife, because half-conscious of having taken up a position he could not justify?

We cannot tell what passed through that much-tried heart during those long hours. But this, at least, we recognize; that this is in line with the discipline through which we all have to pass. Hours of waiting for God! Days of watching! Nights of sleepless vigil! Looking for the outposts of the relief that tarries! But all in vain! Nay, but it is not in vain. For these long waiting hours are building up the fabric of the spirit-life, so as to become a thing of beauty, and a joy for evermore.

Only let us see to it that we never relax our attitude of patience, but wait to the end for the grace to be brought unto us.

The Horror of a Great Darkness

The sun at last went down, and the swift Eastern night cast its heavy veil over the scene. Worn out with the mental conflict, the watchings, and the exertions of the day, Abraham fell into a deep sleep. And "Lo, a horror of great darkness fell upon him" (v. 12).

It was a long and dark prospect which unfolded itself before Abraham. He beheld the history of his people through coming centuries, strangers in a foreign land, enslaved and afflicted. Treasure-city, cemented by blood and suffering? It was, indeed, enough to fill him with darkness that could be felt.

And yet the sombre woof was crossed by the warp of silver threads. The enslaved were to come out, and to come out with great substance, their oppresors being overwhelmed with crushing judgment. They were to come into that land again. While, as for himself, he should go to his fathers in peace, and be buried in a good old age.

It is thus that human life is made up: brightness and gloom; shadow and sun; long tracks of cloud, succeeded by brilliant glints of light. And amid all, Divine justice is working out its own schemes, affecting others equally with the individual soul which seems the subject of especial discipline.

Oh, ye who are filled with the horror of great darkness because of God's dealings with mankind, learn to trust that infallible wisdom which is co-assessor with immutable justice; and know that He who passed through the horror of the darkness of Calvary, with the cry of forsakenness, is ready to bear you company through the valley of the shadow of death, till you see the sun shining upon its further side.

The Ratification of the Covenant

When Abraham awoke, the sun was down. Darkness reigned supreme. A solemn stillness brooded over the world. Then came the awful act of ratification. For the first time since man left the gates of Eden there appeared the symbol of the glory of God; that awful light which was afterwards to shine in the pillar of cloud, and the Shekinah gleam.

In the thick darkness, that mysterious light—a lamp of fire—passed slowly and majestically between the divided pieces; and, as it did so, a voice said: "Unto thy seed have I given this land, from the river of Egypt unto the great river, the river Euphrates" (v. 18).

Remember that promise: made with the most solemn sanctions, never repealed since, and never perfectly fulfilled. For a few years during the reign of Solomon the dominions of Israel almost touched these limits, but only for a very brief period. The perfect fulfillment is yet in the future. Somehow the descendants of Abraham shall yet inherit their own land, secured to them by the covenant of God. Those rivers shall yet form their boundary lines: for "the mouth of the Lord hath spoken it."

As we turn from this scene—in which God bound Himself by such solemn sanctions, to strengthen the ground of His servant's faith—we may carry with us exalted conceptions of His great goodness, which will humble itself so low in order to secure the trust of one poor heart. By two immutable things, His word and oath, God has given strong assurance to us who are menaced by the storm, drawing us on to a rock-bound shore. Let us, by our Forerunner, send forward our anchor, Hope, within the vail that parts us from the unseen: where it will grapple in ground that will not yield, but hold until the day dawn, and we follow it into the haven guaranteed to us by God's immutable counsel (Heb. 6:19, 20).

12

Hagar, the Slave Girl

Genesis 16

There is here a very startling manifestation of the tenacity with which Abraham's self-life still survived. We might have expected that by this time it had been extinguished: the long waiting of ten slow-moving years: the repeated promises of God: the habit of contact with God Himself—all this had surely been enough to eradicate and burn out all confidence in the flesh; all trust in the activities of the self-life; all desire to help himself to the realization of the promises of God. Surely, now, this much-tried man will wait until, in His own time and way, God shall do as He has said.

Instead of this he listened to *the reasoning of expediency,* which happened to chime in with his own thoughts, and sought to gratify the promptings of his spirit by doing something to secure the result of which God had spoken. Simple-hearted faith waits for God to unfold His purpose, sure that He will not fail.

Sarah's Temptation

"Sarai said unto Abram" (v. 2). Poor Sarah! It was clear that Abraham should have a son; but it was not definitely said by God that the child would be hers. Abraham was a strict monogamist; but the laxer notions of those days warranted the filling of the harem with others, who occupied an inferior rank to that of the principal wife, and whose children, according to common practice, were reckoned as if they were her own. Why should not her husband fall in with those laxer notions of the marriage vow?

It was an heroic sacrifice for her to make. She was willing to forego a woman's dearest prerogative; to put another in her own place; and to surrender a position to which she had a perfect right to cling, even though it seemed to clash with the direct promise of God. But her love to Abraham; her despair of having a child of her own; and her inability to conceive of God fulfilling His word by other than natural means—all these things combined to make the proposal from which, in another aspect, her wifely nature must have shrunk.

No one else could have approached Abraham with such a proposition, with the slightest hope of success. But when Sarah made it, the case was altered. It was supported by the susceptibilities of natural instinct. It was consistent with the whisperings of doubt. It seemed to be a likely expedient for realizing God's promise. And without demur, or reference to God, he fell in with the proposal. "Abram hearkened to the voice of Sarai."

It is always hard to resist temptation when it appeals to natural instinct or to distrusting fear. But the temptation is still more perilous when it is presented by some object of our love; who, like Sarah, has been the partner of our pilgrimage, and who is willing to sacrifice all in order to obtain a blessing which God has promised, but has not yet bestowed.

The Resulting Sorrow

As soon as the end was obtained, the results, like a crop of nettles, began to appear in that home, which had been the abode of purity and bliss; but which was now destined to be the scene of discord.

If any should read these words who are tempted to use any expedients of human devising for the attainment of ends, which in themselves may be quite legitimate, let them stand still, and take to heart the teachings of this narrative. For, as surely as God reigns, shall every selfish expedient involve us in unutterable and heartrending sorrow.

Hagar's Comfort
We cannot be surprised at the insolent bearing of the untutored slave-girl. But, taken as she was from her true station, and put into a position in which she was a mother without being a lawful wife, what could her lot be but misery in the home in which she had no proper status, and where the irate mistress dealt so bitterly with the girl that she fled from her face, and took the road, trodden by the caravans, towards her native land.

"The angel of the Lord" (and here, for the first time, that significant expression is used, which is held by many to express some evident manifestation of the Son of God in angel-guise) "found her by a well of water" (v. 7) which was familiarly known in the days of Moses. There, worn, and weary, and lonely, she sat down to rest. There followed the distinct command, "Return, and submit." The day would come when God Himself would open the door, and send Hagar out of that house (Gen. 21:12-14). But until that moment should come, after thirteen years had rolled away, she must return to the place which she had left, bearing her burden and fulfilling her duty as best she might.

Meanwhile the heart of the prodigal is cheered by promise (v. 10). The Angel of the Lord unfolds all the blessed results of obedience. And as the spirit considers these, it finds the homeward way no longer lined by flints, but soft with flowers.

Nor is this all: in addition to promise, there breaks on the soul the conception of One who lives and sees: who lives to avenge the wronged, and to defend the helpless; and who sees each tear and pang of the afflicted soul.

Let us often stay the whirr of life's shuttles to say softly to ourselves, "God is here; God is near; God sees—He will provide; He will defend; He will avenge." "The eyes of the

Lord run to and fro throughout the whole earth, to show Himself strong in the behalf of them whose heart is perfect toward Him" (2 Chron. 16:9; Zech. 4:10).

13

Be Thou Perfect!

Genesis 17

Thirteen long years passed slowly on after the return of Hagar to Abraham's camp. The child Ishmael was born, and grew up in the patriarch's house—the acknowledged heir of the camp, and yet showing symptoms of the wild-ass nature of which the angel had spoken (Gen. 16:12). Not a little perplexed must Abraham have been with those strange manifestations; and yet the heart of the old man warmed to the lad, and clung to him, often asking that Ishmael might live before God.

And throughout that long period there was no fresh appearance, no new announcement. Never since God had spoken to him in Charran had there been so long a pause. And it must have been a terrible ordeal, driving him back on the promise which had been given, and searching his heart to ascertain if the cause lay within himself. Such silences have always exercised the hearts of God's saints, leading them to say with the Psalmist: "Be not silent to me; lest, if Thou be silent to me, I become like them that go down into the pit" (Ps. 28:1). And yet they are to the heart what the long silence of winter is to the world of nature, in preparing it for the outburst of spring.

At last, "when Abram was ninety years old and nine," the Lord appeared unto him again, and gave him a new revelation of Himself; unfolded the terms of His covenant; and addressed to him that memorable charge, which rings its summons in the ear and heart of every believer still: "Walk before Me, and be thou perfect" (v. 1).

The Divine Summons

"Walk before Me, and be thou perfect." "Perfection" is often supposed to denote sinlessness of moral character, which at the best is only a negative conception, and fails to bring out the positive force of this mighty word. Surely perfection means more than—sinlessness. And if this be admitted, and the further admission be made, that it contains the thought of moral completeness, then it becomes yet more absurd for any mortal to assert it of himself.

Besides all this, the word "perfect" bears very different renderings from those often given to it. For instance, when we are told that the man of God must be *perfect* (2 Tim. 3:17), the underlying thought, as any scholar would affirm, is that of a workman being "thoroughly equipped for his work," as when a carpenter comes to the house, bearing in his hand the bag in which all necessary tools are readily available. Again, when we join in the prayer that the God of Peace would make us *perfect* in every good work to do His will, we are, in fact, asking that we may be "put in joint" with the blessed Lord; so that the glorious Head may freely secure through us the doing of His will (Heb. 13:20, 21). Again, when our Lord bids us be *perfect* as our Father in heaven is perfect, He simply incites us to that "impartiality of mercy" which knows no distinctions of evil and good, of unjust and just, but distributes its favors with bountiful and equal hand (Matt. 5:48).

What, then, is the true force and significance of this word in that stirring command which lies before us here, "Walk before Me, and be thou perfect"? A comparison of the various passages where it occurs establishes its meaning beyond a doubt, and compels us to think into it the conception of "whole heartedness."

This quality of wholehearted devotion has ever been dear to God. It was this that He considered in Job, and loved in

David. It is in favor of this that His eyes run to and fro to show Himself strong (2 Chron. 16:9). It is for this that He pleads with Abraham; and it was because He met with it to so large an extent in his character and obedience that He entered into eternal covenant bond with him and his.

And such an attitude can only be *maintained by a very careful walk.* "Walk before Me, and be thou perfect." We must seek to realize constantly the presence of God. We must cultivate the habit of feeling Him near, as the Friend from whom we would never be separated, in work, in prayer, in recreation, in repose. We must guard against the restlessness and impetuosity, the excessive eagerness and impatience, which drowns the accents of His still, small voice. We must abjure all expedients He does not inspire, all actions He does not promote. We must often turn from the friend, the poem, the landscape, or the task, to look up into His face with a smile of loving recognition. And yet we shall not live forced or unnatural lives. All the circles of our daily life will move on in unbroken order and beauty; just as each shining moon circles around its planet, because the planet obeys the law of gravitation to the sun. Would you walk before God? Then let there be nothing in heart or life which you would not open to the inspection of His holy and pitiful eye.

The Divine Revelation

"I am the Almighty God" (*'El-shaddai'*). In God's dealings with men you will invariably find that some transcendent revelation precedes the Divine summons to new and difficult duty; promise opens the door to precept: He gives what He commands, ere He commands what He wills. And on this principle God acted here. It was no child's play to which He called His servant. To walk always before Him—when heart was weak, and strength was frail, and the temptation strong to swerve to right or left. To be perfect in devotion and obedience, when so many crosslights distracted, and per-plexed, and fascinated the soul. To forego all methods of self-help, however tempting. To be separated from all alliances that others permitted or followed. This was much. And it was only possible through the might of the Almighty. And, therefore, it was that there broke on him the assurance: "I am the Almighty God."

All this is as true today as ever. And if any will dare venture forth on the path of separation, cutting themselves aloof from all creature aid, and from all self-originated effort; content to walk alone with God, with no help from any but Him—such will find that all the resources of the Divine Almightiness will be placed at their disposal, and that the resources of Omnipotence must be exhausted ere their cause can fail for want of help.

The Divine Covenant

"I will make My covenant between Me and thee" (v. 2). A covenant is a promise made under the most solemn sanctions, and binding the consenting parties in the most definite and impressive way. What mortal would not consent when the Almighty God proposed to enter into an everlasting covenant with His creature, ordered in all things and sure, and more stable than the everlasting hills!

And there was a marked advance. In Haran it ran thus, "I will make of thee a great nation." At Bethel, thus, "Thy seed shall be as the dust of the earth." At Mamre, thus, "Tell the stars; so shall thy seed be." But now, three times over, the patriarch is told that he should be the father of many nations, a phrase explained by the Apostle as including all, of every land, who share Abraham's faith, though not sprung from him in the line of natural descent (Gal. 3:7-29). *We* are included in the golden circle of those words, if we believe; and we may claim the spiritual part, at least, of this covenant, which was made with Abraham before he was circumcised.

"I will give unto thee, and to thy seed after thee, the land wherein thou art a stranger, all the land of Canaan, for an everlasting possession" (v. 8). This promise has been partially fulfilled by the foundation of Israel.

Till then Abraham had no other thought than that Ishmael

should be his heir. But this could not be: (1) because he was slave born; and the slave abideth not in the house for ever; (2) because he was a child of the flesh, and not the direct gift of God. Abraham had been left to wait till the hope of children had become as remote from him as it had been for years from his wife; so that the heir should be evidently the creation of the Almighty God, whose name was disclosed, ere this astounding announcement was made. This is why we are kept waiting till all human and natural hope has died from our hearts, so that God may be All in all. "And God said, Sarah thy wife shall bear thee a son indeed; and thou shalt call his name Isaac" (v. 19).

For us there is yet a crowning sweetness in the words, "I will be a God unto thee, and to thy seed"; words repeated, in Hebrews 8:10, so as certainly to include us all, if we believe. Who can unfold all the wealth of meaning of these words? All light, and no darkness at all. All love, and no shadow of change. All strength, and no sign of weakness. Beauty, sweetness, glory, majesty, all are in God, and all these will be thine and mine, if God saith to us, "I will be a God unto thee."

14

The Sign of the Covenant

Genesis 17

Three times over in Scripture Abraham is called "the friend of God" (II Chron. 20:7; James 2:23; Isaiah 41:8). And it would almost appear as if these two chapters, Genesis 17 and 18, had been written for this, among other things: to show the familiarity and intimacy which existed between the Eternal God and the man who was honored to be called His "friend." But it is surely also intended as a specimen of the way in which the Eternal God is willing to deal with true-hearted saints in all ages. To hundreds, and perhaps thousands, of His saints, God has been all that He was to Abraham; and He is willing to be all that to us still.

Oh, *friends of God!* why do you not make more of your transcendent privileges? Why do you not talk to Him about all that wearies and worries you, as freely as Abraham did, telling Him about your Ishmaels, your Lots, and His dealings? Why do you not fall on your faces while God talks with you (v. 3)? Life should be one long talk between God and us. No day at least should close without our talking over its history with our patient and loving Lord; entering into His confessional; relieving our hearts of half their sorrow, and all their bitterness, in the act of telling Him all. And if only we get low enough, and be still enough, we shall hear His accents sweet and thrilling, soft and low, opening depths which eye hath not seen, nor ear heard; but which He has prepared for those who love and wait for Him.

There are, however, three conditions to be fulfilled by us if we would enjoy this blessed friendship: *separation, purity,* and *obedience,* each of which was set forth in the rite of circumcision, which was given to Abraham for himself and his descendants at this time.

We are all of us more or less dependent on outward symbols and signs; and Abraham and his children were no exception to this rule; and it therefore seemed good to God to carve in the flesh of His people an unmistakable reminder and sacrament of that holy relationship into which they had entered. A similar function, in the Christian Church, is met by the sacraments of baptism and the Lord's Supper.

As in so many other Jewish rites, there was an inner spirit, which passed on into the Christian Church, and is our heritage today. St. Paul, the deadly foe of the empty rite, speaks of the spiritual circumcision, and says it is made without human hands, by the direct interposition of the Holy Spirit: and that it consists in "the putting-off of the body of the sins of the flesh" (Col. 2:11). "For we are the circumcision, which worship God in the Spirit, and rejoice in Christ Jesus, and have no confidence in the flesh" (Phil. 3:3).

It is only in proportion as we know the spiritual meaning of circumcision that we can enter into the joyous appropriation of the friendship of God. But if we are willing, our Lord and Saviour is both able and willing to effect in us this blessed spiritual result.

Separation

Abraham and his seed were marked out by this rite as a separated people. And it is only as such that any of us can be admitted into the friendship of God. Blood-shedding and death—the cross and the grave—must lie between us and our own past life; yea, between us and all complicity with evil. The only trysting place for Christ and His followers is outside the camp, where the ground is still freshly trodden by the feet of the exiled King.

This was the key to Abraham's life; and is the inner meaning of the rite of circumcision.

Purity

"Putting off of the body of the flesh by the circumcision of Christ" (Col. 2:11). Purity can be attained only by the special grace of the Holy Spirit; and by doing two things: first, by our turning instantly from paragraphs in papers, or pictures on the walls, and all things else, which excite impure imaginations; secondly, by our seeking immediate forgiveness, when we are conscious of having yielded, even for a moment, to the deadly and insidious fascinations of the flesh.

There are some who sigh after the white rose of chastity, with a kind of despair that it should ever become their own. They forget that it is only possible to us by the grace of Christ, and through the Holy Spirit; whose temples we profess ourselves to be. Let us trust Him to keep His own property in the perfect loveliness of that purity and chastity which are so dear to God; this is the circumcision of Christ.

Obedience

For Abraham this rite might have seemed less necessary than for some in his camp. But no sooner was it commanded than it was undergone. "In the self-same day was Abraham circumcised, and Ishmael his son" (v. 26). Does it not remind us of Him who said, "Ye are My friends, if ye do whatsoever I command you"? (John 11:14). Instant obedience to known duty is an indispensable condition of all intimacy with God: and if the duty be irksome and difficult, then remember to claim all the more of the Divine grace; for there is no duty, to which we are called, for the discharge of which there is not strength enough within reach, if only we will put forth our hands to take it.

We do not obey in order to become friends; but having become friends we hasten to obey. Love is more inexorable than law. And for the love of Him who calls us by so dear a title, we are glad to undertake and accomplish what Sinai with all its thunders would fail to nerve us to attempt.

15

The Divine Guest

Genesis 18

There is no doubt as to the august character of one of the
three who, on that memorable afternoon, when every living
thing was seeking shelter during the heat of the day, visited
the tent of the patriarch. In the first verse we are expressly
told that Jehovah appeared unto Abraham in the plains of
Mamre, as he sat in the tent door in the heat of the day. And
in the tenth verse there is the accent of Deity, who alone can
create life, and to whom nothing is too hard, in the words of
promise which tell how certainly Sarah should have a son.
And, besides, we are told that two angels came to Sodom at
even. Evidently they were two of the three who had sat as
Abraham's guests beneath the tree which sheltered his tent
in the blazing noon. But as for the other, who throughout the
wondrous hours had been the only spokesman, His dignity
is disclosed in the amazing colloquy which took place on the
heights of Mamre, when Abraham stood yet before the Lord,
and pleaded with Him as the Judge of all the earth.

It was thus that the Son of God anticipated His incarnation; and was found in fashion as a man before He became
flesh. He loved to come *incognito* into the homes of those He
cherished as His friends, even before He came across the
slopes of Olivet to make His home in the favored cottage,
where His spirit rested from the din of the great city, and
girded itself for the cross and the tomb. "He rejoiced in the

habitable part of the earth, and His delights were with the sons of men" (Prov. 8:31).

Abraham evidently, at the outset, did not realize the full meaning of the episode in which he was taking part. Even so do we often fail to value aright characters with whom we come in contact. It is only as they pass away from us for ever, and we look back upon them, that we realize that we have been entertaining angels unawares. Let us so act always and everywhere, that as we review the past we may have nothing to regret; and may not have to reproach ourselves with having omitted to do something or other, which we would have inserted in our program had we only realized our opportunities.

Abraham's Hospitality

Abraham treated his visitors with true Eastern hospitality. He *ran* to meet them, and bowed himself toward the ground. He proposed water for their feet, and rest for their tired frames, beneath the spreading shadow. He started his wife to the immediate kneading of the meal for baking on the scorching stones. He ran to choose his tenderest calf, refusing to delegate the work to another's hand. He served his visitors himself, and stood as a servant by their side, under the tree, while they did eat. Christians have not much to boast of—and a good deal to learn—as they consider the action of this old-time saint, and his dealings with the three strangers who came to his tent. The faith which he had towards God had a very winsome aspect towards men. There was nothing in him which was austere or forbidding; but much that was exceedingly lovely, and brimming with the milk of human kindness.

Christ in Disguise

But we are too busy, or too tired, or too much afraid of making a mistake; and, therefore, we either refuse Him altogether, or we treat Him so badly that He passes unobserved away, to carry to some one else the blessing which He would have left with us had we only shown ourselves worthy.

There was much truth in the simplicity of the little German lad, who left the door open for the Lord to enter and sit with his mother and himself at their frugal supper table; and who, as a beggar stood within the portal, asking alms, remarked: "Perhaps the Lord could not come Himself, and had therefore sent this poor man as His representative."

God's Largess

He takes care to pay for His entertainment, royally and divinely. He uses Peter's fishing smack, and gives it back, nearly submerged by the weight of the fish which He had driven into the nets. He sits down with His friends to a country marriage feast, and pays for their simple fare by jars brimming with water turned to wine. He uses the five barley loaves and two small fishes; but He fills the lad with an ample meal. He sends His prophet to lodge with a widow, and provides meal and oil for him and her for many days. And Abraham was no loser by his ready hospitality; for, as they sat at meat, the Lord foretold the birth of Sarah's child: "I will certainly return unto thee; and Sarah thy wife shall have a son" (v. 10).

Sarah was sitting inside the flimsy curtain of camel's hair, secluded after the Eastern fashion for those of high rank; and as she heard the words, she laughed within herself the laugh of incredulity. That laugh was at once noticed by Him from whom nothing can be hid, and whose eyes are as a flame of fire. "And the Lord said unto Abraham, Wherefore did Sarah laugh, saying, Shall I of a surety bear a child, which am old? Is anything too hard for the Lord?" (vv. 13, 14).

These were the only audible words which we know to have passed between God and Abraham's wife; and they reveal the superficiality and unbelief of her nature. But we must not judge her too harshly, for she had not had the opportunities of her husband. However, she seems to have been led by these words into a true faith; for it is said, "By faith also Sarah herself received strength to conceive seed, and was delivered of a child when she was past age, because she judged Him faithful who had promised" (Heb. 11:11).

The True Law of Faith
Do not look at your faith or at your feelings; but look away to the word of promise, and, above all, to the Promiser.

Has He ever failed to keep His word? Is there any conceivable reason why He should not keep it? His power is omnipotent; and would He ever have pledged Himself to do what He could not effect? "He is faithful that promised." Look from faith to the promise, and from the promise to the Promiser. And as we become conscious of possessing the power of vision while we look on any object to which we may direct our gaze, so we shall become conscious of the presence and growth of faith as we look away to our faithful God.

God's Power
"Is anything too hard for the Lord?" That is one of God's unanswered questions. It has lain there for three thousand years, perused by myriads, answered by none; unless, indeed, those words of Jeremiah are the only answer which mortal men can give: "Ah, Lord God! behold, Thou hast made the heaven and the earth by Thy great power and stretched-out arm; and there is nothing too hard for Thee" (Jer. 32:17).

The one thing that hinders God is our unbelief. Sarah must believe, and Abraham also, ere the child of promise could be born. And so must it be with us. As soon as we believe, then, according to our faith it is done to us; yea, exceeding abundantly beyond all we had asked or thought.

You ask how to obtain this faith. Remember that faith is the receptive attitude of the soul, begotten and maintained by the grace of God. Christ is the Author and Finisher of faith; not only in the abstract, but in the personal experience of the soul. Faith is the gift of God. If, then, you would receive it, put your will on the side of Christ; not a passing wish, but the whole will of your being: will to believe patiently, persistently, yearningly; let your eyes be ever toward the Lord; study the promises of God; consider the nature of God; be prepared to be rid of everything that grieves His Holy Spirit; and it is as certain as the truth of Christ, that you will have begotten and maintained in you the faith that can move mountains, and laugh at impossibilities.

16

Pleading for Sodom

Genesis 18

As the day wore on, Abraham's mysterious guests went off across the hills towards Sodom; and Abraham went with them to bring them on their way. But all three did not reach the guilty city, over which the thunderclouds had already commenced to gather. That evening two angels entered it alone. And where was their companion? Ah! He had stayed behind to talk yet further with His friend.

Abraham was the "friend of God"; and friendship constitutes a claim to be entrusted with secrets hidden from all beside. "The secret of the Lord is with them that fear Him." "Henceforth," said the Master to His disciples, "I call you not servants; for the servant knoweth not what his lord doeth; but I have called you friends; for all things that I have heard of My Father I have made known unto you" (John 15:15). If we live near God, we shall have many things revealed to us which are hidden from the wise and prudent.

But the words which follow point to a yet further reason for the full disclosures that were made: "For I know him, that he will command his children and his household after him; and they shall keep the way of the Lord, to do justice and judgment" (v. 19). Was there a fear lest Abraham and his children might doubt the justice of the judgment of God if the righteous were summarily cut off with the wicked; and if the cities of the plain were destroyed without a revelation of their sin on the one hand, and the display of the Divine

mercy on the other? Certainly it has placed the Divine character in an altogether different light, in that we have been
permitted, in such a case as this, to understand some of the
motives which have actuated God in His goodness or severity.

The Divine Announcement

"The cry of Sodom and Gomorrah is great" (v. 20). Quiet
though Sodom seemed in the far distance, and in the hush of
the closing day; yet to God there was a cry. The cry of the
earth compelled to carry such a scar. The cry of inanimate
creation, groaning and travailing in pain. The cry of the oppressed, the downtrodden—the victims of human violence
and lust. These were the cries which had entered into the
ears of the Lord God of Sabaoth. And each sin has a cry. And,
if each sin has a cry, what must not be the volume of sound
for a life, and for a city! Must not God still have to say of our
great cities, one by one?—"Its cry is great; and its sin is very
grievous."

"I will go down now, and see" (v. 21). God always narrowly investigates the true condition of the case, before He
awards or executes His sentences. He comes seeking fruit for
three years, before He gives the order for the cutting down of
the tree that cumbered the vineyard soil. He walks our streets
day and night. He patrols our thoroughfares, marking everything, missing nothing. He glides unasked into our most
sacred privacy; for all things are naked and open unto the
eyes of Him with whom we have to do. He is prepared, nay,
eager to give us the benefit of any excuse. But flagrant sin,
like that which broke out in Sodom that very night, is
enough to settle for ever the fate of a Godless community
when standing at the bar of Him who is Judge and Witness
both.

The Impact of the Announcement

So soon as the angels had gone on, leaving Abraham alone
with the Lord, he was thoroughly aroused by the revelation

which had broken upon him; and his mind was filled with a tumult of emotion. He hardly dared expostulate with God. And yet he was impelled to make some attempt to avert the doom that threatened the cities of the plain.

The motives that prompted him were twofold: 1) *There was a natural anxiety about his kinsman, Lot.* Twenty years had passed since Lot had left him; but he had never ceased to follow him with the most tender affection. And now the strong impulse of natural affection stirred him to make one strenuous effort to save Sodom, lest his nephew might be overwhelmed in its overthrow. Real religion tends not to destroy, but to fulfil all the impulses of true natural love.

2) *There was also a fear lest the total destruction of the cities of the plain might prejudice the character of God in the minds of the neighboring peoples.* Abraham did not deny that the fate which was about to overtake them was deserved by many of the people of that enervating and luxuriant valley: but he feared that if all were summarily swept away, the surrounding nations would have a handle of reproach against the justice of his God, and would accuse Him of unrighteousness, inasmuch as He destroyed the righteous with the wicked.

The character of God has ever been dear to His true-hearted servants of every age. Moses was prepared to forego the honor of being the ancestor of the chosen people, rather than that the nations which had heard of the Divine fame should be able to say that God was not able to bring them into the Land of Promise. And when the men of Israel fled before Ai, Joshua and the elders appear to have thought less of the danger of an immediate rising to cut them off than of what God would do for His great name. Oh for more of this chivalrous devotion to the interests and glory of our God!

This passion for the glory of God burnt with a clear strong flame in Abraham's heart; and it was out of this that there arose his wondrous intercession. And when we become as closely identified with the interests of God as he was, we shall come to feel as he did; and shall be eager that the Divine character should be vindicated amongst the children of men.

Abraham's Intercession

It was lonely prayer. He waited till on all that wide plateau, and beneath those arching skies, there was no living man to overhear this marvelous outpouring of a soul overcharged, as are the pools, when, after the rains of spring, they overflow their banks. "He stood before the Lord." It is fatal to all the intensest, strongest devotion to pray always in the presence of another, even the dearest. Every saint must have a closet, of which he can shut the door, and in which he can pray to the Father which is in secret.

It was prolonged prayer. "Abraham stood yet before the Lord" (v. 22). The story takes but a few moments to read; but the scene may have lasted for the space of hours. We cannot climb the more elevated pinnacles of prayer in a hasty rush. They demand patience, toil, prolonged endeavor, ere the lower slopes can be left, and the brooding cloud line passed, and the aspiring soul can reach that cleft in the mountain side, where Moses stood beneath the shadow of God's hand. Of course, our God is ever on the alert to hear and answer those prayers which, like machine guns, we fire throughout the day; but we cannot maintain this posture of ejaculatory prayer unless we cultivate the prolonged occasions.

It was very humble prayer. "Behold, now, I have taken upon me to speak unto the Lord, which am but dust and ashes" (v. 27). The nearer we get to God, the more conscious are we of our own unworthiness. The man who lives in touch with God does not think of taking any other position than that of lowliest humiliation and prostration in His presence. Before Him angels veil their faces, and the heavens are not clean in His sight. And is it not remarkable that our sense of weakness is one of our strongest claims and arguments with God? "He forgetteth not the cry of the humble." "To that man will I look who trembleth."

This prayer was persevering. *Six times* Abraham returned to the charge, and as each petition was granted, his faith and courage grew; and, finding he had struck a right vein, he worked it again, and yet again. It looks at first sight as if he forced God back from point to point, and wrung his petitions from an unwilling hand. But this is a mistake. In point of fact, *God was drawing him on;* and if he had dared to ask at first what he asked at the last, he would have got more than all that he asked or thought at the very commencement of his intercession. This was the time of his education.

It is so that God educates us still. In ever-widening circles, He tempts His new-fledged eaglets to try the sustaining elasticity of the air. He forces us to ask one thing; and then another, and yet another. And when we have asked our utmost, there are always unexplored remainders behind; and He does exceeding abundantly above all. There were not ten righteous men in Sodom; but Lot and his wife, and his two daughters, were saved, though three of them were deeply infected with the moral contagion of the place. And God's righteousness was clearly established and vindicated in the eyes of the surrounding peoples.

In closing, we remark *one of the great principles in the Divine government of the world.* A whole city had been spared, if ten righteous men had been found within its walls. Ah, how little the world realizes the debt it owes to its saints, the salt to stay its corruption, the light to arrest the reinstitution of the reign of chaos and night! We cannot but yearn over the world, as it rolls on its way towards its sad dark doom. Let us plead for it from the heights above Mamre. And may we and our beloved ones be led out from it into safety, ere the last plagues break full upon it in inevitable destruction!

17
A Bit of the Old Nature
Genesis 20

For long years an evil may lurk in our hearts, permitted and unjudged, breeding failure and sorrow in our lives. But that which escapes our ken is patent in all its naked deformity to the eye of God. "The darkness and the light are both alike to Him" (Ps. 139:12). And He will so direct the discipline of our lives as to set in clear prominence the deadly evil which He hates; so that, when He has laid bare the cancerous growth, He may bring us to long for and invite the knife which shall set us free from it forever.

These words have been suggested by the thirteenth verse of this chapter, which indicates an evil compact, into which Abraham had entered with Sarah some thirty years before the time of which we write. "And it came to pass, when God caused me to wander from my father's house, that I said unto my wife, This is thy kindness which thou shalt show unto me; at every place whither we shall come, say of me, He is my brother."

This secret compact between Abraham and his wife, in the earliest days of his exodus, was due to his slender faith in God's power to take care of them, which again sprang from his limited experience of his Almighty Friend. In this we may find its sole excuse. But it ought long before this to have been cancelled by mutual consent.

The judgment and eradication of this lurking evil were therefore necessary, and were brought about in this wise.

The day before Sodom's fall, the Almighty told Abraham that, at a set time in the following year, he should have a son and heir. And we should have expected that he would have spent the slow-moving months beneath the oak of Mamre, already hallowed by so many associations. But such was not the case. It has been suggested that he was too horrified at the overthrow of the cities of the plain, to be able to remain any longer in the vicinity. All further association with the spot was distasteful to him. Or it may have been that another famine was threatening. But in any case "he journeyed from hence towards the south country, and dwelled between Kadesh and Shur, and sojourned in Gerar" (Gen. 20:1).

Here, the almost forgotten agreement between Sarah and himself offered itself as a ready expedient, behind which Abraham's unbelief took shelter. He knew the ungoverned license of his time, unbridled by the fear of God (v. 11). He dreaded, lest the heathen monarch, enamored with Sarah's beauty, or ambitious to get her into his power for purposes of state policy, might slay him for his wife's sake. And so he again resorted to the paltry policy of calling her his sister. As if God could not have defended him and her, screening them from all evil; as He had done so often in days gone by.

Abraham's Cowardice

He risked Sarah's virtue, and the purity of the promised seed. And, even if we accept the justification of his conduct proposed by some, who argue that he was so sure of the seed promised him by God that he could dare to risk what otherwise he would have more carefully guarded, his faith leading him into the license of presumption, yet, it was surely very mean on his part to permit Sarah to pass through any ordeal of the sort. If he had such superabundant faith, he might have risked his own safety at the hand of Abimelech rather than Sarah's virtue.

It was also very dishonoring to God. Among those untutored tribes Abraham was well known as the servant of Jehovah. And they could not but judge of the character of

Him whom they could not see, by the traits they discerned in His servant, whom they knew in familiar intercourse. Alas that Abraham's standard was lower than their own! so much so that Abimelech was able to rebuke him, saying: "Thou hast brought on me and on my kingdom a great sin: thou hast done deeds unto me that ought not to be done" (v. 9).

It is heart breaking, when the healthen rebukes a profesor of superior godliness for speaking lies. Yet it is lamentable to confess that such men often enough have higher standards of morality than those who profess godliness. Even if they do not fulfil their own conceptions, yet the beauty of their ideal is undeniable, and is a remarkable vindication of the universal vitality of conscience. Let us walk circumspectly towards them that are without; adorning in all things the Gospel of Jesus Christ; and giving no occasion to the enemy to blaspheme, save as it concerns the law of our God.

Abraham and Abimelech

As to his original character, Abimelech commends himself to us as the nobler of the two. He rises early in the morning, prompt to set the great wrong right. He warns his people. He restores Sarah with munificent presents. His reproach and rebuke are spoken in the gentlest, kindest tones. He simply tells Sarah that her position as the wife of a prophet would, not in Philistia only, but wherever they might come, be a sufficient security and veil (v. 16). There is the air of high-minded nobility in his behavior throughout this crisis which is exceedingly winsome.

It would almost appear as if the Spirit of God took delight in showing that the original texture of God's saints was not higher than that of other men, nor indeed so high. He seems to delight to secure His choicest results in natures which men of the world might reject as hopelessly bad. He demands no assistance from us, so sure is He that when once faith is admitted as the root principle of character, all other things will be added to it.

Oh, critics of God's handiwork, we do not deny the incon-

sistencies of a David, a Peter, or an Abraham; but we insist
that those inconsistencies were not the result of God's work,
but in spite of it.

And you, on the other hand, who aspire for the crown of
saintliness, to which ye are truly called, take heart! There is
nothing which God has done for any soul that He will not do
for you. And there is no soil so unpromising that He will not
compel it to yield His fairest results. Only cease from your
own works, and keep always on God's "lift," refusing each
solicitation to step off its ascending energy, or to do for yourself what He will do for you so much better than you can ask
or think.

18

Hagar and Ishmael Cast Out

Genesis 21

Even though we were hearing this story for the first time, and did not know of the grave crisis to which we were approaching in the next chapter, we might be sure that something of the sort was imminent; and we should rest our conclusion on the fact of the stern discipline through which the great patriarch was called to pass.

In what way the presence of Hagar and Ishmael hindered the development of Abraham's noblest life of faith, we cannot entirely understand. Did his heart still cling to the girl who had given him his firstborn son? Was there any secret satisfaction in the arrangement, which had at least achieved one cherished purpose, though it had been unblessed by God? Was there any fear that if he were summoned to surrender Isaac, he would find it easier to do so, because, at any moment, he could fall back on Ishmael, as both son and heir? We cannot read all that was in Abraham's mind; but surely some such thoughts are suggested by the expressions which to this hour record the history of the anguish of this torn and lonely heart, as one darling idol after another was rent away, that he himself might be cast naked and helpless on the omnipotence of the Eternal God. "The thing was very grievous in Abraham's sight" (v. 11).

The final separation from Abraham of ingredients which would have been prejudicial to the exercise of a supreme faith was brought about by the birth of the long-promised child, which is alluded to at the commencement of this chapter, and which led up to the crisis with which we are now dealing.

"The Lord visited Sarah as He had said, and the Lord did unto Sarah as He had spoken" (v. 1). It is impossible to trust God too absolutely. God's least word is a spar of imperishable wood driven into the Rock of Ages, which will never give, and on which you may hang your entire weight for evermore. "The counsel of the Lord standeth for ever; the thoughts of His heart to all generations" (Psalm 33:11).

Awaiting God's Time

"Sarah bare Abraham a son in his old age, *at the set time* of which God had spoken unto him" (v. 2). God has His set times. It is not for us to know them; indeed, we cannot know them; we must wait for them. If God had told Abraham in Haran that he must wait for thirty years until he pressed the promised child to his bosom, his heart would have failed him. So, in gracious love, the length of the weary years was hidden, and only as they were nearly spent, and there were only a few more months to wait, God told them that "according to the time of life, Sarah shall have a son" (Gen. 18:14). The set time came at last; and then the laughter that filled the patriarch's home made the aged pair forget the long and weary vigil. "And Abraham called the name of his son that was born unto him, whom Sarah bare unto him, Isaac" (that is, Laughter) (v. 3). Take heart, waiting one, thou waitest for One who cannot disappoint thee; and who will not be five minutes behind the appointed moment: ere long "your sorrow shall be turned into joy."

The peace of Abraham's house remained at first unbroken, though there may have been some slight symptoms of the rupture which was at hand. The dislike which Sarah had manifested to Hagar, long years before, had never been extinguished. Nor had the warm passionate nature of Hagar ever forgotten those hard dealings which had driven her forth, to fare as best she might in the inhospitable desert. At last the women's quarters could conceal the quarrel no longer, and the scandal broke out into the open day.

The immediate occasion of this open rupture was the weaning of the young Isaac. "The child grew, and was weaned: and Abraham made a great feast the day that Isaac was weaned" (v. 8). But amid all the bright joy of that happy occasion, one shadow suddenly stole over the scene, and brooded on the mother's soul. Sarah's jealous eye saw Ishmael mocking. The lad had recently suffered a severe disappointment.

It must have been very difficult to view with equanimity the preparations made in honor of the child who was destined to supersede him: and so, under the appearance of sportive jesting, he jeered at Isaac. This awoke all Sarah's slumbering jealousy. Why should she, the chieftain's wife, and mother of his heir, brook the insolence of a slave? And so she said unto Abraham with a sneer and the sting of the old jealousy, "Cast out this bondwoman and her son; for the son of this bondwoman shall not be heir with my son, even with Isaac" (v. 10).

We cannot but recall the use which the great apostle makes of this incident. In his days the Jews, priding themselves on being the lineal descendants of Abraham, refused to consider it possible that any but themselves could be children of God, and the heirs of promise. And when large numbers of Gentiles were born into the Christian Church under the first preaching of the Gospel, and claimed to be the spiritual seed, with all the rights pertaining thereunto; they who, like Ishmael, were simply born after the flesh, persecuted them which, like Isaac, were born after the Spirit. And ere long the Jewish nation was rejected; put aside; cast out. Succeeding ages have seen the building up of the Church from among the once-persecuted ones, while the children of Abraham have wandered in the wilderness fainting for the true water of life (Gal. 4:29).

But there is a still deeper reference. Hagar, the slave, who may even have been born in the Sinaitic Desert, with which she seems to have been so familiar, is a fit representative of the spirit of legalism and bondage, seeking to win life by the observance of the law. Sarah, the free woman, on the other hand, represents the covenant of free grace. Her children are love, and faith, and hope; they are not bound by the spirit of "must," but by the promptings of spontaneous gratitude. Now, argues the Apostle, there was no room for Hagar and Sarah, with their respective children, in Abraham's tent. If Ishmael was there, it was because Isaac was not born. But as soon as Isaac came in, Ishmael must go out. So the two principles—of legalism, which insists on the performance of the finished work of the Savior—cannot coexist in one heart. So, addressing the Galatian converts, who were being tempted by Judaizing teachers to mingle legalism and faith, the Apostle bade them follow the example of Abraham, and cast out the spirit of bondage which keeps the soul in one perpetual agony of unrest.

You, my readers, are trusting Christ; but, perhaps, you are living in perpetual bondage to your scruples; or, perhaps, you are always endeavoring to add some acts of obedience, by way of completing and assuring your salvation. Ah! it is a great mistake. Do not always imagine that God's love to you depends on the performance of many minute acts, concerning which there are no definite instructions given. Trust Christ. Realize His wonderful and complete salvation. Work not towards sonship, but from it. Live the free, happy life of Isaac, whose position is assured; and not that of Ishmael, whose position is dependent on his good behavior.

The remaining history is briefly told. With many a pang—as the vine which bleeds copiously when the pruning knife is doing its work—Abraham sent Hagar and her child forth from his home, bidding them a last sad farewell. In the dim twilight they fared forth, before the camp was astir. The strong man must have suffered keenly as he put the bread into her hand, and with his own fingers bound the bottle of water on her shoulder, and kissed Ishmael once more. And yet he must not let Sarah guess how much he felt it. How many passages in our lives are only known to God!

Yet it was better so. And God provided for them both. When the mother's hopes were on the point of expiring, and the lad lay dying of thirst in the scorching noon, under the slender shade of a desert shrub, the Angel of God stayed her sobs, pointed out the well of water to which her tears had made her blind, and promised that her child should become a great nation. Ishmael would never have developed to his full stature if he had perpetually lived in the enervating luxury of Abraham's camp. There was not room enough there for him to grow. For him, as for us all, there was need of the free air of the desert, in which he should match himself with his peers, becoming strong by privation and want. That which seems like to break our hearts at the moment, turns out in after years to have been of God. "And God said unto Abraham, Let it not be grievous in thy sight; in all that Sarah hath said unto thee, hearken unto her voice" (v. 12).

One more weight was laid aside, and one more step taken in the preparation of God's "friend" for the supreme victory of his faith; for which his whole life had been a preparation, and which was now at hand.

19

The Greatest Trial of All

Genesis 22

So long as men live in the world, they will turn to this story with unwaning interest. There is only one scene in history by which it is surpassed; that where the Great Father gave His Isaac to a death from which there was no deliverance. God and Abraham were friends in a common sorrow up to a certain point; though the infinite love of God stepped in to stay the hand of Abraham at the critical moment, sparing His friend what He would not spare Himself.

God's Trials
"God did tempt Abraham." A better rendering might be, "God did put Abraham to the test." Satan tempts us that he may bring out the evil that is in our hearts; God tries or tests us that He may bring out all the good. In the fiery trial through which the believer is called to pass, ingredients of evil which had counteracted his true development drop away, shriveled and consumed; while latent qualities—produced by grace, but not yet brought into exercise—are called to the front; receive due recognition; and acquire a fixity of position and influence which nothing else could possibly have given them. In the agony of sorrow we say words and assume positions, which otherwise we should never have dreamed of, but from which we never again recede.

But God sends us no trial, whether great or small, without first preparing us. He "will with the temptation also make a

way to escape, that ye may be able to bear it" (I Cor. 10:13).
Trials are, therefore, God's vote of confidence in us. Many a
trifling event is sent to test us, ere a greater trial is permitted
to break on our heads. We are set to climb the lower peaks
before urged to the loftiest summits with their virgin snows;
are made to run with footmen before contending with
horses; are taught to wade in the shallows, before venturing
into the swell of the ocean waves. So it is written: "It came to
pass *after these things*, that God did tempt Abraham" (v. 1).

The trial came very suddenly. As we have seen, life was
flowing smoothly with the patriarch—courted by Abimelech;
secure of his wells; gladdened with the presence of Isaac; the
everlasting God his friend. "Ah, happy man," we might well
have exclaimed, "thou hast entered upon thy land of Beulah;
thy sun shall no more go down, nor thy moon withdraw
itself; before thee lie the sunlit years, in an unbroken chain of
blessing." But this was not to be. And just at that moment,
like a bolt out of a clear sky, there burst upon him the
severest trial of his life.

The trial touched Abraham in his tenderest point. It concerned his Isaac. Nothing else in the circumference of his life
could have been such a test as anything connected with the
heir of promise, the child of his old age, the laughter of his
life. *His love was tested.* For love of God, he had done much.
But at whatever cost, he had ever put God first, glad to sacrifice all, for very love of Him.

Would not you like to love God like this? Then tell Him
you are willing to pay the cost, if only He will create that love
within you. And, remember: though at first He may ask you
to give up Isaac to Him, it is only that you may take up your
true position, and evince to the world your choice; for He
will give your beloved back again from the altar on which
you have laid him. "Take now thy son, thine only son Isaac,
whom thou lovest, and offer him for a burnt offering" (v.2).

A Great Test of Faith

Isaac was the child of promise. "In Isaac shall thy seed be

called." With reiterated emphasis this lad had been indicated as the one essential link between the aged pair and the vast posterity which was promised them. And now the father was asked to sacrifice his life. It was a tremendous test to his faith. How could God keep His word, and let Isaac die? One thought, however, as the Epistle to the Hebrews tells us, filled the old man's mind, "God is able." He "accounted that God was able to raise him up, even from the dead" (Heb. 11:19). He felt sure that somehow God would keep His word. He had already seen Divine power giving life where all was as good as dead; why should it not do it again? In any case he must go straight on, doing as he was told, and calculating on the unexhausted stores in the secret hand of God. Oh for faith like this!—simply to believe what God says.

It was a test of Abraham's obedience. It was in the visions of the night that the word of the Lord must have come to him: and early the next morning the patriarch was on his way. The night before, as he lay down, he had not the least idea of the mission on which he would be started when the early beams of dawn had broken up the short Eastern night. But he acted immediately. "And Abraham rose up early in the morning" (v. 3). He "saddled his ass, and clave the wood for the burnt-offering, and rose up, and went unto the place of which God had told him." This promptness was his safe-guard. I do not think he confided his secret to a single soul, not even to Sarah. Why should he? The lad and he would enter that camp again, when the short but awful journey was over. "I and the lad will go yonder and worship, and come again to you."

This test did not outrage the natural instincts of his soul. He was too familiar with God's voice to mistake it. Too often had he listened to it to make a mistake in this solemn crisis. And he was sure that God had some way of deliverance; which, though he might not be able to forecast it, would secure the sparing of Isaac's life.

What those three days of quiet traveling must have been to Abraham, we can never know. It is always so much easier to act immediately and precipitately, than to wait through long days, and even years; but it is in this process of waiting upon God that souls are drawn out to a strength of purpose and nobility of daring, which become their sacred inheritance for all after time. And yet, despite the patriarch's preoccupation with his own special sorrow, the necessity was laid upon him to hide it under an appearance of resignation, and even gladsomeness; so that neither his son nor his servants might guess the agony which was gnawing at his heart.

As soon as the mountain had loomed into view, Abraham said unto his young men: "Abide ye here with the ass; and I and the lad will go yonder and worship, and come again to you" (v. 5). What a significant expression, in this connection, is that word *worship!* It reflects the mood of the patriarch's mind. He was preoccupied with that Being, at whose command he had gone forth on this sorrowful errand. He looked upon his God, at the moment when He was asking so great a gift, as only deserving adoration and worship. The loftiest sentiment that can fill the heart of man swayed his whole nature; and it seemed to him as if his costliest and dearest treasure was not too great to give to that great and glorious God who was the one object of his life.

It is of the utmost importance that we should emphasize the words of *assured confidence,* which Abraham addressed to his young men before he left them. "I and the lad will go yonder and worship, and come again to you." This was something more than unconscious prophecy: it was the assurance of an unwavering faith, that somehow or other God would interpose to spare his son; or at least, if necessary, to raise him from the dead. God is bound to be as good as His word. And even though He ask you to do the one thing that might seem to make deliverance impossible; yet if you dare to do it, you will find not only that you shall obtain the promise, but that you shall also receive some crowning and unexpected mark of His love.

Isaac's Lesson

The influence of Abraham's behavior was felt by his son. He

caught his father's spirit. We do not know how old he was; he was at least old enough to sustain the toil of a long march on foot, and strong enough to carry up hill the faggots, laid upon his shoulders by his father, but he gladly bent his youthful strength under the weight of the wood, just as through the *Via Dolorosa* a greater than he carried His cross. Probably this was not the first time that Abraham and Isaac had gone on such an errand; but it is beautiful to see the evident interest the lad took in the proceedings as they went, "both of them together."

At all previous sacrifices, Abraham had taken with him a lamb; but on this occasion Isaac's wondering attention was drawn to the omission of that constant appendage to their acts of sacrifice; and with a simplicity which must have touched Abraham to the quick, he said, "My father, behold the fire and the wood! but where is the lamb for a burnt offering?" (v. 7). What a stab was this to that sorely tried heart, which dared not even reveal the secret beneath which it bowed; and which eagerly caught at a subterfuge to enable it to postpone the answer. Thus with a gleam of prophetic insight, mingled with unwavering faith in Him for whose sake he was suffering, the father answered, "My son, God will Himself provide a lamb for a burnt offering." So they went both of them together.

Can we wonder that Abraham shrank from disclosing all the facts? We all have our treasures whom we fondly love. Our dear ones depart in spite of all we do to keep them; but in Abraham's case there was this added anguish, that he was to inflict the blow. The last thought that Isaac would have of him would be, holding the uplifted knife; and even though the lad might be restored to him—yet would it not be a revelation to the young heart to discover that it was possible for his father to do to him an act of violence like that?

But at last the discovery could no longer be withheld. Suppose they stood on this side, and He on that side: would we go with Him, though it cost us the loss of all? You think you would. Aye, it is a great thing to say. The air upon this height is too rare to breathe with comfort. The one explanation of it is to be found in the words of our Lord: "He that loveth father or mother, son or daughter, more than Me, is not worthy of Me" (Matt. 10:37).

The blade was raised high, flashing in the rays of the morning sun; but it was not permitted to fall. With the temptation God also made a way of escape. "And the angel of the Lord called unto him out of heaven, and said, 'Abraham!' " With what avidity would that much-tried soul seize at anything that offered the chance of respite or of pause! and he said, his uplifted hand returning gladly to his side, "Here am I!" Would that we could more constantly live in the spirit of that response, so that God might always know where to find us; and so that we might be always ready to fulfil His will. Then followed words that spoke release and deliverance: "Lay not thine hand upon the lad, neither do thou anything unto him: for now I know that thou fearest God, seeing thou hast not withheld thy son, thine only son, from Me" (v. 12).

When we have given our best and costliest to God, passing our gifts through the fire, surrendering them to His will, He will give them back to us as gold refined. But it is also quite likely that He will not do so until we have almost lost all heart and hope. "Abraham called the name of that place Jehovah-Jireh," "The Lord will provide." And so it passed into a proverb, and men said one to another, "In the mount of the Lord deliverance shall be seen." It is a true word. Deliverance is not seen till we come to the mount of sacrifice. God does not provide deliverance until we have reached the point of our extremest need.

Near by the altar there was a thicket; and, as Abraham lifted up his eyes and looked around, he beheld a ram caught there by its horns. Nothing could be more opportune. He had wanted to show his gratitude, and the fulness of his heart's devotion; and he gladly went and took the ram, and offered him up for a burnt offering instead of his son. Here, surely, is the great doctrine of substitution; and we are taught how life can only be preserved at the cost of life given.

All through this marvelous story there is an evident setting forth of the mysteries of Calvary. Abraham's act enables us better to understand the sacrifice which God made to save us. The gentle submission of Isaac gives us a better insight into Christ's obedience to death. Isaac's restoration to life, as from the dead, and after having been three days dead in his father's purpose, suggests the resurrection from Joseph's tomb. Yet the reality surpasses the shadow. Isaac suffers with a clear apprehension of his father's presence. Christ, bereft of the consciousness of His Father's love, complains of His forsakenness. All was done that love could do to alleviate Isaac's anguish; but Christ suffered the rudeness of coarse soldiery, and the upbraidings of Pharisee and Scribe. Isaac was spared death; but Christ drank the bitter cup to its dregs.

Before they left the mountain brow, the angel of Jehovah once more addressed the patriarch. God had often promised: now for the first time He sware; and since He could swear by no greater He sware by Himself, and said: "By Myself have I sworn, because thou hast done this thing, and hast not withheld thy son, thine only son; that in blessing I will bless thee; . . ." (vv. 16, 17).

20
Machpelah and His First Tenant

Genesis 23

When Abraham came down the slopes of Mount Moriah, hand in hand with Isaac, fifty years of his long life still lay before him. Of those fifty years, twenty-five passed away before the event recorded in this chapter. What happened in those serene and untroubled years we do not know. The river of Abraham's life had passed the rapids and narrows of its earlier course, and now broadened into reaches of still water, over which its current glided with an almost imperceptible movement.

Abraham's Tears

"And Sarah died in Kirjath-Arba; the same is Hebron in the land of Canaan" (v. 2). Abraham seems to have been away from home, perhaps at Beersheba, when she breathed her last; but he came at once "to mourn for Sarah, and to weep for her." This is the first time we read of Abraham weeping. We do not read that he wept when he crossed the Euphrates, and left for ever home and kindred. There is no record of his tears when tidings came to him that his nephew Lot was carried into captivity. He does not seem to have bedewed his pathway to Mount Moriah with the tears of his heart.

What made the difference? Ah! there is all the difference between *doing* God's will and *suffering* it. So long as we have something to do for God—whether it be a toilsome march; or a battle; or a sacrifice—we can keep back our tears, and bear up.

Abraham's Confession

"Abraham stood up from before his dead, and spake unto the sons of Heth, saying, I am a stranger and a sojourner with you; give me a possession of a burying-place with you" (vv. 3, 4). See how sorrow reveals the heart. To look at Abraham as the great and wealthy patriarch, the emir, the chieftain of a mighty clan, we cannot guess his secret thoughts. He has been in the land for sixty-two years; and surely by this time he must have lost his first feelings of loneliness.

Abraham's Faith

It is very beautiful to remark the action of Abraham's faith in the matter of Sarah's burial place; and to see its outcome in his utter refusal to receive the land as a gift from any hand but that of God. When the chieftains to whom he made his appeal heard it, they instantly offered him the choice of their sepulchre affirming that none of them would withhold his sepulchre from so mighty a prince. And afterwards, when he sought their intercession with Ephron the son of Zohar, for the obtaining of the cave of Machpelah, which was at the end of his field, and Ephron proposed to give it him in the presence of the sons of his people, Abraham steadfastly refused. It was all his as the gift of God; it would be all his some day in fact; and in the meanwhile he would purchase the temporary use of that which he could never accept as a gift from any but his Almighty Friend.

21

Gathered to His People

Genesis 25

No human name can vie with Abraham's for the widespread reverence which it has evoked among all races and throughout all time. What was the secret of this widespread renown? It is not because he headed one of the greatest movements of the human family; nor yet because he evinced manly and intellectual vigor; nor because he possessed vast wealth. It was rather the remarkable nobility and grandeur of his religious life that has made him the object of veneration to all generations of mankind.

At the basis of his character was a mighty faith. "Abraham believed God." In that faith he left his native land, and traveled to one which was promised, but not clearly indicated. In that faith he let Lot choose the best he could for himself; because he was sure that none could do better for himself than God was prepared to do for the one who trusted Him. In that faith he waited through long years, sure that God would give him the promised child. In that faith he lived a nomad life, making no attempt to return to the settled country from which he had come out. Indeed, his soul was consumed with the passionate expectancy of the city of God. In that faith he was prepared to offer Isaac, and buried Sarah.

To faith he added virtue, or manly courage. What could have been more manly than the speed with which he armed his trained servants; or than the heroism with which he, with a train of undisciplined shepherds, broke on the disciplined bands of Assyria.

And to manly courage he added knowledge. Year by year fresh revelations of the character and attributes of God broke upon his soul. An unknown country grew beneath his gaze; as he climbed through the years into closer fellowship with God, and from the summit looked down upon its lengths and breadths, its depths and heights, its oceans, mountain-ranges, and plains.

And to knowledge he added temperance, or self-control. That he was master of himself is evident from the way in which he repelled the offer of the King of Sodom; and curbed his spirit amid the irritations caused by Lot's herdsmen. There is no type of character more splendid than that of the man who is master of himself, because he is the servant of God; and who can rule others rightly because he can rule himself well.

And to temperance, patience. No ordinary patience was that which waited through the long years, not murmuring or complaining, but prepared to abide God's time.

And to his patience he added godliness. One of his chief characteristics was his piety—a constant sense of the presence of God in his life, and a love and devotion to Him. Wherever he pitched his tent, there his first care was to rear an altar. In every time of trouble he turned as naturally to God as a child to its father; and there was such holy intercourse between his spirit and that of God, that the name by which he is now best known throughout the East is "the friend."

And to godliness he added brotherly kindness. Some men who are devoted towards God are lacking in the tenderer qualities towards those most closely knit with them in family bonds. Not so was it with Abraham. He was full of affection. Beneath the calm exterior and the erect bearing of the mighty chieftain there beat a warm and affectionate heart. Listen to that passionate cry, "Oh that Ishmael might live before Thee!" Remember God's own testimony to the affection he bore towards Isaac, "Thy son, thine only son, whom thou lovest."

And to brotherly kindness he added charity, or love. In his

dealings with men he could afford to be generous, open-
hearted, openhanded; willing to pay down the large price
demanded for Machpelah's cave without haggling or complaint; destitute of petty pride; affable, courteous, able to
break out into sunny laughter; right with God, and therefore
able to shed upon men the rays of a genial, restful noble
heart.

All these things were in him and abounded, and they
made him neither barren nor unfruitful; they made his calling and election sure; they prepared for him an abundant
entrance into the everlasting kingdom of God our Saviour.
The words denote the welcome given by choral songs and
joyous greetings to the conqueror who, laden with spoils,
returned to his native city; a welcome so exuberant, so bois-
terous in its unutterable joy, so royally demonstrative, as to
resemble that given in all times to those who have conferred
great benefits, or who have learned the art of stirring the
loyal devotion of their fellows.

"Abraham gave up the ghost." There was no reluctance in
his death; he did not cling to life—he was glad to be gone;
and when the angel messenger summoned him, without a
struggle, nay, with the readiness of glad consent, his spirit
returned to God who gave it.

He was gathered to his people. What a lovely synonym for
death! *To die* is to rejoin our people; to pass into a world
where the great clan is gathering, welcoming with shouts
each newcomer through the shadows. Where are your
people? I trust they are God's people; and if so, those that
bear your name, standing on the other shore, are more
numerous than the handful gathered around you here. But
remember, if your people are God's people, you cannot be
gathered to them unless first in faith and love you are
gathered to Him.

"And his sons, Isaac and Ishmael, buried him in the cave
of Machpelah" (v. 9). There were great differences between
these two. Ishmael, the child of his slave: Isaac, of the wed-
ded wife. Ishmael, the offspring of expediency: Isaac, of

promise. Ishmael, wild and masterful; strongly marked in his individuality; proud, independent, swift to take an insult, swift to avenge it: Isaac, quiet and retiring, submissive and meek, willing to carry wood, to be kept in the dark, to be bound, to yield up his wells, and to let his wife govern his house. And yet all differences were wiped out in that moment of supreme sorrow.

Out of materials which were by no means extraordinary, God built up a character with which He could hold fellowship as friend with friend; and a life which has exerted a profound influence on all after-time. It would seem as if He can raise any crop He chooses, when the soil of the heart and life are entirely surrendered to Him. Why should not we henceforth yield ourselves utterly to His divine husbandry, asking Him to fulfil in us the good pleasure of His goodness, and the work of faith with power? Only let us trust Him fully, and obey Him instantly and utterly; and as the years pass by, they shall witness results which shall bring glory to God in the highest, while they fill us with ceaseless praise.

Book II: Joseph

1

Early Days

Genesis 37

Seventeen years before our story opens, a little child was borne by Rachel, the favorite wife of Jacob. The latter was then living as manager for his uncle Laban, on the ancient pastureland of Charran, situated in the valley of the Euphrates and the Tigris, from which his grandfather Abraham had been called by God. The child received an eager welcome from its parents, and from the first gave unusual promise. He was like one of those children, whom we sometimes meet in large families, who bear a marked contrast to the rest; and who grow up like some fair Saxon child amid the swarthy natives of a tent of gypsies who have made it their prize.

When yet a child he was hastily caught up by his mother, and sustained in her arms on the back of a swift camel, urged to its highest speed, in the flight across the desert that lay with only one oasis between the bank of the Euphrates and the green prairies of Gilead. He could just remember the panic that spread through the camp when tidings came that Esau, the dread uncle, was on his march, with four hundred followers. Nor could he ever forget the evening full of preparation, the night of solemn expectancy, and the morning when his father limped into the camp, maimed in body, but with the look of a prince upon his face.

More recently still, he could recall the hurried flight from the enraged idolaters of Shechem; and those solemn hours at Bethel where his father had probably showed him the very spot on which the foot of the mystic ladder had rested, and where the whole family formally entered into a new covenant with God. It may be that this was the turning point of his life. The other sons of Jacob may have been unmoved spectators; but there was a deep response in the susceptible heart of the lad, who may have felt, "This God shall be my God for ever and ever; He shall be my Guide, even unto death" (Ps. 48:14).

If this were so, these impressions were soon deepened by three deaths. When they reached the family settlement, they found the old nurse Deborah dying. She was the last link to those bright days when her young mistress Rebekah came across the desert to be Isaac's bride; and they buried her with many tears under an ancient but splendid oak. And he could never forget the next. The long caravan was moving slowly up to the narrow ridge along which lay the ancient village of Bethlehem: suddenly a halt was called; the beloved Rachel could not go another step; there Rachel, Joseph's mother, died. This was the greatest loss that he had ever known. A little while after, the lad stood with his father and brethren before Machpelah's venerable grave, to lay Isaac where Abraham and Sarah and Rebekah awaited him.

These things made Joseph what he was. And the little sympathy that he received from his family only drove him more apart, and compelled him to strike his roots deeper into the life of God.

It may be that these words will be read by youths of seventeen who have passed through experiences not unlike Joseph's. They have lost sainted friends. They feel lonely in the midst of their home. Have you put your hand into the hand of "the mighty God of Jacob"? The answer may mark the crisis of your lives. Choose Christ; and, in choosing Him, choose life, and blessedness, and heaven. And when you have chosen Him, cleave close to Him, and send the rootlets of your existence deep down into the hidden wells of communion and fellowship.

Joseph was endowed with very remarkable intelligence.

The Rabbis describe him as a wise son, endowed with knowledge beyond his years. It was this, combined with the sweetness of his disposition, and the memory of his mother, that won for him his father's peculiar love. "Israel loved Joseph more than all his children" (v. 3).

And this love provided the coat of many colors. The Hebrew word means simply a tunic reaching to the extremities, and describes a garment commonly worn in Egypt and the adjacent lands. Imagine a long white linen robe extending to the ankles and wrists, and embroidered with a narrow stripe of color round the edge of the skirt and sleeves, and you will have a very fair conception of this famous coat.

Now we can understand the envy of his brothers. This sort of robe was worn only by the opulent and noble, by kings' sons, and by those who had no need to toil for their living. All who had to win their bread by labor wore short, colored garments that did not show stain, or cramp the free movement of the limbs. Such was the lot of Jacob's sons, and such the garments they wore. They had to wade through morasses, to clamber up hills, to carry wandering sheep home on their shoulders, to fight with robbers and beasts of prey; and for such toils the flowing robe would have been quite unfit. But when Jacob gave such a robe to Joseph, he declared in effect that from such hardships and toils his favorite son should be exempt. Now in those times the father's will was law. When, therefore, they saw Joseph tricked out in his robe of state, the brethren felt that in all likelihood *he* would have the rich inheritance, while *they* must follow a life of toil. "And when his brethren saw that their father loved him more than all his brethren, they hated him, and could not speak peaceably unto him" (v. 4).

The case was aggravated by his plain speaking. "He brought unto his father their evil report" (v. 2). He was jealous for the family name, which they had already "made to stink among the inhabitants of the land." He was eager for the glory of God, whose name was continually blasphemed through their means.

This was enough to make them hate him. "Every one that doeth evil hateth the light." As soon as our lives become a strong contrast and reproof, we shall arouse its undying hate.

Further, Joseph dreamed that he should become the center of the family life. All young people dream. But there was this in Joseph's dreams, they foretold not only his exaltation, but his brothers' humiliation. If he were the central sheaf, their sheaves must do obeisance, by falling to the earth around it. If he were on the throne, sun, moon, and stars must do him homage. This was more than the proud spirits of his brethren could take, and "they hated him yet the more" (v. 5).

2
The Pit
Genesis 37

The cross of our Lord Jesus Christ is the center of human history. It is the sun around which the firmament circles; the key to all Scripture history and type; the fact which gives meaning and beauty to all other facts. To ignore the cross is to repeat the error of the old philosophers; who thought that the earth, and not the sun, was the center of our system, and to whom therefore the very heavens were in confusion. To know and love the cross is to obtain a deep insight into the harmonies of all things in heaven and earth.

It is remarkable to learn that, on the day of our Savior's passion, it being equinox, the whole habitable world was lit up between the hours of nine a.m. and six p.m. Could an angel have poised himself in midair during those memorable hours, he would have seen each continent bathed in successive sunshine. At nine a.m. it was noon in India, and all Asia was in light to its far eastern fringes; at noon all Europe and all Africa was in light; at 6 p.m. the whole continent of America had passed into the golden glory. This may serve as a parable. Poise yourself above the cross; look back to the morning of earth's history, and onward to its evening—and all will be light. The radiance that streams from the cross illumines all events, and banishes all darkness.

The sun which now shines, so to speak, from the other side of the cross, so as to fling its shadow forward clear and sharp on the canvas of the present, once shone from where we now stand, and flung its shadow backward upon the canvas of the past. One of these shadows is caught and photographed for us in this sweet story of Joseph.

"Jacob dwelt in the land of his father's sojournings" (v. 1). When he had buried his old father he continued to reside in the Vale of Hebron. This was the headquarters of his vast encampment. But rich as were the pasture lands of Hebron, they were not sufficient to support the whole of the flocks and herds. The sons were compelled to drive these by slow stages to distant parts of the land; and were even forced, by stern necessity, to brave the anger of the people of Shechem, whom they had grievously wronged, and who had vowed vengeance on them for their foul behavior.

It was this that gave point to Jacob's question, "Do not thy brethren feed the flock at Shechem?" (v. 13).

He was alone in Hebron with Joseph and Benjamin: they were his darlings; his heart loved them with something of the intense devotion which he had felt towards their mother. Benjamin was young; but Joseph was seventeen years old. The old man kept them with him, reluctant to lose them from his sight. Hebron means fellowship, and was a fitting residence for hearts so closely knit as theirs. But still, on the other hand, the old man yearned with anxious love over his absent sons; and at last, after many battlings and hesitations, he suddenly said to the dearly loved Joseph, "Come, I will send thee: go, I pray thee, and see whether it be well with thy brethren, and bring me word again" (v. 14).

On Joseph's part there was not a moment's hesitation. In the flash of a thought he realized the perils of the mission— perils of waters, perils of robbers, perils of wild beasts, perils in the lonely nights, perils among false brethren, who bitterly hated him. But "none of these things moved him, neither counted he his life dear unto himself." As soon as he knew his father's will, he said, "Here am I." "So Jacob sent him; and he came."

But Joseph did not go in search of his brethren simply because his father sent him. Had this been the case, he would have returned home when he found that they had safely left the dreaded Shechem. But instead of that he sought them, because he loved them, and went after them until he found them.

Our Lord never wearied of calling Himself the Sent of the Father. There is hardly a page in the Gospel of John in which He does not say more than once, "I came not of Myself, but My Father sent Me."

It must have cost Jacob something to part with the beloved Joseph: and this can be gauged by those who have lost their beloved. But who can estimate how much it cost the Infinite God to send His only-begotten Son, who had dwelt in His bosom, and who was His Fellow from everlasting? Truly God *so* loved the world! But who shall fathom the depths of that one small word?

But our Savior did not come solely because He was sent. He came because He loved His mission. He came to seek and to save that which was lost. And He especially came in search of His brethren, His own, the children of the Hebrew race. Nor was He content with only *seeking* the lost; He went after them *until* He found them. "Joseph went after his brethren until he found them in Dothan" (v. 17).

"They saw him afar off, even before he came near unto them, and they conspired against him to slay him" (v. 18). And he would doubtless have been ruthlessly slain, and his body flung into some pit, away from the haunts of men, if it had not been for the merciful pleadings of Reuben, the eldest brother. "And it came to pass, when Joseph was come unto his brethren, that they stripped him of his coat, his coat of many colors, and they took him, and cast him into a pit." Our mother earth has seen many dark crimes committed on her surface by her children; but she has never seen a darker one than this.

The confession of those cruel men, made to one another after the lapse of twenty-five years, enables us to supply the missing coloring for this deed of horror.

Years after they said one to another, "We are verily guilty

concerning our brother, in that we saw the anguish of his soul, when he besought us and we would not hear." We seem to see Joseph, in those rude hands, like a fleecy lamb in the jaws of a tiger. He struggles to get free. He entreats them with bitter tears to let him go. He implores them for the sake of his old father, and by the tie of brotherhood. The anguish of his soul is clearly evident in his bitter cries, and tears, and prayers.

There was a time when the germ of this sin alighted on their hearts in the form of a ruffled feeling of jealousy against the young dreamer. Take care how you permit a single germ of sin to alight and remain upon your heart. Treat that germ as you would the first germ of fever that entered your home. At the first consciousness of sin, seek instant cleansing in the precious blood of Christ.

Unforgiven sin is a fearful scourge. They tried to lock up the skeleton in their most secret cupboard, but it contrived to come forth to confront them even in their guarded hours. Sometimes they thought they saw that agonized young face in their dreams, and heard that piteous voice wailing in the night wind. The men who carry with them the sense of unforgiven sin, will be the first to believe in a vulture for ever tearing out the vitals, a worm that never dies, a fire that is never quenched.

But Joseph's grief was a true anticipation of Christ's. "He came to His own, but His own received Him not" (John 1:11). They said, "This is the heir, come let us kill Him, and the inheritance shall be ours" (Matt. 21:38). "They caught Him, and cast Him out, and slew Him." "They parted His raiment among them" (Ps. 22:18). They sold Him to the Gentiles. They sat down to watch Him die. The anguish of Joseph's soul reminds us of the strong cryings and tears wrung from the human nature of Christ by the near approach of His unknown sufferings as the scapegoat of the race. The comparative innocence of Joseph reminds us of the spotlessness of the Lamb who was without blemish, and whose blamelessness was again and again attested before He died.

No victim destined for the altar was ever more searchingly inspected for one black hair or defect than was Jesus, by those who were compelled to confess, "This Man hath done nothing amiss" (Luke 23:41).

However, Joseph's sufferings stopped before they reached the point of death; Jesus tasted death. Joseph's sufferings were personal; the sufferings of Jesus were substitutionary and mediatorial; "He died for us"; "He gave Himself for me." Joseph's sufferings had no efficacy in atoning for the sin that caused them; but the sufferings of Jesus atone not only for the guilt of His murderers, but for the guilt of all; "He is the propitiation for our sins; and not for ours only, but also for the whole world" (I John 2:2).

"They sat down to eat bread" (v. 25). With hardened unconcern they took their midday meal. Just at that moment a new and welcome sight struck their gaze. They were sitting on the plain at Dothan, a spot which still retains its ancient name; and anyone stationed there, and looking eastward towards the valley of the Jordan, would be able to trace the main road that led from the fords of the Jordan towards the coast of the Mediterranean. Along this road at that moment a caravan was travelling.

The sight of these travelling merchants gave a sudden turn to the thoughts of the conspirators. They knew that there was in Egypt a great demand for slaves, and that these merchantmen were in the habit of buying slaves in their passage and selling them in that land, which has always been the great slave mart of the world. Why not sell their brother? It would be an easy way of disposing of him. It would save them from fratricide. So, acting upon the suggestion of Judah, they lifted Joseph out of the pit, and, as money was no object to them, they sold him for twenty rings of silver— about three pounds.

Joseph was betrayed by his brothers; Jesus by His friend. Joseph was sold for money; so was our Lord. Joseph followed in the train of captives to slavery; Jesus was numbered with transgressors. The crime of Joseph's brothers fulfilled the Divine plan; and the wicked hands of the crucifiers of Jesus fulfilled the determinate counsel and foreknowledge of God.

God will "make the wrath of man to praise Him; and the remainder of wrath will He restrain." "Oh, the depth of the riches both of the wisdom and of the knowledge of God! how unsearchable His judgments, and His ways past finding out!" (Rom. 11:33).

3

In the House of Potiphar

Genesis 39

The Midianite merchantmen, into whose hands his brethren sold Joseph, brought him down to Egypt—with its ribbon of green pasture land amid the waste of sand.

He was bought by Potiphar, "the captain of the guard." The margin tells us he was the chief of the slaughtermen or executioners. He was, in all likelihood, the chief of the military force employed as the royal bodyguard, in the precincts of the court.

Potiphar was an Egyptian grandee; a member of a proud aristocracy; high in office and in court favor. The young captive, accustomed to the tendernesses of his simple and beloved home, must have trembled as he passed up the pillared avenue, through sphinx-guarded gates, into the recesses of that strange, vast Egyptian palace, where they spoke a language which he could not understand and where all was so new and strange. But "God was with him"; the sense of the presence and guardianship of his father's God pervaded and stilled his soul, and kept him in perfect peace. Who would not rather, after all, choose to be Joseph in Egypt with God, than the brothers with a blood-stained garment in their hands and the sense of guilt on their souls?

Let us consider how Joseph fared in Potiphar's house.

"The Lord was with Joseph; and he was a prosperous man" (v. 2). The older versions of the Bible give a curious rendering here: "The Lord was with Joseph; and he was a luckie fellow." I suppose the meaning is that everything he handled went well. Potiphar and his household got into the way of expecting that this strange Hebrew captive could untie every knot, and bring to successful issues the most intricate arrangements. This arose from two causes.

In the first place, though stripped of his coat, he had not been stripped of his character. See to it, young people, that no one rob you of that: everything else may be replaced but that! He was industrious, prompt, diligent, obedient, reliable. He did his work, not because he was obliged to do it, but because God had given it to him to do, and had called him to do it. He read the will of God in "the daily round, the common task." He said to himself, as he said in afterlife, "God did send me hither" (Gen. 45:5). He felt that he was the servant—not so much of Potiphar as—of the God of Abraham and Isaac. There, in the household of Potiphar, he might live a devout and earnest life as truly as when he spent the long, happy days in Jacob's tent: and he did. And it was this which made him so conscientious and careful, qualities which in business must ensure success.

When his fellow servants were squandering the golden moments, Joseph was filling them with activities. They often pointed at him with envy, and perhaps said, "He is a lucky fellow." They did not think that his luck was his character; and that his character meant God. And if you wish to possess such a character as will insure your success in this life, there is no true basis for it but Jesus Christ.

In the second place: "The Lord made all that he did to prosper. The Lord blessed the Egyptian's house for Joseph's sake; and the blessing of the Lord was upon all that he had in the house, and in the field" (v. 5). This blessing was not the exclusive privilege of Joseph: it is promised to overtake all those "who hearken diligently unto the voice of God, and who observe to do all His commandments" (Deut. 28:1, 2). Such blessing would oft be ours if we walked as near to God as Joseph did.

You will surely be helped by the example of this noble

youth. He did not give himself to useless regrets and unavailing tears. He girded himself manfully to do with his might whatsoever his hand found to do. He believed that God had put him where he was; and in serving his earthly master well he felt that he was really pleasing his great heavenly Friend, who was as near him in those hieroglyphed places as in Jacob's tents. This is the spirit in which all service should be done. "Ye serve the Lord Christ. Whatsoever ye do, do it heartily, as to the Lord, and not unto men" (Col. 3:23). It is not so important what we do as how we do it. A mean man may belittle the most momentous affairs by the paltriness of his spirit. A noble man may greaten trifles by his nobility.

"The Lord blessed the Egyptian's house for Joseph's sake." When we reach heaven, and are able to trace the origin of things, we shall find that many of the choicest blessings of our lives were procured by the prayers or presence of very obscure and unrecognized people who were dear to God.

Years passed on, and Joseph became a prosperous man, the steward and bailiff in his master's house. "He left all that he had in Joseph's hand; and he knew not aught he had, save the bread which he did eat" (v. 6). And it was just here that Joseph encountered the most terrible temptation of his life.

We may expect temptation in days of prosperity and ease rather than in those of privation and toil. But unless we keep armed then, we are lost. "Watch and pray, that ye enter not into temptation. The flesh is weak" (Mark 14:38).

Temptation is hardest to resist when it arises from the least expected quarter. Egyptian women in those days enjoyed as much liberty as English women do now: this is conclusively proved by the Egyptian monuments, which also testify to the extreme laxity of their morals. It may be that Potiphar's wife was not worse than many of her sex, though we blush to read of her infamous proposals. They must have startled Joseph like a shock of earthquake, and filled him with a sudden tumult of thoughts.

It seemed essential to Joseph to stand well with his master's wife. How many would have reasoned that, by yielding for only a moment, they might win influence which they could afterwards use for the very best results! It is this policy which leads many to say, when tempted to do wrong, by master, or mistress, or foreman, or chief customer, "I did not care for it, or wish it. I yielded because my bread depended on it; I did not dare offend them." The only armor against policy is *faith* that looks to the long future, and believes that in the end it will be found better to have done right, and to have waited the vindication and blessing of God.

"Keep thy heart with all diligence; for out of it are the issues of life." There is no sin in having certain tendencies, appetites, and desires; else there would be sin in hunger, and in drowsiness. But the danger lies in the fear that they should be gratified to an immoderate excess, or from wrong and improper sources. Human nature is very liable to this. It is biassed thus; and stolen waters are sweet. Therefore Joseph must have suffered the more.

No thoughtful man, who knows his own weakness, can ever dare to affirm his immunity from temptation, or the impossibility of his yielding. If he stand it is only by the grace of God.

There were peculiar elements of trial in Joseph's case. It was well timed, and if he had yielded, there was not much fear of detection and punishment; the temptress would never publish her own shame. The temptation was also repeated day by day.

Yet Joseph stood firm. He reasoned with her. He urged his master's kindness and trust. He tried to recall her to a sense of what became her as his master's wife. But he did more. He brought the case from the court of reason to that of conscience, and asked in words for ever memorable, and which have given the secret of victory to tempted souls in all ages: "How shall I do this great wickedness, and sin against God!" (v. 9).

There are few subjects which require more notice both from speakers and writers than this great subject of chastity.

There is no one sin which will sooner bring about a nation's fall. If history teaches anything, it teaches that sensual indulgence is the surest way to national ruin. Society in not condemning this sin condemns herself.

It is said that the temptations of our great cities are too many and strong for the young to resist. Refuse to entertain such thoughtlessness and dangerous talk. While the case of Joseph remains on record, it is a standing contradiction to the whole. A young man *can* resist; he *can* overcome; he *can* be pure, and chaste, and sweet. We must, however, obey the dictates of Scripture and common sense. Avoid all places, books, and people which minister to evil thoughts. Resist the first tiny rill of temptation, lest it widen a breach big enough to admit the ocean. Remember that no temptation can master you unless you admit it *within* your nature; and since you are too weak to keep the door shut against it, look to the mighty Savior to place Himself against it. All hell cannot break the door open which you entrust to the safe keeping of Jesus.

What a motto this is for us all! "How can *I* do this great wickedness?" *I*, for whom Christ died. "How can I do this great *wickedness?*" Others call it "gaiety"; "being a little fast"; "sowing wild oats." I call it *sin*. "How can I do this *great* wickedness?" Many wink at it; to me it is a *great* sin. "How can I sin *against God?*" It seems only to concern men; but in effect it is a personal sin against the holy God.

We have no right to expect God to keep us if we voluntarily put ourselves into temptation. But if we are compelled to go there by the circumstances of our life, we may count upon His faithfulness.

Joseph did a wise thing when he fled. Better lose a coat and many a more valuable possession than lose a good conscience. "Flee youthful lusts." Do not linger in its vicinity. Do not stay to look at it. It will master you if you do.

There is no sin in being tempted. The will is the citadel of our manhood. The sin comes in when I assent, and acquiesce and yield. Much better fight it in the first circle of defense— in the first suggestion, or insinuation, or desire. Resist the devil there, and he will flee from you; and you will be saved a struggle within, which will leave its scar on your soul for years to come.

Never forget that we who believe in Jesus are seated with Him at the right hand of power; nor that Satan is already, in the purpose of God, defeated foe beneath our feet. Open your whole being to the subduing grace of the Holy Spirit. And we shall be more than conquerors through Him who loves us.

4
Misunderstood and Imprisoned

Genesis 39, 40. See also Psalm 105:17-19

Between the pit and the prison there was only a transient gleam of sunlight and prosperity. The sky of Joseph's life was again soon overcast. For when Potiphar heard the false but plausible statement of his wife, and saw the garment in her hand, which he recognized as Joseph's, his wrath flamed up; he would hear no words of explanation, but thrust him at once into the state prison.

It was not a prison like those with which we are familiar—airy, well-lit, and conducted by humane men. To use Joseph's own words, in the Hebrew, it was a miserable "hole." "I have done nothing that they should put me into the 'hole' " (Gen. 40:15).

Those who have seen the dreary prison at Tangier will be able to form a better conception of what that "hole" must have been like. Imagine a large gloomy hall, with no windows, paved with flags black with filth, no light or air, save what may struggle through the narrow grated aperture, by which the friends of the wretched inmates, or some pitying strangers, pass in the food and water which are the sole staff of life: no arrangements of any kind being made for cleanliness, or for the separation of the prisoners.

Confinement is intolerable to us all, but especially to youth, and of all youth most so to those in whose veins flows something of that Arab blood which dreads death less than bondage. But in addition to the confinement of the prison, he was bound, and his feet were hurt by fetters.

But besides all this, his religious notions added greatly to his distress. Joseph had tried to be good. Had he not always kept his father's commandments and acted righteously, though his brethren were men of evil report, and tried to make him as bad as themselves? Had he not, in the full flush of youthful passion, resisted the blandishments of the beautiful Egyptian, because he would not sin against God? Had he not always been kind and gentle to his fellow-prisoners, listening to their stories, speaking comfort to their hearts? What had he gained? To judge by what he saw, simply nothing; and he might as well have kept his kindness to himself.

You who have been misunderstood, who have sown seeds of holiness and love to reap nothing but disappointment, loss, suffering, and hate—*you* know something of what Joseph felt in that wretched dungeon hole.

Then, too, disappointment poured her bitter drops into the bitter cup. What had become of those early dreams which had filled his young brain with splendid phantasmagoria? Were these not from God? He had thought so—yes, and his venerable father had thought so too; and *he* should have known, for he had talked with God many a time. Was there no truth, no fidelity, in heaven or earth? Had God forsaken him? Had his father forgotten him? Did his brothers ever think of him? Was he to spend all his days in that dungeon, dragging on a weary life, never again enjoying the bliss of freedom? Do you wonder at the young heart being weighed almost to breaking?

And yet Joseph's experience is not alone. You may have never been confined in a dungeon; and yet you may have often sat in darkness, and felt around you the limitation which forbade your doing as you wished. You may have been doing right, and doing right may have brought you into some unforeseen difficulty; and you are disposed to say, "I have been too honest." Who does not know what it is to be misunderstood, misrepresented, accused falsely, and punished wrongfully?

Each begins life so buoyantly and hopefully. Youth, attempting the solution of the strange problem of existence, fears nothing, forbodes no ill. But presently disappointment, sorrow, and disaster overcloud the sky and blot out the sunny prospect; and the young mariner wakes as from a dream, "Can this be I, who imagined that I should never see ill?"

Taken on the lowest ground, this imprisonment served Joseph's temporal interests. That prison was the place where state prisoners were bound. Chief butler and chief baker do not seem much to us, but they were titles for very august people. Such men would talk freely with Joseph; and in doing so would give him a great insight into political parties, and a knowledge of men and things generally, which in after-days must have been of great service to him.

Psalm 105:18, referring to Joseph's imprisonment, has a striking alternative rendering, "His soul entered into iron." Turn that about, and render it in our language, and it reads thus, *Iron entered into his soul*. It is a very profound truth, that sorrow and privation, the yoke borne in the youth, the soul's enforced restraint, are all conducive to an iron tenacity and strength of purpose, an endurance, a fortitude, which are the indispensable foundation and framework of a noble character. Do not flinch from suffering. Bear it silently, patiently, resignedly; and be assured that it is God's way of infusing iron into your spiritual make-up.

As a boy, Joseph's character tended to softness. He was a little spoiled by his father. He lacked strength, grip, power to rule. But what a difference his imprisonment made in him! From that moment he carries himself with a wisdom, modesty, courage, and manly resolution, that never fail him. He acts as a born ruler of men. He carries an alien country through the stress of a great famine, without a symptom of revolt. He holds his own with the proudest aristocracy of the time. He promotes the most radical changes. He had learned to hold his peace and wait. Surely the iron had entered his soul!

It is just this that suffering will do for you. The world wants iron dukes, iron battalions, iron sinews, and thews of steel. God wants iron saints; and since there is no way of imparting iron to the moral nature than by letting His people suffer, He lets them suffer. "No chastening for the present seemeth to be joyous, but grievous; nevertheless afterward it yieldeth the peaceable fruit of righteousness unto them which are exercised thereby" (Heb. 12:11). Are you in prison for doing right? Are the best years of your life slipping away in enforced monotony? The iron crown of suffering precedes the golden crown of glory.

Is some aged eye perusing these words? Why does God sometimes fill a whole life with discipline?

"There is service in the sky." And it may be that God counts a human life of seventy years of suffering not too long an education for a soul which may serve Him through the eternities. If only we could see all that awaits us in the palace of the Great King, we should not be so surprised at certain experiences which befall us in earth's darker cells. You are being trained for service in God's Home, and in the upper spaces of His universe.

"He was there in the prison; but the Lord was with him" (Gen. 39:20, 21). The Lord was with him in the palace of Potiphar; but when Joseph went to prison, the Lord went there too. The only thing which severs us from God is sin. The godly man is much more independent of men and things than others. It is God who makes him blessed. Like the golden city, he has no need of sun or moon, for the Lord God is his everlasting light. If he is in a palace he is glad, not so much because of its delights as because God is there. And if he is in a prison he can sing and give praises, because the God of his love bears him company.

Moreover, "the Lord showed him mercy" (v. 21). Oh, wondrous revelation! He did not stand in a niche on the mountainside, as Moses did, whilst the solemn pomp swept past; and yet the Lord showed him a great sight—He showed him His mercy. That prison cell was the mount of vision,

from the height of which he saw, as he had never seen before, the panorama of Divine loving kindness. When the colored slide is flung upon the screen it is invisible, because the
room is full of light. Darken the room, and instantly the
round circle of light is filled with brilliant color. God our
Father has often to turn down the lights of our life because
He wants to show us mercy. Whenever you get into a prison
of circumstances, be on the watch. Prisons are rare places for
seeing things. It was in prison that Bunyan saw his wondrous allegory, and Paul met the Lord, and John looked
through heaven's open door, and Joseph saw God's mercy.

God can also raise up friends for His servants in most
unlikely places, and of most unlikely people. "The Lord gave
him favor in the sight of the keeper of the prison" (v. 21). All
hearts are open to our King: at His girdle swing the keys by
which the most unlikely door can be unlocked. "When a
man's ways please the Lord, He maketh even his enemies to
be at peace with him." It is as easy for God to turn a man's
heart, as it is for the husbandman to turn the course of a
brook to carry fertility to an arid plot.

There is always alleviation for our troubles in ministry to
others. Joseph found it so. It must have been a welcome relief
to the monotony of his grief when he found himself entrusted with the care of the royal prisoners. A new interest
came into his life, and he almost forgot the heavy pressure of
his own troubles amid the interest of listening to the tales of
those who were more unfortunate than himself. Joseph is the
patron of all prison philanthropists; but he took to this holy
work not primarily because he had an enthusiasm for it, but
because it gave a welcome opiate to his own griefs.

If your life is woven with the dark shades of sorrow, arise
to seek out those who are more miserable than you are, bearing them balm for their wounds and love for their heart-
breaks. And if you are unable to give much practical help,
you need not abandon yourself to the gratification of lonely
sorrow, for you may largely help the children of bitterness by
imitating Joseph in listening to their tales of woe or to their

dreams of foreboding. It is a great art to be a good listener. The burdened heart longs to pour out its tale in a sympathetic ear. There is immense relief in the telling out of pain. But it cannot be hurried; it needs plenty of time; it cannot clear itself of its silt and deposits unless it is allowed leisure to stand. And so the sorrowful turn away from men engaged in the full rush of active life as too busy, and seek out those who, like themselves, have been "winged," and are obliged to go softly, as Joseph was, when the servants of Pharaoh found him in the Egyptian dungeon. If you can do nothing else, listen well, and comfort others with the comfort wherewith you yourself have been comforted by God.

And now some closing words to those who are suffering wrongfully. Do not be surprised. You are the followers of One who was misunderstood from the age of twelve to the day of His ascension; who did not sin, and yet was counted as a sinner; concerning whom the unanimous testimony was, "I find in Him no fault at all"; and yet they called Him Beelzebub! If they spoke thus of the Master of the house, how much more concerning the household! "Think it not strange concerning the fiery trial that is to try you, as though some strange thing happened unto you" (I Pet. 4:12); only be sure that you suffer wrongfully, and as a Christian.

Do not get weary in well doing. Do right, because it is right to do right; because God sees you; because it puts gladness into the heart. And then, when you are misunderstood and ill treated, you will not swerve, or sit down to whine and despair.

Above all, do not avenge yourselves. When Joseph recounted his troubles, he did not recriminate harshly on his brethren, or Potiphar, or Potiphar's wife. He simply said: "I was stolen away out of the land of the Hebrews, and here also have I done nothing that they should put me into the hole." "If when ye do well, and suffer for it, ye take it patiently, this is acceptable with God" (I Pet. 2:20). We make a great mistake in trying always to clear ourselves; we should be much wiser to go straight on, humbly doing the next thing, and leaving God to vindicate us. "He will bring forth our righteousness as the light, and our judgment as the noonday." In Psalm 105:19 there follow words which, rightly rendered, read thus: "The word of the Lord cleared him." What a triumphant clearing did God give His faithful servant!

The believer takes his case into a higher court, and lays it before his God. It is a very little thing for him to be judged adversely at the bar of man: he cares only for the judgment of God, and awaits the moment when the righteous shall shine forth in the kingdom of their Father, as the sun when it breaks from all obscuring mists. Oh, slandered ones, you can afford to await the verdict of eternity.

It is hard to suffer wrong at the hands of man, and to think that perhaps it might have never been. But there is a truer and more restful view, to consider all things as being under the law and rule of God.

Unbroken sunshine would madden our brains; and unsullied prosperity of soul or circumstance would induce a spiritual excitement, which would be in the last degree deleterious. We must descend into the darksome glen, that we may test for ourselves the reliability of the staff and the rod.

> *He sent a man before them,*
>   *Even Joseph, who was sold for a servant,*
> *Whose feet they hurt with fetters;*
>   *He was laid in iron,*
> *Until the time that His word came:*
>   *The word of the Lord tried him.*
> *The king sent and loosed him,*
>   *Even the ruler of the people,*
>   *And let him go free.*
> *He made him lord of his house,*
>   *And ruler of all his substance;*
> *To bind his princes at his pleasure,*
>   *And teach his senators wisdom.*
>   Psalm 105:17-22

5

The Steps of the Throne

Genesis 41

"Remember me when it shall be well with thee" (Gen. 40:14). It was a modest and pathetic prayer that Joseph made to the great officer of state, to whose dream he had given so favorable an interpretation. Some, however, have said he had no right to make it.

The strongest faith has wavered at times. Elijah sank down on the desert sand, and asked that he might die. Many a time when we have professed that our soul waited only upon God, we have either eagerly hinted at or openly shown our needs to those whom we thought likely to assist.

The great man no doubt readily acceded to his request, and promised all he asked. "Remember you," he said; "of course I will." And, doubtless, in the fulness of his heart, he resolved to give Joseph a place among the under butlers, or perhaps in the vineries. And as he passed out, we can imagine him saying, "Good-bye: you will hear from me soon." But he "forgat." Week after week he watched for the message of deliverance. Then he invented ingenious excuses for the delay. But at last it was useless to hide from himself the unpalatable truth, which slowly forced itself upon his mind, that he was forgotten.

It may be that some who read these lines are in perplexity or distress which may be compared to that of Joseph when in the dungeon. There was a woman who went every morning for ten years to the village postmaster to ask for a letter from her son, which he promised to send, but which had never come. It is sad enough to be disappointed; but the sting of disappointment is when we are forgotten.

Men fail us; even the best prove to be less able or less willing than we thought. "Cursed be the man that trusteth in man, and maketh flesh his arm, and whose heart departeth from the Lord" (Jer. 17:5).

"He abideth faithful." He cannot promise and fail to perform. He says Himself: "Thou shalt not be forgotten by Me." A woman may forget her sucking child, and be unmindful of the son of her womb, "yet will I not forget thee." He may allow your prayers to accumulate like unopened letters on the table of an absent friend. But at last He will say, "O man, O woman, great is thy faith: be it unto thee even as thou wilt."

You may have had what Joseph had when still a lad—a vision of power and usefulness and blessedness. But you cannot realize it in fact. All your plans miscarry. Now turn your heart to God; accept His will; tell Him that you leave to Him the realization of your dream. He may keep you waiting a little longer; but you shall find Him verify the words of one who knew by experience His trustworthiness: "The salvation of the righteous is of the Lord; He is their strength in the time of trouble. And the Lord shall help them, and deliver them; He shall deliver them from the wicked and save them, because they trust in Him" (Ps. 37:39, 40).

There are links in the chain of Divine providence. First, the wife of Potiphar makes a baseless charge, which leads to Joseph's imprisonment; then, the young prisoner ingratiates himself with the keeper of the prison, and is allowed to have free access to the prisoners; then it happens at the very time that two state officials are thrown into jail on suspicion of attempting to poison their royal master; then the verification of Joseph's interpretation of their dreams shows that he is possessed of no common power; then that department of memory in which Joseph's face and case are hidden becomes sealed, lest anything premature should be attempted on his behalf; then, after two full years, the king of Egypt dreams.

To the casual observer there might seem a great deal of chance in all this; but the historian, directed by the Holy Spirit, lifts the veil, and shows that God was working out, step by step, His own infinite plans.

The dream was twice repeated, so similarly as to make it evident to the dullest mind that something was intended of unusual importance. The scene in each case was the river bank; first the green margin of grass, next the rich alluvial soil. To say the least, it was a bad omen to see the lean kine devour the fat, and the withered ears devour the full: nor can we wonder that the monarch of a people who attached special importance to omens and portents should send in hot haste for the army of priests who were always in close attendance upon him. But there was none that could interpret the dream of Pharaoh. "God made foolish the wisdom of this world."

Then the butler suddenly remembered his prison experiences, and told the king of the young captive Hebrew. Pharaoh eagerly caught at the suggestion: he sent and called Joseph; and they brought him hastily out of the dungeon—the margin says, "they made him run." Still the king's impetuous speed was compelled to wait till he had shaved himself and changed his prison garb. Perfect cleanliness and propriety of dress were so important in the eyes of Egyptians that the most urgent matters were postponed until they were properly attended to. Alas, that men should be so careful of their appearance before one another, and so careless of their appearance before God! Many a man who would not think of entering a drawing room if his linen were not snowy white is quite content to carry within his breast a heart as black as ink.

It is beautiful to notice Joseph's reverent references to God in his first interview with Pharaoh. "It is not in me: God shall give Pharaoh an answer of peace." "God hath showed Pharaoh what He is about to do" (v. 16). "The thing is established by God; and God will shortly bring it to pass" (v. 32). When the heart is full of God, the tongue will be almost obliged to speak of Him; and all such references will be easy and natural as flowers in May. Joseph was not ashamed to speak of his God amid the throng of idolaters in the court of Egypt.

There was no difficulty in interpreting the consumption of the seven good kine by the seven lean kine, and of the seven full ears by the seven empty ears, blasted by the east wind; or of indicating that the seven years of great plenty should be followed by seven years of famine, so sore that all the plenty should be forgotten in the land of Egypt, and that famine should consume the land.

It seems wonderful, not that Joseph gave it, but that the wise men of Pharaoh's court failed to discover it. This is an illustration of the Divine words, "Thou hast hid these things from the wise and prudent, and hast revealed them unto babes: even so, Father, for so it seemed good in thy sight" (Matt. 11:25).

That dream was framed in a thoroughly Egyptian setting and was connected with the Nile. The river was the object of idolatrous worship. The buffalo, a species of ox, well known anciently in Egypt, delights to stand in the water in hot countries with all the body, except the head, immersed. The sight of horned cattle coming up out of a river would, therefore, not be a rare occurrence; and Joseph had no difficulty in carrying his audience with him, when he said that these seven kine—as also the seven ears of corn on one stalk, after the nature of that species of bearded wheat still known as Egyptian wheat—were emblems of seven years of great plenty throughout all the land of Egypt.

But perhaps the thing which gave Joseph most influence in that court was not his interpretation, but the wise and statesmanlike policy on which he insisted. As he detailed his successive recommendations: the appointment of a man discreet and wise with this exclusive business as his lifework; of the creation of a new department of public business for the purpose of gathering up the resources of Egypt in anticipation of the coming need; of the vast system of storage in the

cities of the land—it was evident that he was speaking beneath the glow of a spirit not his own; and with a power
which commanded the instant assent of the monarch and his
chief advisers. "The thing was good in the eyes of Pharaoh,
and in the eyes of all his servants. And Pharaoh said unto his
servants, Can we find such an one as this is, a man in whom
the Spirit of God is?" Oh that we might carry with us, even
into business relationship, the evident stamp of the Spirit of
God! "Ask and have; seek and find; open your heart and
receive."

There is an interesting illustration given to us here of the
words, "Them that honor Me, I will honor." When Joseph
had finished, Pharaoh said unto his servants, "Can we find
such an one as this is, a man in whom is the Spirit of God?"
(v. 28). Then he turned to Joseph and said, "Forasmuch as
God hath showed thee this, there is none so discreet and
wise as thou art; thou shalt be over my house, and according
to thy word shall all my people be ruled: only in the throne
will I be greater than thou. . . . See, I have set thee over the
whole land of Egypt" (vv. 38-41).

All of this happened because one day, for the sake of God,
Joseph resisted a temptation to one act of sin. If he had
yielded, we should probably never have heard of him again;
he would have been slain by the siren who has slain so many
more strong men. Let us seek first the kingdom of God and
His righteousness. He will turn again and have mercy upon
us, and will exalt us to inherit the earth.

And when that day comes, let us ascribe all to God. I admire the names which Joseph gave to his sons. They show
the temper of his heart when in the zenith of his prosperity.
Manasseh means "forgetting"—God had made him forget
his toils. Ephraim means "fruitfulness"—God had caused
him to be fruitful. Be true! *you* shall forget your sorrow and
long waiting; *you* shall be fruitful. Then be sure and give
God the praise.

The parallel between the life of Joseph and the life of the
Lord Jesus is surely more than a coincidence. The Holy
Spirit, enamored with the mystery of love which was com-

ing, anticipated its most striking features in the life of Joseph. Joseph was rejected by his brethren; Jesus by the Jews, His brethren according to the flesh. Joseph was sold for twenty pieces of silver to the Ishmaelites; Jesus was sold by the treachery of Judas for thirty pieces, and then handed over to the Gentiles. Joseph was cast into prison: Jesus abode in the grave. Joseph in prison was able to preach the gospel of deliverance to the butler; Jesus went and preached the gospel to the spirits in the prison. The two malefactors of the cross find their counterpart in Joseph's two fellow prisoners. Joseph, though a Jew by birth and rejected by his own brethren, nevertheless was raised to supreme power in a Gentile state, and saved myriads of them from death; Jesus, of Jewish birth and yet disowned by Jews, has nevertheless been exalted to the supreme seat of power, and is now enthroned in the hearts of myriads of Gentiles, to whom He has brought salvation from death, and spiritual bread for their hunger. The very name that Pharaoh gave to Joseph meant "Savior of the world"—our Savior's title. Yes, and we must carry the parallel still farther. After Joseph had been for some time ruling and blessing Egypt, his very brethren came to him for forgiveness and help; so in days not far away we shall see the Jews retracing their steps and exclaiming—as thousands are now doing in Russia—"Jesus is our Brother." So all Israel shall be saved!

We have now, therefore, to think of Jesus as seated on His throne, Prime Minister of the universe, the Interpreter of His Father's will, the Organ and Executor of the Divine decrees. On His head are many crowns; on His finger is the ring of sovereignty; on His loins the girdle of power. Glistening robes of light envelop Him. And this is the cry which precedes Him, "Bow the knee!" Have *you* ever bowed the knee at His feet? The tongue of malice and envy may traduce Him, and refuse to let Him reign. But nothing can upset the Father's decree and plan. "Yet have I set My Son upon My holy hill" (Ps. 2:6). "In His name every knee shall bow, and every tongue shall confess that He is Lord" (Phil. 2:11). Agree with Him quickly. "Kiss the Son, lest He be angry" (Ps. 2:12).

6

Joseph's First Interview
With His Brethren

Genesis 42

The life of Joseph, as the Prime Minister of Egypt, was a very
splendid one. Everything that could please the sense or
minister to the taste was his. The walls of Egyptian palaces
still exist in the rainless air to attest the magnificent provision that was made for all necessaries and luxuries. In point
of fact, the civilization of our time in many points has nothing of which to boast over that of the age in which he lived.
His palaces would consist of numberless rooms opening into
spacious courts, where palms, sycamores, and acacia trees
grew in rare luxuriance. Rare perfumes rose from vases of
gold and bronze and alabaster; and the foot sank deep in
carpets covering the floors. Choirs of musicians filled the air
with sweet melody.

But though one of rare splendor, his life must have been
one of considerable anxiety. He had to deal with a proud
hereditary nobility, jealous of his power, and with a
populace mad with hunger. During the first seven years of
his premiership he went throughout all the land of Egypt
superintending the dykes and ditches which should utilize
as much as possible the unusual rise of the Nile; building
vast granaries, and buying up a fifth of the vast profusion of
grain. "The earth brought forth by handfuls; and Joseph
gathered corn as the sand of the sea, very much, until he left

numbering, for it was without number" (Gen. 41:47, 49). It must have been difficult for this young foreigner to carry out his wide-reaching plans in face of the stolid apathy or the active opposition of great officials and vested interests.

He was, however, eminently qualified for this work. As Pharaoh had said most truly, "He was a man in whom was the Spirit of God." Oh, when will men learn that the Spirit of God may be in them when they are buying and selling, and arranging all the details of business or home?

All these events took time. Joseph was a lad of seventeen summers when he was torn away from his home; and he was a young man of thirty when he stood for the first time before Pharaoh. Seven years for the golden time of plenty must be added; and perhaps two more while the stores of the granaries were being slowly exhausted: so that probably twenty-five years had passed between the tragedy at the pit's mouth and the time of which we are thinking now. During those years the life in Jacob's camp had flowed uneventfully and quietly. The chief sign of the number of the slow passing years was the growing weakness in the old father's step and the increasing infirmity of his form. He pathetically speaks much of his "grey hairs." He bore in his heart the scars of many wounds, the chief of which was grief for his beloved Joseph. He went step by down step towards the grave "mourning for his son."

Meanwhile, the sons had become middle-aged men, with families of their own. They probably never mentioned that deed of violence to each other. They did their best to banish the thought from their minds. Sometimes in their dreams they may have caught a glimpse of that young face in its agony, or heard the beseechings of his anguished soul; but they sought to drown such painful memories by deep draughts of the Lethe-stream of forgetfulness. Conscience slept. Yet the time had come when God meant to use these men to found a nation. And in order to fit them for their high destiny it was necessary to bring them into a right condition of soul. The great Physician never heals over a wound from above. The foundations of noble character must touch the rock of genuine repentance. But it seemed almost impossible to secure repentance in those obtuse and darkened hearts.

This, then, is our theme: God's gracious methods of awakening the consciences of these men from their long and apparently endless sleep. And it is a theme well worth our study for if there is one thing more than another that is needed in Christian congregations and in the world, it is the deep conviction of sin.

The first step towards their conviction was the pressure of want. There was dearth in all lands; and the famine reached even to the land of Canaan. Often before, in the lives of the patriarchs, had they been driven by famine down to Egypt; and Jacob aroused his sons from the hopeless lethargy into which they were sinking by saying, "Why look ye on one another? Behold, I have heard that there is corn in Egypt; get you down there and buy for us, that we may live and not die. And Joseph's ten brethren went down to buy corn in Egypt" (vv. 1-3). When the mighty famine came, the hearts of these men were opened to conviction; their carnal security was shattered; and they were prepared for certain spiritual experiences of which they would never have dreamed. Yes; and they were being prepared for the meeting with Joseph.

It is so that God deals with us. He breaks up our nest. He loosens our roots. He sends a mighty famine which cuts away the whole staff of bread. And at such times, weary, worn, and sad, we are prepared to confess our sins, and to receive the words of Christ, when He says, "Come unto Me, all ye that labor and are heavy-laden, and I will give you rest" (Matt. 11:28). In after days those men looked back upon that time of sore straitness as the best thing that could have happened to them: nothing less would have brought them to Joseph. Yes, and the time is coming when you will bless God for your times of sorrow and misfortune. You will say, "Before I was afflicted I went astray; but now have I kept Thy Word" (Ps. 119:67).

The second step was the rough usage they received at the

hands of Joseph. It would seem that in some of the larger markets he superintended the sale of the corn himself. He was standing as usual at his post, surrounded by all the confusion and noise of an Eastern bazaar, when suddenly his attention was attracted by the entrance of those ten men. He looked with a fixed, eager look for a moment, his heart throbbing quickly all the while; and he needed no further assurance: "he knew them."

Evidently, however, they did not know him. He had grown from a lad of seventeen to a man of forty. He was clothed in pure white linen, with ornaments of gold to indicate his rank. He was governor of the land. So, in unconscious fulfilment of his own boyish dream, they bowed down themselves before him with their faces to the earth.

Joseph instantly saw that they failed to recognize him; and partly to ascertain if his brethren were repentant, partly in order to know why Benjamin was not with them, he made himself strange unto them. He spake roughly to them. He accused them of being spies. He refused to believe their statements, and put them in prison until they could be verified. He kept Simeon bound.

In all this, I believe he repeated exactly the scene at the pit's mouth. It is likely that when they saw him coming towards them, in his princelike dress, they had rushed at him, accusing him of having come to spy out their corrupt behavior, and take back an evil report to their father, as he had done before: if so, this will explain why he now suddenly accused them of being spies. No doubt the lad protested that he was no spy—that he had only come to inquire after their welfare; but they had met his protestations with rude violence in much the same way as the rough-speaking governor now treated them. It may be that they had even thrust him into the pit with the threat to keep him there until his statements could be verified, in much the same way as Joseph now dealt with them; and Simeon may have been the ringleader. If this were the case—and it seems most credible—it is obvious that it was a powerful appeal to their conscience and memory, and one that could not fail to awaken both.

We remember all things: there is a record of everything that ever we saw or did, somewhere in the archives of memory; but we cannot always recollect an incident, or recall it at the required moment.

So is it with sin. Long years ago, you may have committed some sin; you have tried to forget it. It has not been forgiven and put away; you have almost succeeded in dropping it from your thoughts: but believe me, it is still there; and the most trivial incident may at any moment bring it all back upon your conscience, as vividly as if committed only yesterday. If sin is forgiven, it is indeed forgotten: God says, "I will remember it no more." But if only forgotten, and not forgiven, it may have a most unexpected and terrible awakening.

This was the case with Joseph's brethren. They said one to another, as they heard the reiterated demand of the strange governor for evidence that they were not spies, "We are verily guilty concerning our brother; in that we saw the anguish of his soul, when he besought us, and we would not hear: therefore is this distress come upon us" (v. 21).

The third step towards conviction was the giving of time for them to listen to God's Spirit, speaking to them. It is not enough to feel that sin is a blunder and a mistake, but not guilt. This sense of sin, however, is the prerogative of the Spirit of God. He alone can convict of sin. When He is at work, the soul cries out, "Woe is me, I am a sinful man!" "We are verily *guilty* concerning our brother."

Are *you* not verily guilty? In early life you may have wronged some man or some woman. You may have taught some young lad to swear. You may have laughed away the early impressions from some anxious seeker, until they fled to return no more. You may not have done your best to save those committed to your care. And now others seem to be treating you as you treated the associates of earlier days. You now are eager for salvation; and you learn the bitterness of being ridiculed, thwarted, tempted, and opposed. You recall the past; it flashes before you with terrible intensity. You cry, "God forgive me! I am verily guilty concerning that soul whom I betrayed or wronged." And this is the work of the Holy Spirit. Let Him have His blessed way with you.

There is at least one Brother whom you have wronged. He is not ashamed to call you brother; but you have been ashamed of Him. He did not withhold Himself from the cross; but you have never thanked Him. He has freely offered you the greatest gifts; but you have trampled them beneath your feet, and done despite to Him, and crucified Him afresh. There is, no doubt, a time coming when the Jews shall say of Him, whom they once rejected and put into the pit of death, but who has since been giving corn to the Gentiles, "We are verily guilty concerning our Brother." But these words may also be humbly and sorrowfully appropriated by many of us.

While these men spoke thus, Joseph stood by them. There was no emotion on those compressed features, no response in those quiet eyes. "They wist not that he understood them." Ah, how often do anguished souls go to priests, ministers, and friends, with the bitter tale of anguish! They wist not that One is standing by who hears and understands all, and longs to throw aside every barrier in order to bring them aid. True, He speaks to them by an interpreter; but if they would only speak straight to Him, He would speak directly to their waiting hearts.

There is a curious contrast in the twenty-fourth verse. First, we learn that "he turned himself about from them and wept"; and next we are told that he "took Simeon and bound him before their eyes." The brethren saw only the latter of these two actions, and must have thought him rough and unkind. They could not guess that the retention of Simeon was intended to act as a silken cord to bring the brothers back to him, and as part of the process of awakening the memory of another brother, whom they had lost years before.

The sacks were filled with corn; provision was given for

the journey home, so that they needed not to come on the stores they were carrying back for their households; and every man's money was returned in his sack's mouth (v. 25). All this was meant in tender love; but their hearts failed them with fear. A guilty conscience misinterprets the kindest gifts and mercies which God sends to us. How often we cry, "What hath God done to us?" and are filled with fear, when, in point of fact, God's dealings are working out a purpose of mercy which shall make us rejoice all our days.

7

Joseph's Second Interview
With His Brethren

Genesis 43

Where is there such another story as this of Joseph? It seems sometimes impossible to believe that the events happened thirty-five centuries ago, in the solemn, rainless land of the Nile and the Pyramids. They might have occurred within our own memory, the experience is so natural, so lifelike, so like our own. And yet orientalists assure us that, in its minutest details, it is verified by the paintings which, to this day, exist on the walls of palaces and temples, unimparied and fresh.

Jacob had never turned his thoughts to Egypt if there had been plenty in Canaan. The famine drove the sons of Israel into Egypt to buy corn. And even though poor Simeon was bound in Egypt, the brothers had not gone a second time if it had not been for the rigor of that necessity.

There is a touching picture given of the conversation between the old man and his sons. Reuben seems already to have lost the priority which his birthright would have secured, and Judah held the place of spokesman and leader amongst the brethren. At the outset, Jacob's request that they should go down to buy food was met with the most distinct refusal, unless Benjamin was permitted to accompany them. And when he complained of their having betrayed the existence of another brother, the whole of them vindicated their action, and declared that they could not have done otherwise. At last Judah made himself personally responsible for the lad's safety, a pledge which, as we shall see, he nobly redeemed. And so, at last, the old man yielded, proposing only that they should take a present to mollify the ruler's heart, a double money to replace what had been returned in their sacks, and uttering a fervent prayer to the Almighty on their behalf. Thus God in His mercy shut up every other door but the one through which they might find their way to plenty and blessedness.

So is your life. You have had all that this world could give. You have had all that man could wish. But what has been your state of heart meanwhile? Have you set your affections upon things above? Have you lived for that world which lies beyond the narrow horizon of the visible? You know you have not. So God has called for a famine on your land, and broken the whole staff of your bread. Everything has been against you.

In the first burst of the tempest, you say stubbornly, "I will not go down; I will not yield; I will stand out to the last." But, beware! It is a fatal mistake to wrestle against the love of God. Jacob tried it by the Jabbok ford; and he limped on a halting thigh until he gathered his feet up into his deathbed. The famine must continue until the wanderer arises to return to the Father, with words of penitent contrition on his lips. Oh that your reply might be!—"Come, and let us return unto the Lord; for He hath torn, and He will heal us; He hath smitten, and He will bind us up."

For twenty years conscience had slept. And as long as this was the case there could be no real peace between Joseph and his brethren. *They* could never feel sure that he had forgiven them. *He* would always feel that there was a padlock on the treasure-store of his love.

Men will best learn what is the true nature of their own iniquities when they experience the treatment which they meted out to others. And Joseph's device was a success. Listen to their moan, "We are verily guilty because of our brother."

Here again is a clue to the mysteries of our lives. God sometimes allows us to be treated as we have treated Him, that we may see our offence in its true character, and may be obliged to turn to Him with words of genuine contrition.

Then Joseph displays much tender love towards his brethren. As soon as Joseph espied them he invited them to his own table to feast with him. They were brought into his house, where every kindness was shown to them. Their fears as to the return of the money were allayed by the pious, though prevaricating, assurance of the steward that if they had discovered it in their sacks it must have been put there by God. And when Joseph came they prostrated themselves before him in striking fulfilment of his own boyish dream. He asked them tenderly about the well-being of their father; and there must have been a pathos in his words to Benjamin which would have revealed the whole secret if they had not been so utterly unprepared to find Joseph beneath the strange guise of the great Egyptian governor.

Joseph's heart welled up into his eyes, so that he needed to make haste to conceal the bursting emotions, which threatened to overmaster him. "He sought where to weep, and he entered into his chamber, and wept there. And he washed his face, and went out, and refrained himself; and said, Set on bread."

There may be prophetic touches here. And we may yet see the counterpart of this scene literally fulfilled, when the Lord comes forward to recognize and receive His ancient people. But in the meanwhile what shall we say of His love to ourselves? He loves us with a love in which is concentrated the love of all parents to their children, and of all friends for their beloved. And that love is constantly devising means of expressing itself. It takes a tender interest in those we love; it wishes us grace from God; it adjusts itself to our temperaments and puts us at our ease, so that gleams of light as to the love of Jesus strike into our hearts! He feels yearnings over us which He restrains, and dares not betray till the work of conviction is complete, and He can pour the full tides of affection on us, without injury to others or harm to ourselves.

There was the destruction of their self-confidence. They thought their *word* was good; but when they told their family history, Joseph refused to believe it, and said it must be proved. They were confident in their *money*. But when they reached their first halting-place on their way home, "as one of them opened his sack to give his ass provender, he espied his money; for, behold, it was in the sack's mouth: and he said unto his brethren, My money is restored; and lo, it is even in my sack: and their heart failed them, and they were afraid, saying one to another, What is this that God hath done unto us?" (Gen. 42:27, 28).

They were confident also in their *integrity*. They were in high spirits. Simeon was with them; so was Benjamin, notwithstanding the nervous forebodings of the old father. They were evidently in high favor with the governor, else they had not been treated to so grand a feast on the previous day. But they had hardly got clear of the city gate, when they were arrested by the steward's voice. "Stop! Stop! Why have ye rewarded evil for good?" And they said, "Wherefore saith my lord these words? Behold, the money which we found in our sacks' mouths we brought again unto thee: how then should we steal silver or gold out of thy lord's house?" And, "With whomsoever they master's cup is found, let him die, and we also will be my lord's bondmen." And the steward searched them there on the bare road, beginning with the eldest to the youngest, "*and the cup was found in Benjamin's sack.*" Well might Judah and his brethren come to Joseph's house and fall before him on the ground, and say, "What shall we say unto my lord? What shall we speak? or how shall we clear ourselves? God hath found out the iniquity of thy servants" (Gen. 44:4-9, 16). They were stripped of every rag of self-confidence, and were shut up to his uncovenanted mercy.

Some men resemble Benjamin. They are naturally guileless and beautiful. Some faint traces of original innocence linger about them. Their type is shown forth in the young man whom Jesus loved, as he stood before Him breathless with haste, protesting that he had kept all the commandments blameless from his youth. We do not reckon sin to such; and they do not reckon it to themselves. The publican and the sinner may stand in urgent need of the blood of Christ; but surely nitre and soap will suffice for them. But this reasoning is full of flaws. Such people seem good, only because they are compared with sinners of a blacker dye. Compare them with the only standard of infinite purity; and they are infinitely condemned. "If I wash myself with snow-water, and make my hands never so clean, yet shalt Thou plunge me in the ditch, and mine own clothes shall abhor me."

There is a stolen cup in your sack, my respectable, reputable, moral friend. You are probably unconscious of it. You pride yourself upon your blameless life. You suppose that Christ Himself has no controversy with you. But if you only knew, you would see that you are robbing Him of His own. You use for yourself time and money and talents which He bought with His own precious blood, and which He meant to be a chosen vessel unto Himself. It is remarkable that you, who are so scrupulous in paying every man his dues, should be so careless of the daily treachery of which you are guilty in defrauding the Lord of His own purchase. But if you hide the unwelcome truth from yourself, you cannot hide it from your Lord. "Wot ye not that such an one as He can certainly divine?" "He searcheth the hearts and trieth the reins of the children of men" (Jer. 17:10). And "he that is first in his own cause seemeth just; but his neighbor cometh and searcheth him."

How then shall we act? First, Do not linger. "Except we had lingered, surely now ere this we should have returned twice" (v. 10). Except you had lingered, ere this you would have become an earnest, happy Christian. The entrance is nearly bricked up. The hourglass is nearly run out, and when its last grain has gone the court of mercy will close.

Secondly, Make full confession or restitution. "They came

near to the steward of Joseph's house and communed with him," and told him all about the finding of the money, and offered it back in full weight. Commune with Christ as you close this story. Tell Him all that is in your heart. "When I kept silence, my bones waxed old through my roaring all the day long; for day and night thy hand was heavy upon me; my moisture was turned into the drought of summer. I acknowledged my sin unto Thee, and mine iniquity have I not hid. And Thou forgavest the iniquity of my sin" (Ps. 32:5). "He that covereth his sins shall not prosper; but whoso confesseth and forsaketh them shall have mercy" (Prov. 28:13).

Thirdly, Throw yourself on the mercy of Christ. Judah did not excuse himself or his brethren. He adopted a wiser course—he pleaded for mercy. Try that plea with your Lord. You will find that it will not fail you. Say, as you beat upon your breast, "Be merciful unto me, *the* sinner!" He will not be able to refrain. He will say, in broken accents, "Come near unto Me; I am Jesus your Brother: your sins nailed Me to the cross, but speak of it no more; grieve not for it. God has overruled it for good, that I might save your lives by a great deliverance."

8
Joseph Making Himself Known

Genesis 45

"The cup was found in Benjamin's sack" (Gen. 44:12). There in the open road, in the early morning light, as the villagers were passing into the city with melons and leeks and onions, and as the city was beginning to bestir itself, the cup of the great Premier, in whose hands was the power of life and death, was found lying in the corn, half hidden, as by stealth. But how did it come there? The brothers could not tell.

Each brother must have wished that the cup could have been found in any sack rather than in Benjamin's. They all remembered their father's strange unwillingness to let him come. When first they returned from Egypt he said decisively, "My son shall not go down with you; for his brother is dead, and he is left alone: if mischief befall him by the way in which ye go, then shall ye bring down my grey hairs with sorrow to the grave" (Gen. 42:38). And when the pressure of famine compelled them, the last words of the timid and stricken parent were, "God Almighty give you mercy before the man, that he may send away your other brother, and Benjamin. If I be bereaved of my children, I am bereaved" (Gen. 43:14). Each of those men must have thought to himself, as he followed in the sad procession back, "How dare I face my father?" But there was nothing for it except to reload their asses and return.

Notice the circumstances in which they found themselves.

Their conscience was now awakened, and it was ill at ease. The first words uttered by Judah their spokesman as they entered the audience chamber of Joseph, betrayed the dark forebodings of their thoughts: "What shall we say unto my Lord? What shall we speak? or how shall we clear ourselves? God hath found out the iniquity of thy servants" (Gen. 44:16).

God will always find out our iniquity. "Be sure your sin will find you out." If all sin is not traced home to its authors in *this* world, at least there is enough to show how terrible that moment will be, when, at the "great white throne," the secrets of all hearts will be disclosed, and God will bring to light the hidden things of darkness. There is absolutely no chance of escape for a man, save in the wounds of Jesus; these are the city of refuge into which the pursuer cannot enter, and in which the fugitive is safe.

But, in addition, they felt that they were absolutely in Joseph's power. And the counterpart of this must surely be an alarming thought to the awakened sinner—that he is entirely at the mercy of the Judge of the quick and the dead.

There was no doubt that the cup had been found in Benjamin's sack; and though they were certainly innocent of the theft, they were unable to clear or excuse themselves.

The divining cup is familiar enough to all students of ancient literature. It was sometimes made of crystal and of precious stones; and it was supposed that all secrets would be reflected by the liquid it contained. Homer sings of the cup of Nestor. And Spenser tells us how the royal maiden, Britomart, found Merlin's cup in her father's closet, and used it to discover a secret which closely concerned her. We, of course, do not believe that Joseph used such a cup for such a purpose; but it was his desire to maintain the character of an Egyptian of high rank. All Egyptian noblemen used such a cup. In their conscience-stricken condition, the brothers were too depressed to contest its decisions, or to ask for one more decisive test of their innocence or guilt.

Notice their behavior. "They fell before him on the

ground." Here were their sheaves making obeisance to his sheaf, standing erect in the midst.

But who was to be their spokesman? Reuben had always had something to say in self-justification, and had been so sure that all would be right that he had pledged the lives of his children to his father for the safety of Benjamin; but *he* is dumb. Simeon was probably the cruel one, the instigator of the crime against Joseph; but *he* dares not utter a word. Benjamin, the blameless one, the prototype of the young man whom Jesus loved, is convicted of sin, and has nought to say. Who then is to speak? There is only one, Judah, who at the pit's mouth had diverted the brothers from their first thought of murder. And notice how he speaks. He does not attempt to hold up any extenuating circumstances, or to explain the past, or to excuse Benjamin or themselves. He throws himself helplessly on Joseph's mercy: "What shall we say unto my lord? what shall we speak? or how shall we clear ourselves?"

This is a good example for us to follow still. There is no doubt about our guilt. If we try to extenuate our faults to excuse ourselves we shall be brought face to face with the damning evidence of our guilt. But if we throw ourselves on His mercy, we cannot fail.

We stand on surer ground than ever they did. They had no idea of the gentleness of Joseph's heart; they had not seen him turn aside to weep; they had not understood why on one occasion he had hastened from their presence. But we know the gentleness of the Lord Jesus. We have seen His tears over Jerusalem; we have listened to His tender invitations to come to Him; we have stood beneath His cross and heard His last prayers for His murderers, and His words of invitation to the dying thief; we know that He will not break the bruised reed, nor quench the smoking flax. We need not look nervously towards His throne to see if the golden sceptre of His grace is extended towards us. Failure and rejection are alike impossible to the soul that pleads guilty, and that casts itself on the mercy of God which is in Jesus Christ our Lord.

In all literature, there is nothing more pathetic than this

appeal of Judah. The eagerness that made him draw near; the humility that confessed Joseph's anger might righteously burn, since he was as Pharaoh; the picture of the old man, their father, bereft of one son, and clinging to this little one, the only relic of his mother; the recital of the strain which the governor had imposed on them, by demanding that they should bring their youngest brother down; the story of their father's dread, only overmastered by the imperious demand of a hunger that knew no law, and brooked no check; the vivid picture of the father's eagerness again to see the lad, in whose life his own was bound up; the heart-breaking grief at not seeing him amongst them; the heroic offer to stay there a slave, as Benjamin's substitute, if only the lad might go home; the preference of a life of slavery rather than to behold the old man sinking with sorrow into his grave—all this is touched with master-hand. How much of poetry and pathos lie behind some of the roughest men, only waiting for some great sorrow to smite open the upper crust, and bore the Artesian well! But if a rough man could plead like this, think, what must not those pleadings be which Jesus offers before the throne! We have an Advocate in the Court of King's Bench who never lost a case: let us put ourselves into His hands, and trust Him when He says, "I have prayed for thee." "Such a High-Priest became us."

Thus Joseph's object was attained. He had wished to restore them to perfect rest and peace; but he knew that these were impossible so long as their sin was unconfessed and unforgiven. Then, too, he had been anxious to see how they felt toward Benjamin. With this object in view he had given him five times as much as he had given them. Some think that he did this to show his special love. It may have been so; but probably there was something deeper. It was his dream of superiority that aroused their hatred against himself: how would they feel toward Benjamin, if he, the younger, were treated better than them all? Besides, he wanted to see if they could forgive. It was Benjamin who had brought them into all this trouble: had they treated him in the spirit of former days, they would have abandoned him to his fate; but if so, they could not have been forgiven. "If ye forgive not men their trespasses, neither will your Heavenly Father forgive you" (Matt. 6:15). But they had no malice against this young lad. Evidently then all Joseph's purposes were accomplished.

"Then Joseph could not refrain himself" (v. 1). It was only because he studied their lasting welfare, that he refrained himself so long. It may be that some one will read this who has been disposed to think that our Savior is hard to please. Ah, it is the other way! He is gentle and easy to be entreated; it is not for want of love. He loved the dear inmates of the home in Bethany, but He refrained Himself, and abode two days still in the same place where He was, so that Lazarus died; and then He went that He might work his greatest miracle at the grave in which hope itself lay buried.

And Joseph cried, "Cause every man to go out from me." There was great delicacy here. "And so there stood no man with him, while Joseph made himself known unto his brethren" (v. 1). We must stand alone before Christ, if we would know Him. As Peter met our Lord alone on the resurrection morning, for "He was seen of Cephas"—so alone must each man meet Christ. Why not at once?

And he wept aloud. His mind had been on the stretch; and now that the tension was removed, and that there was no further necessity for it, he wept aloud. Ah, sinner, the heart of Christ is on the stretch for thee!

And he said, "I am Joseph." He spoke in deep emotion; yet the words must have fallen on them like a thunderbolt. "Joseph!" Had they been dealing all the while with their long-lost brother? "Joseph!" Then they had fallen into a lion's den indeed. Astonishment as at one risen from the dead, terror for the consequences, fear lest he would repay them the longstanding debt—all these emotions made them dumb. So he said again, "I am Joseph, *your brother*, whom ye sold into Egypt" (v. 4); and he added very lovingly, "Be not grieved, nor angry, for God did send me" (v. 5). How much this reminds us of another scene, not far from the gates of

Damascus, when Jesus arrested the young persecutor with the words, "Saul, why persecutest thou Me?" And he said, "Who art Thou, Lord?" And the answer came back, "I am Jesus, whom thou persecutest" (Acts 9:4, 5). Penitent sinner! it is thus that thy Savior speaks to thee. "I am Jesus, your brother, whom thou hast sold and crucified; yet grieve not for that. I was delivered by the determinate counsel and foreknowledge of God; though the hands have been none the less wicked by whom I have been crucified and slain. But if you repent, your sins shall be blotted out. All manner of sin shall be forgiven unto the sons of men, and the blasphemies wherewith soever they may have blasphemed."

"And Joseph said unto his brethren, come near unto me" (v. 4). They had gone farther and farther back from him; but now he bids them approach. This is a beautiful illustration of the way in which a sinner may be reinstated in the loving favor of God. Once "far off," but now "made nigh" by the blood of Jesus. One moment the rugged road of repentance; the next the Father's kiss and the banquet in the Father's home.

A moment more saw him and Benjamin locked in each other's arms, their tears freely flowing. And he kissed *all* his *brethren.* Simeon? Yes. Reuben? Yes. Those who had tied his hands and mocked his cries? So shall it be one day. The Jews are back in Palestine in unbelief. Sore troubles await them there, to prepare them to recognize their rejected Messiah. But the time is not far distant when they shall be prepared to hear Him say, "I am Jesus, your brother, whom ye crucified; but be not grieved with yourselves, for God has brought good out of evil, both for Gentile and for Jew, by saving life with a great deliverance." "And they shall look upon Him whom they pierced, and mourn because of Him" (Zech. 12:10). "And so all Israel shall be saved."

9

Joseph's Administration of Egypt

Genesis 47

While all the domestic details on which we have been meditating were transpiring, Joseph was carrying his adopted country through a great crisis—I might almost call it a revolution. When he became Prime Minister, the Egyptian monarchy was comparatively weak; but after he had administered affairs for some thirteen years, Pharaoh was absolute owner of all the land of Egypt. Nor is this the only instance of a Hebrew conducting his adopted country through extraordinary perils by the exercise of extraordinary genius.

During the seven years of plenty, Joseph caused one-fifth of all the produce of every district to be hoarded up in its town; so that each town would contain, within immense granaries, the redundant produce of its own district. At last the years of famine came. And recent sad experiences in India will help us to realize something of the meaning of the words: "There was no bread in all the land, for the famine was very sore; so that the land of Egypt, and all the land of Canaan, fainted by reason of the famine" (v. 13). No doubt, had there been no provision made by Joseph, the streets would have been filled by emaciated skeletons picking their way feebly amid the heaps of the dying and the dead; men, women, and children would have fallen before the scythe of famine fever; and it would have taken years for the country to be repopulated to its former extent.

The slender stores of the Egyptians were soon exhausted;

and when all the land of Egypt was famished, the people cried unto Pharaoh, saying: "Bread! bread! give us bread!" Did they invade the palace precincts, flow into the corridors, and force their way into the royal presence, as the Parisian mob had done more than once in the awful days of revolution? We do not know. But Pharaoh had a ready answer: "Go unto Joseph; and what *he* saith unto you, do." "Then Joseph opened all the storehouses and *sold* unto the Egyptians." This was right and wise. It would have been a great mistake to *give*. In the Irish famine the Government set the people to earn their bread by making the roads, since it would have done them lasting injury to have allowed them to receive help without rendering some kind of equivalent. And it is not too much to say that it would have taken the Egyptians one or two generations to recover their moral tone if, instead of selling, Joseph had given the corn. Joseph's policy was in exact accord with the maxims of modern political economy.

But the money was soon exhausted: it lasted just one year. What was to be done now? There was nothing left but persons and lands; the people were naturally loth to pledge these, but there was no alternative; and so they came to Joseph, and said, "Why should we die? Buy us and our land for bread" (v. 19). In other words, they became Pharaoh's tenant farmers, and paid him twenty per cent, or one-fifth of their returns, as rent. This may seem a heavy tax; but it is not heavier than the rentage in almost every European country in the present day.

Let us study the spirit of Joseph's administration. It is summed up in three brief sentences: He was "diligent in business, fervent in spirit, serving the Lord."

Of his *diligence in business* there is ample proof. When first raised to the proud position of Premier, "he went out through all the land of Egypt" Joseph bought the whole land for Pharaoh; and Joseph superintended the removal of the people into the cities from one end of the country to the other for the easier distribution of food. Joseph made the laws. "Seest thou a man diligent in his business, he shall stand before kings, he shall not stand before mean men" (Prov. 22:29). Young men, make Joseph your model in this. Some men do their lifework as if every joint were stiff with rheumatism. Others are somnambulists, not able to find their work, or, having found it, not able to find their tools; taking their passage when the ship has sailed; insuring their furniture when the house is in flames. First choose a pursuit, however humble, into which you can rightly throw your energy, and then put into it all your forces.

Make the most of your time. Be miserly over the moments, and redeem the gold-dust of time, and they will make a golden fortune of leisure. Be punctual. Some men do not miss their appointments; but they always arrive five minutes late. Be methodical. Arrange, so far as you can, your daily work, as postmen do their letters, in streets and districts; subject always, of course, to those special calls which the Almighty may put in your way. Be prompt. If your work must be done, do it at once: well-earned rest is sweet. Be energetic. An admirer of Thomas Carlyle met him once in Hyde Park, and broke in upon his reverie with an earnest request for a motto. The old man stood still for a moment, and then said, "There is no better motto for a young man than the words of the old book: 'Whatsoever thy hand findeth to do, do it with thy might' " (Eccl. 9:10).

But Joseph was also fervent in spirit. "He was a fruitful bough by a well, whose branches ran over the wall" (Gen. 49:22). It is almost impossible to exaggerate the beauty of this similitude. Yonder is the scorched land. Suddenly you descry greenery, and far-reaching boughs laden with luscious grapes. Why? Ah! down there lies a deep, deep well, and the rootlets of the vine go down into those cool depths, and draw up a moisture which the torrid heat cannot exhaust. Joseph's life was spent in a dry and thirsty land; there was not much in Egypt to nourish his spiritual life, yet to its close he bore fruit, which refreshed man and pleased God. Love, joy, peace, longsuffering, meekness, goodness, self-control, all these were in him even to abounding. It is related of a grand vizier, who in early life had been a shepherd, that he set apart one room in his palace for his exclusive use. It was filled with the simple furniture of his early home, and the implements of his humble calling. And he entered it each day for quiet meditation on what he had been, that he might not be proud. So, surely, in Joseph's palace there was a retired room, where he spent many hours each week in communion with the God of his fathers, to whom he owed everything he had.

It is not enough to light a fire—we must feed it. And yet how many of my readers may have gradually sunk into habits of carelessness in private devotion, such as are bound to reduce and extinguish fervor of soul! There is the well of God's own word! Get near it; strike deep into it; draw up from it by loving habitual study.

But Joseph was also a *servant of God.* "I fear God," was his motto. "It was not you that sent me hither, but God; and *He* hath made me . . . ruler throughout all the land of Egypt" (Gen. 45:8): this was the inspiration of his life. In saying that, he showed that he felt accountable to God for all he was and did. So many live in business on one set of principles—and put on another set with their Sunday clothes. Where is the principle that will bring all our life beneath one blessed rule? I know of no other principle than that laid down by the good centurion, when he said, "A man under authority." We must feel hour by hour that we are men and women under the authority of the Lord Jesus Christ. If there is anything in your life, any habit, any dress, any pursuit, which Christ cannot approve, it must be laid aside. His name must be written upon all the bells of life, or they must cease to ring. The Apostle invested with new dignity the existence of the poor slaves of his time, by saying, "Ye are servants of Christ: do service with a will, not as unto men, but as unto Christ." And it is of no consequence how menial your position is, you may do it for your dear Lord, whispering again and again, "This is for Thee, gracious Master, all for Thee." What a check this would put on hurried and superficial work!

Every room you enter is a room in His temple. Every act is as closely noticed by Him as the breaking of the alabaster box. On every fragment of your life you may write, "Sacred to the memory of Jesus Christ." All life reaches its true unity and ideal just in so far as He is its Head and Lord (1 Cor. 7:22).

Notice the confession of the Egyptians. "Thou has saved our lives" (Gen. 47:25). What a splendid endowment is coolness, foresight, presence of mind! They are the gift of God; and they have enabled many men to be the saviors of their fellows.

But there is something higher than this. As I see these Egyptians crowding round Joseph with these words upon their lips, it makes me think of Him of whom Joseph was but a type. Jesus lay in the grave; and from its dark abyss He was raised to give salvation to His brethren the Jews, and to the millions of Gentile people. Already I hear the sound of countless myriads, as they fall before the sapphire throne, and cry, "Thou hast saved us!" The Egyptian name of Joseph meant, "the Savior of the world"; but the salvation wrought by him is hardly to be named in the same breath with that which Jesus has achieved.

Remark the resolve of these Egyptians. "Let us find grace; and we will be Pharaoh's servants." "Thou has saved our lives; and we will be thy servants" (v. 25). How could we state better the great argument for our consecration to our Savior? He has saved us: ought we not to be His servants?

There are many arguments by which we might urge acceptance of the yoke of Christ. There is such *dignity* in it: "I bear the marks of the Lord Jesus." There is such *happiness* in it; it is perfect freedom. To be free of Christ is to grind in slavery. To obey Christ—is to go forth into the glorious liberty of the sons of God.

But I pass by these arguments now to present one more. It is this: Jesus has saved you—will you not serve Him? These are the successive steps: mark them well! Recognize that Jesus bought you to be His by shedding His own blood as your ransom price, and by giving His flesh for you and for the life of the world. Then give yourself entirely to Him, saying, humbly, lovingly, trustfully, "I do now, and here, offer a present unto Thee, O Lord, myself, my soul and body, to be a reasonable, holy, and living sacrifice to Thee." Take Jesus to be moment by moment your Savior, Friend, and Lord; and yield to Him an obedience which shall cover the entire area of your being, and shall comprehend every second of your time.

10
Joseph's Father

Genesis 47:1-11

From the first moment that Joseph saw his brethren among
the crowd of all nationalities that gathered in the corn-mart,
it was evident that his love to his father burnt with undiminished fervor. And when his brethren came the second
time, they must have been surprised to notice the delicate
tenderness with which he asked them of their welfare, and
said, "Is your father well, the old man of whom ye spake? is
he yet alive?" (Gen. 43:27). Yes; and Judah little realized
what a tender chord he struck, when he spoke again and
again of the father at home, an old man, who so tenderly
loved the young lad, the only memorial of his mother. It was
this repeated allusion to his father that wrought on Joseph's
feelings so greatly as to break him down. "He could not
refrain himself." And so the very next thing he said, after the
astounding announcement, "I am Joseph," was, "Doth my
father yet live?" (Gen. 45:3). And in the tumultuous words
which followed, words throbbing with passion and pathos,
sentences about the absent father came rolling out along with
utterances of reconciliation and forgiveness to his brethren.
"Haste ye, and go up to my father and say unto him: Thus
saith thy son Joseph, 'God hath made me lord of all Egypt:
come down unto me; tarry not.' . . . And ye shall tell my
father of all my glory in Egypt, and of all that ye have seen;
and ye shall haste, and bring down my father hither" (Gen.
45:9, 13).

When at last he heard that the old man had reached the frontier of Egypt, in one of the wagons which, with thoughtful consideration, he had sent to fetch him, he "made ready his chariot, and went up to meet Israel his father" (Gen. 46:29). I think he would surely dismount, and wait, straining his aged eyes at the approaching company, from out the midst of which there came the bejewelled ruler to fall on his neck and weep there a good while. "Let me die," said he, as he looked at him, from head to foot with glad, proud, satisfied eyes: "Let me die, since I have seen thy face; because thou art yet alive." I wonder how he felt, as he recalled his sad lament, "All these things are against me."

When Pharaoh heard of the arrival of his father and brethren, he seemed mightily pleased, and he directed Joseph to see to their welfare. "The land of Egypt is before thee; in the best of the land make thy father and brethren to dwell; in the land of Goshen let them dwell: and if thou knowest any men of activity among them, then let them be rulers over my cattle." After this Joseph brought in Jacob his father, and set him before Pharaoh.

There was a great social gulf fixed between Egypt and Canaan, the court and the tent, the monarch and the shepherd. And if Joseph had been any less noble or simple than he was, he might have shrunk from bringing the two extremes together; might have been ashamed of his relations, who needed to become pensioners on the land of his adoption. But all these thoughts were forgotten in presence of another: this withered, halting, famine-pursued man was *his father*.

There is a great laxity in these respects among children.

With increasing money there comes a change in a man's social position. But what of his aged parents? He is rather ashamed of them. It is a false shame indeed!

Young people, honor your parents! They may have their peculiarities and faults; but it is ungenerous and unkind to dwell on them. It is possible so to fix your attention on these minor points as to become oblivious to many noble qualities, which are more than a compensation.

"How old art thou?" This was Pharaoh's first inquiry, as Jacob entered his presence.

"And Jacob said unto Pharaoh, The days of the years of my pilgrimage are an hundred and thirty years; few and evil have the days of the years of my life been, and have not attained unto the days of the years of the life of my fathers in the days of their pilgrimage" (v. 9). Terah reached the age of 205; Abraham of 175; Isaac of 180. But "the whole age of Jacob was an hundred forty and seven years." They had been evil. As a young man he was wrenched from his dearest associations of home and friends, and went forth alone to spend the best years of his life as a stranger in a strange land.

Arduous and difficult was his service to Laban, consumed in the day by drought, and in the sleepless night-vigils by frost. He escaped from Laban with difficulty; and no sooner had he done so than he had to encounter his incensed and impetuous brother. In the agony of that dread crisis he met with the Angel Wrestler, who touched the sinew of his thigh, so that he halted to the end of his life. Then he was involved in extreme danger with the Canaanites of Shechem, and passed through scenes which have blanched his hair, furrowed his cheeks, and scarred his heart. Thus he came to Luz, and Deborah, Rebekah's nurse, died, and was buried beneath an oak, which was thenceforth called the Oak of Weeping. "And they journeyed from Bethel, and there was but a little way to come to Ephrath, and Rachel (his favorite wife) bare a son; and it came to pass, as her soul was departing, for she died, that she called his name Ben-oni, the son of my sorrow" (Gen. 35:16, 18). A little further on he came to Mamre, arriving just in time to bear the remains of his own father to the grave. And what sorrows befell him after that, have already touched our hearts, as we have studied the wondrous history of his son, Joseph. Reuben involved his name in shameful disgrace. Judah trailed the family honor in the mire of sensual appetite. The dissensions of his sons must have rent his heart. And even after his meeting with his long-lost son he was to linger for seventeen years a pensioner on the bounty of the king of Egypt: far from the glorious heritage which had been promised to his race.

Few have trod a path more paved with jagged flints. Compare it with the lot of Esau; and what a contrast it presents! Esau lost the birthright; but he had all that heart could wish. Wealth, royalty, a line of illustrious sons—these were the portion of his cup. The thirty-sixth chapter of Genesis contains a list of the royal dukes of his line. How often must Esau have pitied his brother! "My poor brother, he was always visionary, counting on the future, building castles in the air; as for myself, I say, make the best of this world while it lasts. Let us eat and drink, for tomorrow we may die."

And yet when this same Jacob stands before Pharaoh, the greatest monarch of the world bends eagerly to catch his blessing. "Jacob blessed Pharaoh." Esau would never have been able to bless Pharaoh. "Without contradiction, the less is blessed of the greater." Evidently, then, Jacob was a greater man than the greatest monarch of his time. There is, therefore, a greatness which is wholly independent of those adventitious circumstances which we sometimes associate with it. The ermine does not make a judge; a crown does not make a king; nor does wealth, or rank, or birth make a great man. Jacob was one of the truly great. He was a royal man with a Divine patent of royalty. God Himself said, "Thy name shall be no more called Jacob, but Israel (a prince of God), for as a prince hast thou power with God, and with men."

Three things made Jacob royal; and will do as much for us.

Prayer. On the moorland, strewn with boulders, he saw in his dreams the mighty rocks pile themselves into a heaven-touching ladder. This struck the keynote of his life. He ever after lived at the foot of the ladder of prayer, up which the angels sped to carry his petitions, and down which they came, with beautiful feet, to bring the golden handfuls of blessing. Learn to pray without ceasing. It is the secret of greatness. He who is oft in the audience-chamber of the great King becomes kinglike.

JOSEPH   163

Suffering. His nature was marred by selfish, base, and carnal elements. He took unlawful advantage of his famished brother; deceived his aged father; increased his property at the expense of his uncle; worked his ends by mean and crafty means. But sorrow ate away all these things, and gave him a new dignity. So does it work still on those who have received the new nature, and who meekly learn the lesson which God's love designs to teach them. Do not shrink from pain and sorrow; they come to crown you. The Lamb sits on the throne today because He was slain; and the throne is reserved for those who have learned to suffer with Him, with Him to die.

Contact with Christ. "There wrestled a man with him until the breaking of the day." Who was He? Surely none less than the Angel Jehovah, whose face may not be seen, or His name known. And from that hour Jacob was "Israel." Jesus, the immortal lover of souls, is wrestling with you, longing to rid you of littleness and selfishness, and to lift you also to a royal life. Yield to Him, lest He be compelled to touch the sinew of your strength. He will make you truly Princes with God; and even those above you in this world's rank will gladly gather round you for the sake of the spiritual blessings you shall bestow.

11

Joseph at the Deathbed of Jacob

Genesis 47:27-31

Jacob dwelt in the land of Goshen. "They grew and multiplied exceedingly" (v. 27). So seventeen uneventful years went by. And as the old man became more and more infirm, his spirit was cheered and sustained by the love of Joseph. Evidently Joseph was the stay of that waning life; and it is not remarkable therefore that the patriarch summoned him not once, or even twice, but thrice, to his deathbed.

The Bible is a book of life. Single verses are enough for dying words. Whenever, therefore, a death scene is described with some minuteness, we may be sure that there is something which demands our attentive heed. So it is here.

"The time drew nigh that Israel must die" (v. 29). But his death was a rift in the dark clouds that veiled the future world from his sons and their children, giving them a glimpse of its reality and beauty.

One of the most sublime verses in the New Testament declares that "Christ has abolished death, and brought life and immortality to light through the Gospel." There is a most inspiring rhythm in the words; but we must not suppose that the Gospel has revealed that concerning which nothing was previously known. Long before our Lord walked this world, carrying at His girdle the keys of Resurrection and Life, men cherished the hope of eternal life: the Gospel simply threw fuller light on that which had been before partially hidden.

Daniel teaches in plainest language the truth of a general

resurrection to endless life or endless shame. The book of
Job, whatever date may be assigned to it, has been called a
very hymn of immortality: he knew at least that his "Redeemer lived, and that he should stand up at the last upon
the earth, and after his skin had been destroyed, yet from his
flesh he should see God" (Job 19:25, 26). In the Book of
Psalms we have no uncertain evidence of the tenacity with
which pious Jews clung to these hopes. "Thou wilt not leave
my soul in sheol; neither wilt thou suffer thine Holy One to
see corruption. Thou wilt show me the path of life" (Ps.
16:10, 11).

Why did Abraham dwell with Isaac and Jacob in frail,
shifting tents, rather than in towns like Sodom and Gomorrah? What did Abraham mean when he said to the sons of
Heth, "I am a stranger and a sojourner with you?" (Gen.
23:4). And what was the thought in Jacob's mind, when, in
the presence of the haughty Pharaoh, he described his life as
a "pilgrimage?" The answer is clearly given in the roll call of
God's heroes contained in Hebrews 11: "They sought a country, a fatherland." And they were so absorbed with this one
thought, that they could not settle for any inheritance in
Canaan.

At first, no doubt, they thought that Canaan was to be the
land of promise. But when they waited for it year after year,
and still it was withheld, they looked into the deed of gift
again, and learned that there were depths in it of which they
had never dreamed. In the dim haze there loomed upon their
vision a land of which the land of milk and honey was a poor
type; and instead of a city built by human hands, there arose
before them the fair vision of the crystal walls and the pearly
gates of the city which hath foundations, whose builder and
maker is God, and which He hath prepared for them that
love Him.

"These all died in faith, not having received the promises,
but having seen them afar off (as the minarets and parapets
of some distant city), and were persuaded of them and embraced them" (Heb. 11:13). The Revised Version says, "They

greeted them from afar," as the wanderer greets his longed-for home, when he sees it from afar. Well might Jacob, on this his deathbed, stay the progress of his parting exhortations to say, "I have waited for thy salvation, O Lord" (Gen. 49:18). This took the bitterness out of his death.

And notice, Jacob did not regard the future life as a mere state of existence stript of all those associations which make life worth the having. Indeed, in this he seems to have had truer thoughts than many who are found in Christian churches. He said, "I am to be gathered unto my people" (Gen. 49:29). He surely did not mean simply that he was to be buried in their tomb, for he expresses that thought afterwards in the words, "Bury me with my fathers in the cave of Machpelah." Nay, he meant to say that for him the city to which he went was the gathering place of his clan, the rendezvous of elect souls, the home of all who were *his* people because they were *God's*.

Year after year the people have been gathering there. And when we leave this world, it will not be to go into a cold, unsympathizing, gravelike realm, where no voice shall greet, no smile welcome us. But we shall go to our people; those whom we have loved and lost; those who are awaiting our coming with fond affection, and who will administer a choral entrance to us into that world of everlasting reunion.

But it was not simply to express these hopes that the dying patriarch summoned the beloved Joseph to his side. The father wanted to bind the son by a solemn promise not to have him buried in the land of his exile, but to carry him back to that lone cave. To him interment in the most splendid pyramid in Egypt was not for a moment to be compared with burial in that solitary and humble sepulchre, where the mortal remains of Abraham and Sarah, of Isaac and Rebekah, and of the faithful Leah, lay waiting the day of resurrection.

There was something more than natural sentiment. He was a man of faith. He knew and cherished the ancient promise made by God to His friend, the patriarch Abraham, that Canaan should become the possession of his seed. And

though he could not share the perils and pains and glories of
the exodus, he will be there to meet them when in after-years
their bands enter upon their inheritance.

"If now I have found grace in thy sight, put, I pray thee,
thy hand under my thigh, and deal kindly and truly with me.
Bury me not, I pray thee, in Egypt: but I will lie with my
fathers; and thou shalt carry me out of Egypt and bury me in
their burying place." Joseph was too good and tender to
hesitate for a single moment. "And he said, I will do as thou
hast said" (vv. 29, 30). But the old man was not content with
a mere promise. "And he said, Swear unto me. And he sware
unto him. And Israel bowed himself upon the bed's head"
(v. 31). So ended Joseph's first visit to his dying father.

Tidings came to the Prime Minister of Egypt that his father
was sick and wished to see him. And he went to him without
delay, taking with him his two sons, Manasseh and Ephraim.

When Joseph arrived at his father's dwelling, the aged patriarch seemed to have been lying still, but when someone
there said, "Behold, thy son Joseph is come," the sound of
that loved name revived him, and he made a great effort,
and, propped by pillows, sat up upon the bed.

There was clearly no decay in his power of recollection, as
the old man reviewed the past. And as his recollection embraced the past, it was also vividly alive to more recent incidents in the family history. He did not forget that Joseph,
who leant over his dying form, had two sons; and he announced his intention of adopting them as his own. "Thy
two sons, which were born unto thee in the land of Egypt,
before I came unto thee into Egypt, are mine: as Reuben and
Simeon, they shall be mine" (Gen. 48:5). By that act, while
Joseph's name was expunged from the map of Canaan, yet he
himself became possessed of a double portion of his area,
because Ephraim and Manasseh would henceforth stand
there as his representatives.

Once more Joseph visited that death chamber. This was
the third time and the last. But this time he stood only as one

of twelve strong, bearded men, who gathered around the
aged form of their father, his face shadowed by death, his
spirit aglow with the light of prophecy. How intense the awe
with which they heard their names called, one by one, by the
old man's trembling voice, now pausing for breath, now
speaking with great difficulty! The character of each is
criticized with prophetic insight; the salient points of their
past history are vividly brought to mind; and some
foreshadowing is given them of their future.

This scene is an anticipation of the Judgment seat: where
men shall hear the story of their lives passed under review;
and a sentence passed, against which there shall be no appeal.

But the dying patriarch speaks with peculiar sweetness
and grace, when he comes to touch the destiny of his favorite
son.

A few more sentences to Benjamin, and the venerable patriarch drew up his feet into his bed, and quietly breathed
his last, and was gathered unto his people. But that eager,
much-tried spirit passed up and away into other scenes of
more exalted fellowship and ministry, with no pause in his
life, for in after years God attested his continued existence
and energy when He called Himself "the God of Jacob," for
God is not God of the dead, but of the living. And Joseph fell
upon his father's face, and wept upon him, and pressed his
warm lips on the death-cold clay; and he commanded the
physicians to embalm his body, so cheating death of its immediate victory.

12
Joseph's Last Days and Death

Genesis 50:24, 25

"God will surely visit you, and ye shall carry up my bones from hence" (v. 25). These were the dying words of Joseph. And it is somewhat remarkable that these are the only words in his whole career which are referred to in the subsequent pages of the Scriptures. His life was a noble one, and, with one exception, the most fascinating in the sacred record; but this last dying speech is singled out from all the rest for special notice of the Holy Ghost. Of course, I refer to those words in Heb. 11, where it is said, "By faith Joseph, when he died, made mention of the exodus of the children of Israel; and gave commandment concerning his bones" (Heb. 11:22).

Joseph was now an old man. One hundred and ten years had stolen away his strength, and left deep marks upon his form. It was three and ninety years since he had been lifted from the pit to become a slave. Eighty years had passed since he had first stood before Pharaoh in all the beauty and wisdom of his young manhood. And sixty years had left their papyrus records in the State archives, since, with all the pomp and splendor of Egypt's court, he had carried the remains of his old father to Machpelah's ancient cave. So old was he that he saw the bright young faces of his great-grandchildren: "they were brought up upon Joseph's knees" (v. 23). With long life and many days God had blessed His faithful servant. And now, stooping beneath their weight, he was fast descending to the break-up of natural life.

But the shadows of his own decay were small compared with those which he saw gathering around his beloved people. Sixty years before, when Jacob gathered up his feet upon his bed and died, his favorite son was in the zenith of his glory. The days of mourning for the patriarch, just because he was Joseph's father, were only two less in number than those of a king. There was no difficulty in obtaining from Pharaoh the necessary permission to go three hundred miles to inter the remains beside those of Abraham and Sarah, of Isaac and Rebekah, and of Leah.

And, indeed, that funeral procession must have been of a sort not often seen. The proud and titled magnates of Egypt, the most exclusive aristocracy in the world, were willing to follow the remains of a shepherd and a Jew to their last resting-place, out of honor for his son. "There also went up chariots and horsemen, so that it was a very great company" (v. 9).

But sixty years had brought great changes of which there is evidence in the text. When Joseph died, all was getting dark, and the shadow of a great eclipse was gathering over the destinies of his people. No notice seems to have been taken in Egypt of his death. No splendid obsequies were voted to him at public expense. No pyramid was placed at the disposal of his sons. And he addresses his brethren gathered about him as being sorely in need of help. It is as if he had said: "I have done my best for you, but I am dying; nevertheless God will fill my place, and do for you all, and more than all, that I would have done myself." There is a tone of comfort in these words, which indicates how much they needed an advocate at court, and an assurance of Divine visitation.

Three hundred years before, the great founder of the nation had watched all day beside an altar, scaring away the vultures which, attracted by the flesh that lay upon it, hovered around. At length, as the sun went down, the watcher fell asleep—it is hard to watch with God—and in his sleep he dreamt. A dense and awful gloom seemed to enclose him, and to oppress his soul, and on it, as upon a curtain, passed successive glimpses of the future of his race—glimpses which a Divine voice interpreted to his ear. He saw them exiled to a foreign country, enslaved by the foreigner, and lingering there while three generations of men bloomed as spring flowers, and were cut down before the keen sickle of death. And as he beheld all the terror of that enslavement, the horror of a great darkness fell upon his soul. We know how exactly that horror was justified by the events which were so soon to take place. "The Egyptians made the children of Israel to serve with rigor: and they made their lives bitter with hard bondage, in mortar, and in brick, and in all manner of service in the field; all their service, wherein they made them serve, was with rigor" (Ex. 1:13, 14). The first symptoms of that outburst of popular "Jew-hate" were already, like stormy petrels, settling about the closing hour of the great Egyptian premier.

The twilight of the dark night was gathering in; and it was this which made Joseph's words more splendid: they shone out as stars of hope.

His forgiveness and love to them lasted till the testing-hour by that great assayer, Death. From something narrated in the previous verses of this chapter, it would appear that, for long, his brethren, judging of him by their own dark and implacable hearts, could not believe in the sincerity and genuineness of his forgiveness. And so they feared that, as soon as Jacob was removed, Joseph's just resentment, long concealed with masterly art, would break forth against them. It seemed impossible to believe that he felt no grudge, and would take no action at all with reference to the past; and they said, "Joseph will certainly requite us all the evil which we did unto him" (v. 15). And Joseph wept when they spake; wept that they should have so misunderstood him after his repeated assurances; wept to see them kneeling at his feet for a forgiveness which he had freely given them years before. "Fear not," said he in effect; "do not kneel there; I am not God: ye thought evil against me; but God meant it for good, to save much people alive, as it is this day."

This forgiveness might well be wonderful to these men; because it was not of this world at all. The Lord Jesus, who lighteth every man coming into the world, was in Joseph's heart, though less clearly in Joseph's creed; and his behavior was a foreshadowing of Incarnate Love. Reader! He waits to forgive thee thus. Though thou hast maligned, and refused, and crucified Him afresh, and put Him to an open shame; yet, for all that, He waits to forgive thee so entirely, that not one of these things shall be ever mentioned against thee again; yea, if they are looked for, they shall never be found, any more than a stone can be found which has been cast into the bosom of the Atlantic waves. And remember that when once He forgives, it is unnecessary and distrustful to go to Him again about the same sin.

It is said of the love of the Lord Jesus that, having loved His own, which were in the world, He loved them unto the end; or, as the margin of the Revised Version puts it, "to the uttermost." He is able to save to the uttermost, because He loves to the uttermost. So was it with the love of Joseph; it had outlived the frosts of the early spring, and it bore fruit and looked fresh now in the late autumn of his last days.

Lastly, he was dying. "I die." They were among the last words that he had caught from his father's dying lips and now he appropriates them to himself; yes, and in doing so, he touches the zenith of his noble confidence and hope. There is no better proof of immortality than this: that in us must be a something more than flesh and blood, which, when these are most impaired, is most bright and most alive to the realities of the eternal world. And there must be a sphere appropriate to the ethereal tenant, who stands so keen and eager, reaching forth, with unimpaired vitality and with unquenchable vigor.

It was under all these circumstances that Joseph said, "God will surely visit you; and ye shall carry up my bones from hence."

Let us investigate the full importance of these words. And we may do so best by comparing them with Jacob's dying wish: "Bury me with my fathers in the cave that is in the field of Machpelah." This was most natural. And Jacob knew that there would be no great difficulty in carrying out his wish. But with Joseph it was different. He too wanted to be buried in the land of Canaan; but not at once—not then! There were two things he expected would happen: the one, that the people would go out of Egypt; the other, that they would come into the land of Canaan. He did not know when or how; he was only sure that so it would be: "surely."

To Joseph's natural vision these things were most unlikely. When he spoke, Israel was settled in Goshen, and so increasing in numbers and in wealth that any uprooting was becoming daily more unlikely. And as to the oppression which was perhaps beginning to threaten them, what chance would they have of ever being able to escape from the detaining squadrons of Egypt's chivalry, supposing they wished to go? But his anticipation of the future was not founded on human foresight, but on the distinct announcements of the Almighty. He remembered how God had said to Abraham, as he stood upon his mountain oratory, "Look from the place where thou art, northward, and southward, and eastward, and westward; for all the land that thou seest, to thee will I give it, and to thy seed for ever" (Gen. 13:14, 15). That promise was repeated to Isaac. "Unto thee, and unto thy seed, will I give all these countries; and I will perform the oath which I sware unto Abraham thy father" (Gen. 26:3).

Again was that promise reiterated to Jacob as he lay at the foot of the shining ladder, "The land whereon thou liest, to thee will I give it, and to thy seed" (Gen. 28:13). These promises had been carefully treasured and handed on, as in the old Greek race they handed on the burning torch. Jacob on his deathbed reassured Joseph that God would certainly bring them to the land of their fathers; and now Joseph reanimated the trembling company that gathered around him with the self-same hope. In the memories of all these men the word spoken two hundred years before rang like a peal of silver bells in a moss-grown tower. "They shall come hither again" (Gen. 15:16). And so he commanded that his bones should be unburied, so that at any moment, however hurried, when the trumpet of exodus sounded, they might be ready to be caught up and borne onward in the glad march for Canaan.

What a lesson must those unburied bones have read to Israel! When the taskmasters dealt hardly with the people, so that their hearts fainted, it must have been sweet to go and look at the mummy case which held those moldering remains, waiting there to be carried forward; and, as they did so, this was doubtless their reflection, "Evidently then, Joseph believed that we were not to stay here always, but that we should sooner or later leave for Canaan: let us brace ourselves up to bear a little longer, it may only be a very little while!" Yes, and when some were tempted to settle down content with prospering circumstances, and to feast upon leeks, garlics, and onions, it was a check on them to think of those bones, and say, "Evidently we are not to remain here always: we should do well not to build all our hopes and comfort on the unstable tenure of our sojourn in this place."

We have no unburied bones to animate our faith, or to revive our drooping zeal; but we have something better—we have an empty grave. Oh, what volumes does that mutely tell us! When John the Baptist died, his disciples dispersed; when Jesus died, His disciples not only clung together, but sprang up into an altogether new vigor. And the difference was made by that empty grave in the garden of Joseph of Arimathea. And what it did for them it will do for us. It tells us that He is risen. It tells us that not death, but life, is to be the guardian angel of our desert march. It tells us that this world is not our resting place or home; but that we must seek these above, where Christ sitteth at the right hand of God. It tells us that resurrection is not possible only, but certain; and that ere long we shall be where He is. He will go with us along the desert pathway, till we go to be with Him, where the shadow of death is never flung over flower, or child, or friend.

Let us realize the spirit that underlay and prompted these
words. It was above all a pilgrim spirit. Joseph bore an Egyptian title. He married an Egyptian wife. He shared in Egyptian court life, politics, and trade. But he was as much a
pilgrim as was Abraham pitching his tent outside the walls
of Hebron, or Isaac in the grassy plains of the south country,
or Jacob keeping himself aloof from the families of the land.
"He filled his place at Pharaoh's court; but his dying words
open a window into his soul, and betray how little he had felt
that he belonged to the order of things in the midst of which
he had been content to live."

We sometimes speak as if the pilgrim spirit were impossible for us who live in this settled state of civilization. Our
houses are too substantial; our lives too unromantic; our
movements too closely tethered to one narrow round. But if
that thought should ever cross our hearts again, let us turn to
the life of Joseph, and remind ourselves how evidently he
was animated by the spirit of those "who confessed that they
were pilgrims and strangers on the earth." Ah, friends, what
are we living for? Are our pursuits bounded by the narrow
horizon of earth, and limited to the fleeting moments of
time? Are we constantly engaged in lining as warmly as possible the nest in which we hope to spend our old age and die?
I fear these are the real aims of many professing Christians;
and, if so, it is simply useless for them to claim kinship with
that mighty stream of pilgrims, which is constantly pouring
through the earth, bound to the city which hath foundations,
their true home and mother city. On the other hand, it is
quite conceivable that you may be at the head of a large
establishment, engaged in many permanent undertakings,
closely attached to the present by imperious duties; and yet,
like Joseph, your heart may be detached from things seen
and temporal, and engaged, in all its secret longings, to the
things unseen and eternal.

The pilgrim spirit will not make us unpractical. Joseph was
the most practical man in his time. Who are likely to be as
prompt, as energetic, as thorough, as those who feel that

they are working for eternity, and that they are building up day by day a fabric in which they shall live hereafter?

But the pilgrim spirit will make us simple. There are two sorts of simplicity: that of circumstances; and that of heart. Many a man sits down to bread and milk at a wooden table, with a heart as proud as pride can make it: while many another who eats off a golden plate is as simple as Cincinnatus at his plow. The world cannot understand this. But here in Joseph is an illustration. It is not the unjewelled finger, nor the plain attire, nor the unfurnished room, that constitutes a simple unaffected life: but that vision of the spirit, which looks through the unsubstantial wreath vapors of the morning to the peaks of the everlasting hills beyond and above.

What a contrast there is between the opening and closing words of Genesis! Listen to the opening words: "In the beginning, God." Listen to the closing words, "A coffin in Egypt." And is this all? Is all God's work to end in one poor mummy case? Stay. This is only the end of Genesis, the Book of Beginnings. Turn the leaf, and there are Exodus, and Joshua, and Kings, and Prophets, and Christ. And it is enough for each of us, like Joseph, to have lived a true, pure, strong, and noble life—and to leave Him to see after our bodies; our beloved, whom we leave so reluctantly; and our work. Nor will He fail. "And Moses took the bones of Joseph with him," on the night of the exodus (Exod. 13:19); "and they buried the bones of Joseph in Shechem: . . . and it became the inheritance of the children of Joseph" (Josh. 24:32).

BOOK III: MOSES

1
Moses' Early Life
Hebrews 11:23

The writer of the Epistle to the Hebrews lays bare the secret of the marvels effected by the heroes of Hebrew story.

We make a profound mistake in attributing to these men extraordinary qualities of courage, and strength of body or soul. To do so is to miss the whole point of the reiterated teaching of Scripture. They were not different from ordinary men, except in their faith. In many respects it is most likely that they were inferior to ourselves. We should probably be much surprised if we were to encounter them in the daily walks of modern life, and should find it almost impossible to believe that they wrought such prodigies of valor, endurance, and deliverance.

The same truth is repeatedly corroborated in the teaching of our Lord. He never stops to ask what may be the specific quantity of power, or wisdom, or enthusiasm, which exists in His disciples. In His judgment these things are as the small dust of the balance, not to be taken into serious consideration, and not likely to affect the aggregate results of a man's life. But His incessant demand is for *faith*.

The believer is the God-filled, the God-moved, the God-possessed man; and the work which he effects in the world is not his, but God's through him.

His faith made Moses all he was. We shall see this more clearly as we proceed. For it is our eager desire to learn exactly how such a faith as his was produced. Why should we not have it? God's methods are never out of date. It is certain that we shall have his faith, if we but pay the price of enduring his discipline. And if only we possessed his faith, why should we not see another Exodus?—seas seamed with paths of salvation; foes defied; chains snapped; captives emancipated; and Jehovah worshipped with songs of triumph! Surely there is no limit to the possibilities of a life through which God can pour Himself forth.

It was on a very unfriendly world that the little babe opened his eyes. Without, all was as fair as nature and art could make it. Hard by the mean cottage, which for a brief space was to shelter him, the mighty Nile rolled between its reedy banks, reflecting on its broad bosom the deep azure of the arching heavens by day, and the starry constellations of the night. Within the easy distance of a maiden's morning walk stood the great city of Memphis, metropolis of Egypt and seat of the Court; center of trade, art, war, religion; the focus to which the national life converged.

Past that cottage home would go royal processions, as in solemn state the monarch went forth to war, or came down to the Nile brink to worship. Priests from all parts of the land would pass it on their way to the mighty Temple of Phthah, whose pillared avenues, and sculptured galleries, and hieroglyphed chambers, were the result of centuries of industry, and told the story of the generations that had built them; but how little would they dream that the site of that humble cottage would attract the interest of generations to the end of time, when their lordly temple had fallen into an indistinguishable heap!

Moses the Alien

More than three hundred years before, the forefathers of his people had emigrated from Palestine, at the invitation of the Prime Minister of the time, who was connected with them by the ties of kinship and race. The king had welcomed them as likely to be valuable allies; for he also belonged to a foreign race, and sat on an unstable throne. At his command they

had settled in the best of the land, a strip of green, called
Goshen, situated amid vast tracts of sand. There they pros-
pered and multiplied, till they numbered near upon two million souls. But they remained as distinct a people as they are
now in every nation under heaven, and as such were open to
suspicious hate.

The Oppressed Hebrews

A different dynasty had succeeded to that which welcomed
them, and one to whom the name of Joseph had no charm.

Suddenly, the shepherds of Goshen found themselves
drafted for service in the brickfields, under the eye and whip
of cruel taskmasters, who exacted from them daily a certain
tale of bricks; or they performed service in the field, drawing
water from the river for the irrigation of the land, and toiling
in the cultivation of the soil.

The father of the little household was, probably, compelled
to bear his share in the bondage and blows which made the
existence of his people so bitter. From morning to night he
would toil, naked, beneath the burning sun, returning often
with bleeding wounds torn open by the scourge, and inclined to question the very existence of God and His character for mercy. Very dark was the night which lay heavily on
the chosen people in these years of cruel enslavement.

Troublous Times

The household consisted of father and mother, of an elder
sister, some fifteen years of age, marvelously gifted with the
power of song, and of a little brother, Aaron, a bright and
merry boy of three years of age. When the latter was born,
there was apparently no special need of secrecy; for the king
was trying to attain his object by the vigorous policy we have
above described. But during the interval, he had discovered
that it was not stringent enough to attain his end; and he
had, therefore, added to it a scheme for the destruction of all
the male children, by casting them into the river as they were
born.

It is not likely that this decree was in active operation for more than a few months.

Generally, the birth of a child, and especially of a boy, was heralded with unstinted joy: but now it was the subject of anxiety, and almost of dread. There was no glad anticipation, no welcome, no rapture, to compensate for the mother's anguish, in the thought that a man was born into the world. Yet in spite of all, "the people multiplied and became very mighty." The edict remained in operation for but a short time, but it was during its enforcement that Moses was born. This is God's way. In the darkest hours of the night His tread draws near across the billows.

A Child of Believing Parents

We know but little of them. The father is said to have been "a man of the house of Levi" (Exod. 2:1), and we learn afterwards that his name was Amram, and descended from Kohath, the son of Levi; but the tribe of Levi had then no special importance—in fact, it seemed destined to be divided in Jacob, and scattered in Israel. The mother, Jochebed, belonged to the same tribe, and, indeed, was related to her husband in a closer consanguinity than was afterwards permitted. They were humble folk, glad enough to receive "wages" from the hand of wealth and royalty; but they preserved the best religious traditions of their nation, and in this contrasted favorably with many others of their race.

There are clear evidences in the later Scriptures that the people participated in the idolatrous rites of the land of their adoption.

But evidently there were some families who remained faithful amid the prevalent corruption. Among these was that into which this child was born. The sacred covenant between God and their race was reverently remembered, and held by a faith which dared to believe that, sooner or later, God must interpose. The treasured stories which are preserved to us in the book of Genesis would be carefully taught to the children as soon as their hearts could appreciate, and their memories preserve them.

We have often been furnished with a picture depicting the anxiety with which his parents received their newborn babe, the distress of Amram, and the fears of Jochebed. Such a picture may be true of others of the Hebrew parents, but it is not true of them. "They were not afraid." When it was announced to Jochebed that she had borne a boy, she was enabled to cast the care of him on God, and to receive the assurance that he should come to no hurt. And as the couple bent over their child, in that peasant's hut, and saw his exceeding goodliness, the conviction grew in their hearts that a great destiny awaited him; and that in some way he would live to see the expiration of the time of slavery, foretold centuries before in words which had passed from lip to lip, the one rift of light amid the blackness of their night.

"Know of a surety that thy seed shall be a stranger in a land that is not theirs, and shall serve them, and they shall afflict them four hundred years . . . but in the fourth generation they shall come hither again" (Gen. 15:13, 16). The slow-moving years had at last accumulated to the prescribed number. Four hundred years had nearly, if not quite, elapsed. The promise must be on the point of fulfilment. The words, "they shall come out" (Gen. 15:14) rang like a peal of bells in the mother's heart; and there was a confidence nurtured by the Spirit of God, and by the loveliness of her child, that in some way he should share in that Exodus.

Sometimes when her heart grew sick she would betake herself to her knees, and plead the Divine promise on which she had been caused to hope. The whole family lived on that woman's faith, as men live on bread; and God's angels bent over the unconscious babe, shielding it with their tenderest care, and whispering their love words into its ear. Finally, the mother was led by the good Spirit of God to weave the papyrus rushes into a little ark, or boat, coating it with bitumen, to make it impervious to wet. There she put the child with many a kiss, closed the lid upon its sweet face, with her own hands bore it to the water's edge, and placed it tenderly among the flags that grew there. She knew that Pharaoh's daughter came there to bathe, and it might be that she would notice and befriend the little foundling. Or, if not, the God whom she trusted would help her in some other way. But all the while she never lost her simple, steadfast faith. "The Lord was her light and her salvation: whom should she fear?"

Miriam was set to watch, not with any thought of harm that would ensue, whether from unfriendly hand, or from beast of prey, but simply to see "what would be done to him"; and Jochebed went back to her house, fighting a mother's natural anxiety by a faith which had enclasped the very arm of the living God, who could not fail her.

2
Come to Years

Hebrews 11:24

It all befell according to the mother's faith. The princess, accompanied by a train of maidens, came to the river bank to bathe. She saw the ark among the flags, and sent her maid to fetch it. In the midst of the little group the lid was carefully uplifted; and their eyes were charmed with the sight of the beautiful face, while their hearts were touched with the whimper of the babe, who missed its mother.

Quickly the woman's heart guessed the secret. The neighborhood of Hebrew huts, the features and complexion of the babe, the unlikelihood of a mother forgetting her suckling child, the sudden recollection of the stern edict which her father had lately promulgated, all pointed to the inevitable conclusion, "This is one of the Hebrews' children" (Exod. 2:6). The sudden interposition of Miriam, who had eagerly and breathlessly watched the whole scene, with her naive suggestion of fetching a Hebrew nurse, solved the problem of what should be done with the foundling almost as soon as it could have suggested itself. Quickly the child's mother stood before the princess, and received the precious burden from her hands.

The child's life was secure beneath the powerful protection of Pharaoh's own daughter, who had said, "Nurse it for me." And the wages which she had promised would do more than provide for all their need. God had done "exceedingly abundantly."

How long the boy stayed in that lowly home we do not know—perhaps till he was four or five years old: but long enough, in any case, to know something of the perils and hardships of his people's lot; to learn those sacred traditions of their past, which he was afterwards to weave with such majestic simplicity into the Book of Genesis; and to receive into his heart the love of the only God, which was to become the absorbing passion and polestar of his career. Priests, philosophers, and scholars, might do their best afterwards; but these things had been built into the growing structure of his soul, never again to be disintegrated from its fabric. What an encouragement is suggested by this record to mothers—to make the very most of the early years during which children are confided to their charge. The circumstances must be exceptional indeed under which that charge can be entrusted to others.

At last the time arrived when Thermutis claimed for her own the child whom she had rescued. He had now grown so beautiful that, Josephus tells us, passers-by stood still to look at him, and laborers left their work to steal a glance.

He was brought up in the palace, and treated as the grandson of Pharaoh. If he rode forth into the streets, it would be in a princely equipage, amid cries of "Bow the knee." If he floated on the Nile, it would be in a golden barge, amid the strains of voluptuous music. If he wished for aught, the almost illimitable wealth of the treasurers of Egypt was within his reach.

When old enough he was probably sent to be *educated in the college*, which had grown up around the Temple of the Sun, and has been called "the Oxford of Ancient Egypt." There he would learn to read and write the mysterious hieroglyph; there, too, he would be instructed in mathematics, astronomy, and chemistry, in all of which the Egyptians were adepts. There, also, he would acquire a taste for music; so that in after days he could sing glad and triumphant songs of victory, and compose odes which embalmed the history of God's dealings with His people. How wonderfully was God fitting him for his afterlife! Stephen says: "Moses was learned in all the wisdom of the Egyptians" (Acts 7:22). Much of it was undoubtedly the merest folly; but much of it, also, stood him in good stead when he became the founder of a new state.

Thus year followed year till he was forty years of age. Already the foremost positions of the State were open to him; and it seemed as if the river of his life would continue in the same bed, undiverted, and only waxing ever broader and deeper in its flow.

But, beneath all, another thought was always present with him, and gradually dwarfed all others as it grew within his soul. He could not forget that his parents were slaves; that the bondmen who were groaning in the brickfields beneath the lash of the taskmasters were his brethren. He never lost the thought of that God to whom his mother had taught him to pray: and in his gayest, most successful moments, when sipping the intoxicating cup of earthly success, he could not rid himself of the impression that his destiny did not lie amid such surroundings as those, but was in some way to be associated with the fulfillment of that promise which he had heard so often from his mother's lips. Thoughts like these would often cast strange shadows over his face, which baffled those who knew him best.

The Great Resolve
The mystery remained locked in his heart till his vague impressions had become settled resolves; and he broke, as gently as he might, the news to his benefactress that he could no longer hold the position to which she had raised him, or be called her son, but must step back to the lowly lot which was his by birth.

For a palace there would be a hut; for luxury, hard fare and coarse food; for respect and honor, hatred and contempt; for the treasures of Egypt, poverty and want; for the society of the learned and *elite*, association with the ignorant and depraved. But none of these things moved him. He counted them as the small dust of the balance. With deliberate resolution he bowed his head beneath the yoke, rough and heavy.

There is nothing gained in saying that there are no pleasures in sin. There are. The forbidden fruit is pleasant to the eye and luscious to the taste; the first steps along the broad road are over a carpet of velvet grass, enameled with countless flowers. And Moses was not oblivious to all this; yet, in the heyday of his strength, in the prime of his manhood, in a court where continence and purity must have been unknown, he dared to forego it all.

He believed God's promise to Abraham, that after four hundred years of bondage his people would come out; and he knew that that period had nearly expired. He cherished a fervent belief in that promise made to the chosen people, that from their ranks the true Deliverer would arise—a shadowy belief in the coming Messiah, which, notwithstanding its vagueness, he dared not forefeit. He believed that there was a destiny waiting for the chosen people in the long future, which would throw into shadow all the pomp and splendor of the magnificent Pharaoh. He believed that there was a recompense of reward awaiting them beyond Egypt, more glorious than the dazzling splendor of its highest rewards and honors. He evidently believed, what he expected his brethren to believe, that God would deliver them by his hand. And it was this that determined him.

There was true heroism in the act, when Moses stepped down from Pharaoh's throne to share the lot of his brethren. He might have contented himself by sending them money from the treasures of Egypt; but it was a greater and nobler thing to give himself. At the same time there was a great deal for him to learn.

First Attempt at Deliverance

It sprang largely from human sympathy. As soon as he reached Goshen his first act was to go out and see his brethren in the midst of their toils, working amid the conditions of the severest hardship. Brick making in stiff clay pits must always be arduous employment; but how much more so when an Egyptian sun shone vertically above them, and a taskmaster stood by with his heavy whip to punish the least attempt to flinch from toil!

Imagine the accomplished courtier, the child of luxury and fashion, the man of letters and of mighty deeds, as he moves amid these long lines of slaves.

But within a little, that pity for his people turned to indignation against their oppressors. Before he had taken many steps he came on one of the taskmasters cruelly beating a Hebrew; and as he witnessed the horrid spectacle, the heavy blows falling on the unresisting quivering body, he could restrain himself no longer, and felled the caitiff lifeless to the ground, then bore away his body and buried it in the nearest sands.

It was premature. God's time for the deliverance of His people was not due for forty years. The iniquity of the Amorites had not reached its full, though it was nearing the brim of the cup (Gen. 15:16). His own education was very incomplete; it would take at least forty years to drain him of his self-will and self-reliance, and make him a vessel meet for the Master's use. The Hebrew people had not as yet come to the pitch of anguish, which is so touchingly referred to, when the death of their principal oppressor seems to have brought matters to a crisis, and they forsook the false gods to which they had given their allegiance in order to return to the God of their fathers (Exod. 2:23).

One blow struck when the time is fulfilled is worth a thousand struck in premature eagerness.

It was executed in the pride of human strength. It was but natural that Moses should suppose that he could do something for the amelioration of his people's lot. He had always been accustomed to have his way. Crowds of obsequious servants and courtiers had yielded to his slightest whim.

It was a rude surprise when, on the second day, he went out to continue his self-imposed task, and essayed to adjust a difference between two Hebrews, to find himself repulsed from them by the challenge, "Who made thee a prince and a judge over us?" (Exod. 2:14).

We have been disposed to attribute too much of the success of the Exodus to the natural qualities of the great leader; but we must always remember that, like Gideon's host, he was at first too strong for God. God cannot give His glory to another. He dare not entrust His power to men, till they are humbled and emptied, and conscious of their helplessness.

It was too apprehensive of the judgment of other men. We are told that he looked this way and that way before he smote the Egyptian; and when he found that his deed of revenge was known, he feared and fled (Exod. 2:15).

Whenever men look this way and that to see what other men are doing or saying, you may be quite sure they do not know certainly their Master's plan; they are in front of Him, and are acting from the prompting of their own self-will, though perhaps under the cover of religious zeal.

The Flight to the Desert

The news of Moses' first attempt came to the ears of the Pharaoh, and he sought to slay Moses. But Moses feared, and fled from the face of Pharaoh. He was out of touch with God. So he fled, and crossed the desert that lay between him and the eastern frontier; threaded the mountain passes of the Sinaitic peninsula, through which in after years he was to lead his people; and at last sat wearily down by a well in the land of Midian. There his chivalrous interference was suddenly elicited on behalf of the daughters of the priest of Midian, who seem to have suffered daily from the insolence of shepherds appropriating the water which the shepherd-maidens had drawn for their flocks. That day, however, the churls met their match, and were compelled to leave the water troughs to the women; who hurried home, unexpectedly early, to tell, with girls' enthusiasm, of the Egyptian who had delivered them from the hand of the shepherds. It was a good office that could not pass without requital in that hospitable land, and it opened the door to the chieftain's tent; ultimately to marriage with one of those same shepherdesses; and finally to the quiet life of a shepherd in the calm open spaces of that wonderful land, which, on more than one occasion, has served for a divine school.

Such experiences come to us all. We rush forward, thinking to carry all before us; we strike a few blows in vain; we are staggered with disappointment, and reel back; we are afraid at the first breath of human disapprobation; we flee from the scenes of our discomfiture to hide ourselves in chagrin. Then we are hidden in the secret of God's presence from the pride of man. And there our vision clears; our self-life dies down; our spirit drinks of the river of God; our faith begins to grasp His arm, and to be the channel for the manifestation of His power; and thus at last we emerge to be His hand to lead an Exodus.

3

The Burning Bush

Exodus 3:4

A Memorable Day

There are days in all lives which come unannounced, un-
heralded; no angel faces look out of heaven; no angel voices
put us on our guard: but as we look back on them in after
years, we realize that they were the turning points of existence.

Quite ordinary was that morning as it broke. The sheep
browsed as usual on the scant herbage, or they lay panting
beneath the shadow of a great rock; but there was nothing in
their behavior to excite the thought that God was nigh. The
giant forms of the mountains, the spreading heavens, the
awful silence unbroken by song of bird or hum of insect life,
the acacia bushes drooping in the shadeless glare—these
things were as they had been forty years, and as they
threatened to be, after Moses had sunk into an obscure and
forgotten grave. Then, all suddenly, a common bush began
to shine with the emblem of Deity; and from its heart of fire
the voice of God broke the silence of the ages in words that
fell on the shepherd's ear like a double-knock: "Moses,
Moses."

And from that moment all his life was altered. The door
which had been so long in repairing was suddenly put on its
hinges again and opened. The peaceful quiet, the meditative
leisure, the hiding from the strife of tongues, the simple
piety of the homestead—where the priest of Midian minis-

tered, and Zipporah welcomed him with his boys, as he brought the flock home to its fold—suddenly vanished, as a tract of land submerged beneath the ocean. And he went forth, not clearly knowing whither; knowing only that he dared not be disobedient to the heavenly vision, or refuse the voice of Him that spake.

That voice still speaks to those whose hearts are hushed to hear. The main point for each of us is to be able to answer His summons and respond, "Here am I."

Never let the loins be ungirded, or the lamps expire; never throw yourself down at full length by the brook, to drink lazily of the limpid stream. In such an hour as you think not the Lord will come.

Out of the bush came the voice of God, "I have surely seen the affliction of My people which are in Egypt, and have heard their cry by reason of their taskmasters; for I know their sorrows, and I am come down to deliver them." "Come now, therefore, and I will send thee unto Pharaoh" (Exod. 3:6-10).

We are all too apt to run before we are sent, as Moses did in his first well-meant, but ill-timed, endeavors. We put our hands, at our own prompting, to a work that needs doing: we ask God to help us, and we go on very well with the momentum of our own energy for at least a day. But on the morrow, when chiding and rebuke and difficulty arise, as they did to Moses, we are disappointed, and throw it all up; betaking ourselves to flight, finding our refuge in the solitudes of the desert.

Divine Long-Suffering Under Provocation
In the first blush of youthful enthusiasm Moses had been impetuous enough to attempt the emancipation of his people by the blows of his right hand. But now that God proposes to send him to lead an Exodus, he starts back in dismay almost petrified at the proposal. But how true this is to nature! The student, as a precocious schoolboy, thinks that he knows all that can be acquired of a certain branch of science; but

twenty years after he feels as if he had not mastered its elements, though he has never ceased to study. And Moses,
who had run before God in feverish impatience, now lags
fainthearted behind Him.

"Who am I, that I should go to Pharaoh?" There was something more than humility here; there was a tone of self-
deprecation which was inconsistent with a true faith in
God's selection and appointment.

"And God said, Certainly, I will be with thee." "I whose
glory shines here, who am as unimpaired by the flight of the
ages as this fire is by burning; who am independent of
sustenance or fuel from man; who made the fathers what
they were; whose nature is incapable of change—I will be
with thee." What an assurance was here! And yet something
of this kind is said to each of us when we are called to undertake any new charge.

In his next excuse Moses professed his inability to answer if
he were asked the name of God; and this was met by the
proclamation of the spirit-stirring name, *Jehovah:* I AM
THAT I AM. There we have the unity of God to the exclusion
of the many gods of Egypt; the unchangeableness of God,
who lives in an eternal present; the self-sufficiency of God,
who alone is His own equivalent. No other term can describe
Him; when you have said your utmost you must fall back on
this—that God is God.

Moses' third excuse was that the people would not believe
him, nor hearken to his voice. But God graciously met this
also by showing him miracles which he might perform in
Egypt, and which would read deep lessons to himself. "What
is that in thine hand? And he said, A rod." It was probably
only a shepherd's crook. What a history, however, awaited
it! It was to be stretched out over the Red Sea, pointing a
pathway through its depths; to smite the flinty rock; to win
victory over the hosts of Amalek; to be known as the Rod of
God. When God wants an implement for His service He does
not choose the golden scepter, but a shepherd's crook; the
weakest and meanest thing He can find—a ram's horn, a cake

of barley meal, an oxgoad, an earthen pitcher, a shepherd's sling. He employs a worm to thresh the mountains and make the hills as chaff. A rod with God behind it is mightier than the vastest army.

The last excuse that Moses alleged was his lack of eloquence. "O Lord, I am not eloquent; I am slow of speech, and of a slow tongue." But God was willing to meet this also with His patient grace; and if only Moses had been willing to trust Him, it is probable that he would have added the gifts of a persuasive and splendid oratory to the other talents with which he was so copiously endowed. "And the Lord said, Who hath made man's mouth? . . . Have not I?" (Exod. 4:10, 11).

But Moses would not believe it; so at length the Divine anger burned against him, and the Lord ended the conference by saying that He would send Aaron with him, to be his colleague and spokesman. Ah! better a thousand times had it been for him to trust God for speech, than be thus deposed from his premiership! Aaron shaped the golden calf, and wrought folly in Israel, and became a thorn in the side of the saint of God. And probably in the eyes of their contemporaries, Aaron engrossed the greater attention, and had most of the honor and credit of the deliverance.

The Final Assent
It was a very grudging one. "And he said, O my Lord, send, I pray Thee, by the hand of him whom Thou wilt send." It was as much as to say, "Since Thou art determined to send me, and I must undertake the mission, then let it be so; but I would that it might have been another, and I go because I am compelled." So often we shrink back from the sacrifice or obligation to which God calls us, that we think we are going to our doom. We seek every reason for evading the Divine will, little realizing that He is forcing us out from our quiet homes into a career which includes, among other things, the song of victory on the banks of the Red Sea; the two lonely sojourns for forty days in converse with God; the shining

face; the vision of glory; the burial by the hand of Michael; and the supreme honor of standing beside the Lord on the Transfiguration Mount.

4

Failure and Disappointment

Exodus 5:22, 23

In loving interchange of thought, the noble and venerable brothers reached Egypt; and in pursuance of the Divine command proceeded to summon the elders of Israel to a conference, at which they should present their credentials, and give utterance to the Divine message with which they were entrusted.

Interview with the Elders
When all were gathered Aaron recited on the behalf of Moses, who probably stood beside him without a word, the magnificent words spoken at the bush (Exod. 3:16-22). We do not know how they were received. Perhaps Moses' own fear was partly realized when he said to God, "They will not believe me, nor hearken unto my voice; for they will say, the Lord hath not appeared unto thee." The long years of bondage may have so quenched their hopes and quelled their spirits that they were unable to realize that deliverance had come.

At this juncture the brothers would probably give the signs with which God had provided them: the serpent changed into a rod; the leprous hand made natural and whole; the water of the river becoming blood as it was poured out upon the land (Exod. 4:2-9). These won conviction; and from that meeting the tidings spread throughout the nation, whispered from hut to hut, told in under breaths from slave to slave among the brick kilns. "And the people believed; and when they heard that the Lord had visited the children of Israel, and that He had looked upon their affliction, then they bowed their heads and worshipped" (Exod. 4:31).

Audience with Pharaoh

It was probably in an audience-room of some splendid palace, where the lordly Pharaoh received deputations and embassies, that they met him. How mixed must Moses' feelings have been, entering as a suppliant the precincts in which he had played no inconspicuous part in those buried years! And then Aaron and he uttered the words, which pealed as a thunderclap through the audience, "Thus saith the Lord God of Israel, Let My people go, that they may hold a feast unto Me in the wilderness" (Exod. 5:1).

In order to appreciate the audacity of the demand, we must remember the unbridled power and authority which were claimed by the Egyptian monarchs. Each Pharaoh was the child of the sun. He is depicted as fondled by the greatest gods, and sitting with them in the recesses of their temples to receive worship equal to their own. "By the life of Pharaoh," was the supreme oath. Without Pharaoh could no man lift up his hand or foot in all the land of Egypt. For him great Egypt existed. For him all other men lived, suffered, and died. For him the mighty Nile flowed from its unexplored fountains to fructify the soil. For him vast armies of priests, and magicians, and courtiers, wrought and ministered. From his superb throne he looked down on the wretched crowds of subject peoples, careless of their miseries. So that it was in a paroxysm of supercilious scorn that he answered the Divine demand: "Who is the Lord, that I should obey His voice, to let Israel go? I know not the Lord, neither will I let Israel go" (Exod. 5:2).

Turning sharply on the two brethren, he accused them of hindering their people's toils, and bade them begone to their own share in the clay pit, or the brick kiln: "Wherefore do ye,

Moses and Aaron, let the people from their works? Get you
unto your burdens." What a bitter taunt there was in that last
sentence! How the royal lip curled as it was uttered! Already
the heart had begun to harden! And so the audience ended,
and the brothers came down the crowded corridors amid the
titter of the court.

Failure and Disappointment

That same day a new order was issued from the palace,
emanating from Pharaoh himself, to the taskmasters of the
people. And probably, ere the evening fell, the ominous
word had passed from the taskmasters to the head men who
were set over their fellow Hebrews, and were, therefore, responsible for the daily delivery of a certain tale of bricks, that
they must expect no more straw, though the daily returns
must be maintained. "Thus saith Pharaoh, I will not give you
straw; go ye, get you straw where ye can find it. Yet not
aught of your work shall be diminished" (Exod. 5:11).

Soul's Rest

"And Moses returned unto the Lord, and said, Lord, wherefore hast Thou so evil entreated this people? Why is it that
Thou hast sent me?"

The agony of soul through which Moses passed must have
been as death to him. He died to his self-esteem, to his castle
building, to pride in his miracles, to the enthusiasm of his
people, to everything that a popular leader loves. As he lay
there on the ground alone before God, wishing himself back
in Midian, and thinking himself hardly used, he was falling
as a corn of wheat into the ground to die, no longer to abide
alone, but to bear much fruit.

It is a lesson for us all. God must bring us down before He
can raise us up. Emptying must precede filling. We must get
to an end of ourselves before He can begin in us. But what a
beginning He makes! "Then the Lord said unto Moses, Now
thou shalt see what I will do to Pharaoh, for with a strong
hand shall he let them go, and with a strong hand shall he

drive them out of his land" (Exod. 6:1). And as those words of encouragement and promise broke on his ear, he must have forgotten the averted looks and bitter words of the people, and risen into a new world of restful expectation. Deliverance was sure, though he had learned that it did not depend on anything that he could do, but on that all-sufficient God, who had announced Himself as the I AM.

And out of the whole story there comes to us this lesson: we must never suppose that the difficulties which confront us indicate that we are not in God's path, and doing His work. Indeed the contrary is generally the case.

5
The Plagues
Hebrews 3:2

Surely we must believe that Pharaoh was included in the love
that gave Jesus Christ to the world; was embraced within the
compass of His propitiation; and might have shone as a star
in the firmament of blood-bought saints.

It must be possible, therefore, to find a clue which will
reconcile the love of God, which brooded over Pharaoh and
his land, with the apparent harshness that inflicted the successive plagues. And it will help us if we remember that
there is a marked difference between the first four plagues
and the rest. In the commencement of God's dealings with
the tyrant it would almost appear as if He set Himself to
answer the question, "Who is the Lord that I should obey
His voice?" and to remove the ignorance of which he complained when he said, "I know not the Lord."

The Faith of Moses
Though it is quite true that the love of God was at work,
seeking to reveal itself to Pharaoh by the ordering of the
plagues; yet we must always remember that the faith of
Moses played no inconspicuous part in respect to them.

In all probability, throughout the conflict which issued in
the emancipation of Israel, Moses was closely dealing with
God. God was vividly present to the eye of his soul. He
thought much more of the presence and power of Jehovah
than he did of the majesty and might of the greatest king of

the time; and as God disclosed to him each successive stage of His providential dealings with Pharaoh, his faith claimed that He should do even as He had said. It was therefore through *his* faith, as the medium and instrument, that God wrought with His mighty hand and outstretched arm.

The River of Blood

One morning, shortly after the events already described, as the sky would be covered with the roseate hue of dawn's first faint blush, Pharaoh, accompanied by high officials, court functionaries, and priests, came down either to perform his customary ablutions or to worship. Upon the river's brink he found Moses awaiting him, with the rod, with which he was already familiar, in his hand. There was no hesitation now in the premptory summons, "The Lord God of the Hebrews hath sent me unto thee, saying, Let My people go, that they serve Me in the wilderness" (Exod. 7:16). The first revelation of God was to be made in the smitten water flowing blood; in the death of its fish, that formed not only objects of worship, but provided a large part of the food staple; and in the stench that filled the land with loathing.

The summons was met by the curled lip of scorn or imperturbable silence; and as there was no alternative, Aaron smote the water with the rod in the presence of the court. Most certainly, as he did so, the two brothers exercised faith that God would do as He had said; and according to their faith it befell. An instantaneous change passed over the appearance and the nature of the water. It became blood. The fish died, and floated on the surface. The air reeked with corruption. There was no water in all the land, save the scanty supplies obtained by digging shallow wells, and collecting the brackish surface water.

The magicians, in some way, counterfeited the marvel; and Pharaoh probably thought that on the part of Moses and Aaron there was only a superior sort of legerdemain. Therefore he did not set his heart to it, though he must have realized that he was at issue with a power greater than that of the goddess of the Nile.

Frogs

It has been supposed that the plagues followed in rapid succession, so that the impression of one had not passed away before another succeeded it. And thus the whole conflict was probably comprehended within nine or ten months. It may have therefore been but a few days after, that Moses and Aaron renewed their demand for emancipation, and told the king the penalty of refusal. But there was no response, no proposal, and the inevitable blow fell.

The land suddenly swarmed with frogs. They came up from the river in myriads, till the very ground seemed alive with them, and it was impossible to walk far without crushing scores. Frogs in the houses, frogs in the beds, frogs baked with the food in the ovens, frogs in the kneading-troughs worked up with the flour; frogs with their monotonous croak, frogs with their cold, slimy skins, everywhere—from morning to night, from night to morning—frogs. And the aggravation of the plague consisted in the fact of the frog being the emblem of the goddess of fecundity; so that it was sacrilege to destroy it.

Lice

The Egyptians were scrupulously cleanly in their personal habits, anticipating the habits of our own time. And the priests were specially so. They bathed themselves repeatedly, and constantly shaved their persons, that no uncleanliness might unfit them for their sacred duties. What horror, then, must have taken hold of them when the very dust of Egypt seemed breeding lice; and they found that they were not exempted from the plague, which was as painful as it was abhorrent to their delicate sensibility.

Perhaps there is something more than appears at first sight in the words, "there was lice in man and *in beast.*" Not only on the bodies of the priests, but on those of the sacred beasts, was there this odious pest. Each revered shrine boasted its sacred bull or goat, whose glossy skin was cleansed with reverent care; and it was an unheard-of calamity that it should become infested with this most disgusting parasite.

Thus upon the gods of Egypt did God execute judgment, in order that Pharaoh might know that He was God of gods, deserving of the allegiance which He claimed. The magicians themselves seem to have felt that this plague was a symptom of the working of a higher Power than they knew; and even they urged Pharaoh to consider that it was the finger of God. How often do unexpected voices read for us the lessons that God designs to teach!

The Beetle

It is not perfectly certain what is meant by the word translated "flies." And though it is possible that it is rightly rendered "flies," yet it is quite as likely that it stands for a peculiar kind of beetle, which was the emblem of the sun-god. Their most powerful deity seemed now to have turned against them, and to have become their scourge at the behest of the God of these shepherd-slaves. The beetles covered the ground, swarmed into the houses, and spoiled the produce of their land.

Murrain

In the earlier part of his ministry Moses had repeatedly questioned God before he set about the performance of the Divine commissions.

But all that had vanished now. Though he had been at least seven times in the royal presence, and each time the bearer of heavy tidings, increasingly abhorred by Pharaoh and his court, and though so far his appearances there had been unsuccessful in securing the great object which God had set before him, yet there was no hesitancy or questioning, when for the eighth time the Lord bade him present himself in the palace to demand the emancipation of the people on pain of a murrain on the beasts.

The murrain came at the fixed time, "and the cattle of Egypt died." The cattle that fed on the green meadows of the Nile; the horses of the wealthy, for which Egypt was famous; the asses of the poor; the camels that bore the merchandise of

Egypt afar, in exchange for spices and balm and myrrh (Gen.
37:25); the oxen that plowed the fields; the sheep which constituted so large a proportion of their wealth—on all of these
the murrain fell. The land was filled with death; the rich
land-owners were greatly impoverished; the poor suffered
severely; thousands of shepherds and teamsters were thrown
out of work; the routine of business communication was
seriously interrupted; and evidence was given of the increasing severity of the plague: while God's care for His own was
clearly shown in the protection that He placed around
Goshen, concerning which it is said, "Of the cattle of the
children of Israel died not one" (Exod. 9:7).

Boils and Blains
Taking in his hands handfuls of ashes, Moses accosted
Pharaoh on some public occasion, when he and his court of
magicians were assembled in the open air, and sprinkled the
light grey dust up towards heaven; with such immediate
effect that "the magicians could not stand before him because of the boils, for the boil was upon the magicians and
upon all Egyptians" and, perhaps, penetrated also to the sacred precincts of the temples, breaking out in the beasts
which were there zealously kept free from taint, as gods of
the nation (Num. 33:4).

The Hail
As the rod was uplifted, vast thunderclouds drifted up from
the sea, and covered the land, and poured out their contents
in thunder, hail, and fire. Storms of any kind are very rare in
Egypt; and this was "very grievous, such as there was none
like it in all the land of Egypt since it became a nation." There
are several references in the Psalms to this fearful visitation.
The vines torn from their trellises and beaten into the soil;
the sycamore trees blighted as by frost; the forest trees broken down; the crops of flax and barley utterly spoiled, beasts
and herdsmen unsheltered in the open fields in defiance of
the warning given, smitten to death by hailstones, which fell

as thick as rain, and may have weighed (as in exceptional instances hailstones have been known to weigh) from six to eight ounces—such are some of the indications given of the terror of the scene (Psa. 78:47, 48; 105:32). But from all these the land of Goshen was free.

Through the pelting storm, Moses and Aaron were summoned into the royal presence to hear for the first time from those proud lips the confession of sin (Exod. 9:27); with an urgent entreaty that the mighty thunderings and hail which were then shaking palace and city might cease. Moses had no doubt as to the answer which would come to his prayer; but he had grave doubts of the reliableness of the royal word. However, he did as Pharaoh required. Passing uninjured through the storm, he went beyond the city gates into the open country. It was as if he consciously lived in the secret place of the Most High, and abode under the shadow of the Almighty. With outspread hands he interceded for the land of the oppressors of his people; and God hearkened to his request: so that the thunders and hail ceased, and the rain was no more poured out upon the earth.

The Locusts
The tone of Moses rose with every plague. Hitherto he had been content with repeating his demand; but now the failure of the king to keep his royal word had altered the relations between them. Pharaoh had forfeited all claim to his respect. He had made repeated promises and broken them. His confessions of sin had been followed by no efforts at amendment. He was no longer ignorant of Jehovah, but wilfully obstinate and defiant. And Moses altered his tone; not now treating him as a sovereign, but as a sinner, and dealing directly with his proud and obstinate heart: "Thus saith the Lord God of the Hebrews, How long wilt thou refuse to humble thyself before Me?" (Exod. 10:3). The penalty of further delay was to be an infliction of locusts.

The Egyptians well knew what a plague of locusts might mean; and therefore the servants of Pharaoh pleaded with the king to acquiesce in the demand of the Hebrew leaders. Better lose a nation of slaves, said they, than imperil the land. So that from that moment it became a trial of strength between the king of Egypt and God, in whom for the first time in his history he had found more than his match.

Pharaoh, at his servants' suggestion, proposed a compromise. He was willing to let *the men* go, and threatened them with evil if they did not accept this proposition. But there was no hesitation in its instant refusal by the brothers. It could not be. The young and old must go, sons and daughters, flocks and herds—*all*. None was to be absent in that great convocation, which was to assemble somewhere in the desert to hold a feast to Jehovah. The court had never heard the great Pharaoh so addressed; nor could he endure that dauntless speech; so, at a signal from him, they were driven from his presence.

But the locusts came with an east wind, which, blowing straight from the desert, had set in on the land for a whole day and night. "When it was morning, the east wind brought the locusts." Their numbers filled the air, and literally covered the earth. Its green surface was darkened by their brown forms; and every trace of green in the fields, on the fruit trees, and among the plentiful herbs, of which the Egyptians were so fond, instantly disappeared. There was no bud, nor blossom, nor shoot, nor leaf, left anywhere "through all the land of Egypt" (Exod 10:15). The animals had perished, and now the produce of the earth. But again Pharaoh went back from his word.

The Darkness
Unannounced, the darkness fell like a pall upon the land, "even darkness that could be felt." Travelers tell us of darkness caused by sandstorm, so thick that it was impossible to see the hand when placed close against the face. From whatever cause, the darkness of this plague must have been of the same description.

"They saw not one another, neither rose any from his place

for three days" (Exod. 10:23). All the activities of the land were paralyzed. The stoutest hearts were dismayed. It seemed as if their greatest deity had suddenly deserted them, abandoning their case. Perhaps the light would never visit them again. In that land of radiant sunlight it was an awful experience.

When the plague passed away, for the last time the monarch summoned the brothers, and made a final desperate effort at compromise. The nation might go, said he; but the flocks and herds must remain. But Moses penetrated the craft of the proposal, and tore it to shreds. "Our cattle shall go with us, there shall not an hoof be left behind" (Exod. 10:26). Clearly they would be required for sacrifice. Then, again, the proud spirit of the king, uncowed by repeated misfortune, untaught by the stern discipline of pain, broke vehemently forth; "Get thee from me, . . . see my face no more; for in that day thou seest my face thou shalt die" (Exod. 10:28).

The spirit of Moses, also, was swept with that anger which at rare intervals asserted itself in him, as a storm on a tranquil lake (Exod. 11:8); but he made answer with calm dignity, as became the ambassador of God. "And Moses said, Thou hast spoken well; I will see thy face again no more" (Exod. 10:29).

6

Preparing for the Exodus

Exodus 12:41

We have seen how, during those months of agony, Moses had been the organ through which God wrought out His purposes.

Faith Based on Promise
We cannot tell the form in which the Divine Word came to the two brethren. Was it as when a man speaketh to his friend? Should we have heard it, with our uncircumcised ears, had we been in their company? Or was it an impression photographed on the heart of each, upturned towards the source of light? But, howsoever the communication came, in those accents—which first declared what Israel was to do, and then, with unhesitating precision, announced the successive acts which would finally smite the fetters from the captives' hands, and free the nation in a single night—they recognized the voice that had bidden them go to Pharaoh with repeated summonses to surrender.

The directions were substantially these. On the tenth of the following month, the head of each family, whether slave or elder, was to select a firstling lamb, free of disease and defect. Only if the family were too small to need a lamb for itself might it join with some neighboring household. There was no question as to the lamb being too little for the household. Jesus is "enough for all, enough for each, enough for ever more." The lamb was to be kept from the tenth to the

fourteenth of the month, and killed on the latter day, towards
the close of the afternoon. The blood, as it gushed warm from
the wound, was to be carefully caught in a basin, and sprinkled on the two side posts and lintel of the houses where the
Israelites dwelt; the carcass roasted whole, and eaten with
unleavened bread and bitter herbs.

Special instructions were also given as to the attitude in
which the feast was to be eaten. The whole family was to be
gathered around the table, from the grey-headed sire to the
newborn babe. There was to be no symptom of lassitude or
indolence. The men were to have their loins girt as for a long
journey and to grasp their staves. The women were to have
their dough and kneading troughs bound up in little bun-
dles, with their clothes, for easy carriage on their shoulders.
All were to have their feet sandalled. The meal was to be
eaten in haste. And thus, with ears intent to catch the first
note of the trumpet, the whole nation was to await the signal
for its Exodus, sheltered by blood; while strength was stored
for the fatigues that must be endured ere the land of bondage
was left behind for ever.

There was a great contrast, therefore, between the attitude
of the Israelites in the destruction of the firstborn and in the
former plagues. In those they had been perfectly inactive,
only reaping the benefits which accrued from the successive
victories won through the faith of their great leader. But now
they were called upon to appropriate benefits, which might
not accrue if they failed to conform to the conditions laid
down. And in those demands on their obedience and faith,
there surely must have broken, on the minds of the more
intelligent at least, the feeling that there was a deeper meaning in the whole transaction than appeared on the surface;
and that eternal issues were being wrought out, the meaning
of which they could not as yet adequately apprehend.

And when all the provisions had been thus solemnly recited, there followed the words of promise, on which thence-
forward Moses reposed his faith; "I will pass through the
land of Egypt, and will smite all the firstborn in the land of
Egypt, both man and beast; . . . and when I see the blood, I

will pass over you, and the plague shall not be upon you to destroy you, when I smite the land of Egypt" (Exod. 12:12, 13).

Faith and Action

He gathered the elders of Israel, and informed them of the instructions he had received; and whether it was that some prognostications of their coming deliverance had entered their souls, or that they had come to believe in their great leader to an extent which had been previously impossible, it is certain that they offered neither opposition nor suggestion to his proposals. They bowed the head and worshipped, and went their way to do "as the Lord had commanded Moses and Aaron; so did they" (Exod. 12:28).

Oh that such faith were ours! Not arguing, nor questioning, nor reasoning: but believing that the promises of God are Yea and Amen in Christ; and that what He says about accepting all who believe in Christ, making us sit together with Him on His throne, and loving us with the love He bears His Son, He is willing and able to perform.

And such faith becomes contagious. The faith of Moses had kindled faith in three millions of people; who stood ready to plunge the knife into the fleecy victim that awaited it, to sprinkle the blood, to start on the distant march, but with no fear that the firstborn of the house should be left a corpse behind. No father eyed his son with anxiety; no mother trembled to hear the rustle of the angel wing; no boy shuddered at the near approach of death. It was enough that God had said, that, when He saw the blood, He would pass over. But though they could not see it or understand it, or fathom the purposes of God, they knew the blood was there to speak for them; and they believed, therefore, that all must be well. And though no one knew exactly their destination, nor how they would reach it, they had no misgiving as to the issue.

Faith Vindicated

All was still with an almost preternatural silence.

But suddenly the stillness was interrupted by a scream of

anguish, as a mother rushed out into the night to tell that the Angel of Death had begun his work, and she was presently answered by the wail of a mother in agony for her first-born; and this by another, and yet another. It was useless to summon priest or physician, magician or courtier; how could they help others who had not been able to ward off death from their own? The maid grinding at the mill and her lady sleeping under curtains of silk were involved in a common sorrow, which obliterated all social distinctions, and made all one. There was not a house where there was not one dead—even Pharaoh's palace was not exempt. The news spread like wildfire that the heir to the throne was dead. "And there was a great cry in Egypt."

"Then Pharaoh rose up in the night, he and all his servants, and all the Egyptians; and he called for Moses and Aaron by night, and said, 'Rise up, and get you forth from among my people' " (Exod. 12:30, 31). There was no attempt at parley. They, their people, their children, and their property, were to be gone. And the bidding of the palace was repeated by ten thousand tongues. The one eager desire of the Egyptians was to get rid of them at all speed, and at all cost. They were glad to give them anything they asked, and thus bestowed some payment for their long unremunerated labor; and even Pharaoh, the haughty monarch, entreated that they would bless him before they went.

And so the host stepped forth into freedom. For the first time the Israelites realized that they were a nation, and drank the earliest rich deep draught of liberty. A mere horde of slaves, they suddenly crystallized into a people. The spirit of their leader inspired and thrilled them.

7

The Passage of the Red Sea

Exodus 14:29, 30

It was not long after the hour of midnight before the entire
Israelite host was on the move; and as the morning light
suffused the cloudlets with its flush, it beheld them marching, the men five abreast, while wives and children and bag-
gage and cattle followed. From different points the vast
host—which, judging by the fact that the number of the men
amounted to six hundred thousand, could not have been less
than two and a half million—converged towards the central
meeting place at Succoth.

Succoth would be about fifteen miles from their starting-
place, and there they made their first prolonged halt; baked
unleavened cakes of the dough which they had brought with
them; rested the weary women and children in leafy tabernacles hastily improvised from the foliage of that region: so that
the whole host, heartened and refreshed, was able to undertake its second stage, which was Etham, on the edge of the
wilderness, where the green vegetation of Egypt fades into
wastes of sand. There is one episode in this setting forth that
we must not forget to mention, and which shows how largely
the whole Exodus was wrought in faith, at least in the case of
Moses, and perhaps of more. "And Moses took the bones of
Joseph with him" (Exod. 13:19). This great ancestor of their
race had been dead some four hundred years; but on his
deathbed he had made his brethren sware that when God
visited them, as He most surely would, and brought them

out of Egypt, they should bear his bones with them in their march. In his death, and through that weary waiting time, he had been the prophet of the Exodus; and how often must those unburied bones have been the theme of conversation in Hebrew homes! And now that they were accompanying their march, all the people realized that the anticipations of generations were being fulfilled.

The Guiding Pillar

Who has not seen in a summer sky some majestic cumulus cloud sailing slowly through the heavens, as if it had taken the impression of some mighty Alp, whose cliffs, recesses and snows were being reduplicated in its shape and color? Something of this sort must have gathered in the pure morning atmosphere at the head of the vanguard, never again to desert that pilgrim band till the Jordan was crossed and it had settled down to brood over the house of God. But all through the years, when night fell, it burnt with fire at its heart; fire, which was always the symbol of the presence of God.

This served many purposes. It was the guide of their march; it was a shadow from the burning heat of a vertical sun, spreading its folds in fleecy beauty to shelter them in a "weary land," and at night it provided them with a light as it watched over them like the Eye of God.

In the thought of Moses, that cloud by day and night must have been full of reassurance, because it was the very chariot of God, in which He went before His people. And it is very touching to learn that "He took it not away," as if neither sin, nor murmuring, nor disobedience, could ever drive away Him who loves us, not because we are good, but to make us so; and who cannot leave or forsake those whom He has taught to lisp, "Abba, Father."

The Route

The easiest route to Canaan lay through the Isthmus of Suez and the land of the Philistines. A journey of a little over one hundred miles would have conducted them direct to their destination. But God did not permit them to go that way, lest the sight of embattled hosts should unnerve them. In after years, when the education and revelations of the desert were finished, they might behold those scenes undismayed. But as yet they must not know war till they had been more deeply taught in the might and care of God. So is our journey ever adapted to our strength. God is always considering what we are able to bear; never leading into dangers before which heart and flesh would succumb. "God led them about." The leading about tries our patience; but it is the best route for timid hearts and inexperienced feet.

The Pursuit

No sooner had Israel gone than Pharaoh was sorry. The public works stood still for lack of labor. Vast territories were suddenly unoccupied. The labor of this enslaved people was missed on every side, in city and field. There was a sudden loss of revenue and service which he could ill dispense with. And his pride forbade that he should quietly acquiesce in their unhindered Exodus. Besides, in their mad haste to be rid of this people, the Egyptians had laden them with jewels of silver, and jewels of gold, and raiment; so much so that it is distinctly said, "they spoiled the Egyptians." It is clear from the contributions afterwards made to the building of the Tabernacle, that Israel was carrying off a large amount of treasure and valuables. "And the heart of Pharaoh, and of his servants, was turned against the people; and they said, Why have we done this, that we have let Israel go from serving us?" (Exod. 14:5).

At this juncture, the king heard of the extraordinary movement southwards, which seemed to have thrown them again into his power. Surely his gods were recovering their olden power, and were rallying to his aid! And he said, "I will pursue; I will overtake; I will divide the spoil; my lust shall be satisfied upon them!" Then there was great haste, and the marshaling of the chivalry and pride of Egypt, six hundred of the chosen chariots, with cavalry and infantry, horsemen and foot soldiers.

And so as the afternoon closed in, of perhaps the fifth day of the Exodus, the outposts of the fugitive host beheld the dreaded forms of the Egyptian warriors coming over the ridges of the desert hills; and as the night fell they were aware that the whole Egyptian host was encamped in their near vicinity, only waiting for the morning light to swoop down on them, involving them either in a general massacre, or in what was, perhaps, more dreadful, a return to slavery.

It was an awful plight. Terrible, indeed, was the breaking of the news on those craven hearts. They immediately turned on Moses, and spent their fear and anguish on his heart. "Wherefore hast thou dealt thus with us? Were there no graves in Egypt? Better to have perished there than here! Why did you not leave us alone? Where is your God?" (Exod. 14:11).

When God's cloud brings any of His children into a position of unparalleled difficulty, they may always count upon Him to deliver them.

A conspicuous example of this is given here. From His chariot-cloud their Almighty Friend looked down upon the cowering crowd of fugitives in their sore fear as they cried to Him. "In all their affliction He was afflicted, and the angel of His presence saved them; in His love and in His pity He redeemed them; and He bare them, and carried them" throughout that memorable night and day.

The Rod
That rod had already played many parts, but never in all its history had it done, nor would it do, such marvels as awaited it that night, when at the bidding of God it was stretched over the waters of the Red Sea.

The Cloud
Up till now the pillar of cloud had swept in majestic glory through the heavens; but at this juncture it settled down

upon the ground like a great wall of billowy vapor, standing
for a fence between the camp of Egypt and the camp of Israel.

All night through, those heaven-lit beacon fires shone out;
and in after-days the memory of the effect produced by the
mingling of their light with the walls of glassy water,
supplied the inspired seer with the imagery with which to
depict the triumph of the redeemed, who stand on the shores
of the "glassy sea mingled with fire, having the harps of
God" (Rev. 15:2).

The Passage

At this point, following the lead of the Psalmist-historian, it
is clear that a terrific storm broke upon the scene. The earth
shook and trembled; the massy foundations of the mountains rocked; from out the darkness brooding overhead, the
curtains of God's pavilion, came the repeated flash of the
lightning, followed by the long reverberation of the thunder.
The Most High uttered His voice, which was followed by the
pelt of the hailstones and the fall of fireballs. The east wind
rose in fury, driving before it the retreating waters, which
fled at the blast of the breath of his nostrils; then catching
them up in its hands it piled them, wave on wave, until they
stood up a wall of foam and tumult, from base to top, fret-
ting, seething, fuming, chafing at the unexpected restraint,
and wondering at the unwonted posture, but held steadily
and always by the pressure of that mighty blast, that gave
them no respite, but held them as in a vice; and all the water
behind, backed up, leaned upon that rampart, so strangely
built, so marvellously maintained.

And on the other side the tide withdrew back and back
towards the fountains of the great deep behind. It was as if
every wavelet felt the pull, the suction of an abyss opening
somewhere far down in the sea, and hastened to fill it, leaving the foundations of the deep naked in the headlong rush.

Shelving down from the shore between these two walls of
water, a broad thoroughfare lay outspread, which the
prophet compares to those mountain paths by which cattle

descend from the heights on which they graze to the valleys where they rest (Isa. 63:14). Was there ever such a strange comparison? And yet for the moment it seemed almost as natural; and at that moment the word which had sprung from the lips of the leader, and had been caught by those who stood closest around him, passed like prairie fire, though in a whisper, from lip to lip. "Speak unto the children of Israel that they go forward"; and immediately, without precipitate haste, but with glad obedience, the ransomed host stepped down, rank after rank, and passed between the walls of glass and fire amid the rattle of the storm, which made the withdrawal of their hosts inaudible to their foes.

As soon as the Egyptians became aware that Israel was escaping, they followed them, and went on after them into the midst of the sea.

At the bidding of God, Moses stretched out his hand over the sea from that further shore which he and Israel had by this time gained, and the sea returned to its strength. The Egyptians fled against it in vain; they were overwhelmed in the sudden rush of water toppling down on them from either side. They sank as lead in the mighty waters; they went down like a stone into its depths; and in less time than it takes to tell the story, not a trace of their proud array remained.

The Song of Moses
"Then sang Moses" (Exod. 15:1). The morning dawn revealed one of the most memorable spectacles of history. A nation of slaves, fleeing from their masters, had suddenly become a nation of free men, and stood emancipated upon the shores of a new continent. The proud people, which for generations had inflicted such untold griefs upon them, had suffered a humiliation from which it would take them generations to recover. The chivalry of Egypt was overwhelmed in the midst of the sea, there remained not so much as one of them left; and all along the shore lay the bodies of the dead, cast up from the depths of the tide.

And from that ransomed host, congregated there in one vast throng, broke forth an anthem, whose sublime conceptions of language rendered it worthy of the occasion, as it had been the model for triumphal songs in all subsequent times.

Whether or not this ode were composed beforehand in anticipation of this moment we cannot tell. It may have been; else how could it have been sung by those assembled thousands? But this in itself would be a striking token of the faith which dwelt so vigorously in the heart of Moses.

So does God turn our anxieties into occasions of singing—weeping endures for a night, but joy comes in the morning. The redeemed obtain gladness and joy; God puts gladness into their hearts, and new songs into their mouths.

8

The Gift of Manna

Exodus 16:14-16

The Desert Murmurings

It was a great aggravation of the responsibilities which already lay heavily on the heart of Moses, to have to encounter the perpetual murmurings of the people whom he loved so well. It only drove him continually back on his Almighty Friend and Helper, to pour into His most tender and sympathizing ear the entire tale of sorrow. But the repeated outbreak of these murmurings all along the wilderness route only sets in more conspicuous prominence the beauty of his gentle meekness, and the glory of his faith, which probably was the one channel through which the power of God wrought for the salvation and blessing of His people.

Murmurers are short of memory. It was only one short month since the people had come forth out of Egypt—a month crowded with the wonders which the right hand of the Lord had wrought. The chronicler specially notes that it was the fifteenth day of the second month, and adds, "The whole congregation of the children of Israel murmured against Moses and Aaron in the wilderness; and the children of Israel said unto them, Would to God we had died by the hand of the Lord in the land of Egypt, when we sat by the flesh-pots, and when we did eat bread to the full; for ye have brought us forth into this wilderness to kill this whole assembly with hunger" (Exod. 16:2, 3).

They could remember very well the sensual delights of Egypt; but they forgot the lash of the taskmaster, and the anguish of heart with which they wrought at the kneading of the clay. They forgot how graciously God had provided for their needs, ever since they had stood around their tables to eat the flesh of the paschal lamb. Whenever a murmuring fit threatens, let us review the past, and recount the Lord's dealings with us in bygone years.

Murmurers are short of sight. They fail to see that behind all the appearances of things there lie hid the Presence and Providence of God.

Annoyed and apprehensive, it was some relief to expend their spleen on the one man to whom they owed everything. But their faithful leader showed them that their insults were directed not against himself, but against Him whose servant he was, and at whose bidding everything was being wrought. "The Lord heareth your murmurings which ye murmur against Him; and what are we? Your murmurings are not against us, but against the Lord" (Exod. 16:7).

Murmurers are short of faith. It was not so much the hardship that they were at that moment experiencing, but that which they thought to be imminent. Provisions were running short; supplies were becoming exhausted; the slender store refused to be eked out beyond a comparatively short period. It was thus that they came to Moses and murmured.

Too many of God's children despond because of what they dread, and break out into murmurings that they are going to be killed; when if they were to stop to think for a single moment, they would see that God is pledged by the most solemn obligations to provide for them. Why do you murmur? It is because you doubt. Why do you doubt? It is because you will look out on the future, or consider your circumstances, apart from God.

The Wilderness Food
It is not for us to tell here the whole story of the manna, with its wealth of spitiual reference to the true Bread, which is Christ. It is enough to remember: "He gave them bread from heaven to eat." For the believer them are five sources from which help may come; for in addition to the four quarters of

the winds he looks up to the heavens. There came *from heaven* the sound of the rushing of a mighty wind. Look higher, child of God, to the heart and hand of the Father!

Eating the Manna Daily and Early

"They gathered it every morning, and when the sun waxed hot it melted" (Exod. 16:21). There is no time like the early morning hour for feeding on the flesh of Christ by communion with Him, and pondering His words. Once lose that, and the charm is broken by the intrusion of many things, though it may be they are all useful and necessary. You cannot remake the broken reflection of a lake swept by wind. How different is that day from all others, the early prime of which is surrendered to fellowship with Christ! Nor is it possible to live today on the gathered spoils of yesterday. Each man needs all that a new day can yield him of God's grace and comfort. It must be daily bread.

Strength and Blessedness Through Feeding on Christ

If only believers in Christ would realize and appropriate the lesson so clearly taught in this narrative, as well as in the wonderful discourse which our Lord founded upon it (John 6:22-58), they would find themselves the subjects of a marvelous change. It is almost incredible how great a difference is wrought by the prolonged and loving study of what the Scriptures say concerning Him. To sit down to enjoy them; to read two or three chapters, an epistle, or a book, at a sitting; to let the heart and mind steep in it; to do this before other intruders have noisily entered the heart and distracted its attention—ah, how this transforms us!

We are not unfamiliar, in these days, with instances in which the faith of one man avails to procure the daily food of hundreds of orphans and of others. God gives to them that they may give to those with whom they are charged. But all these are dwarfed before the stupendous miracle of a faith that was capable of covering the desert place with food for forty years!

9

The God-ward Aspect

Exodus 18:19

When the Israelite host had left Rephidim, they began to climb up from the coast of the Red Sea into the heart of the mountain range of Sinai.

Tidings in the desert fly fast; and the aged priest, in the fastnesses of Midian, had been kept fully informed of the wonderful series of events of which his relative had been the center. When, therefore, tidings came of the arrival of the vast host in the vicinity of Sinai, he took Zipporah, Moses' wife, and her two sons, who had been entrusted to his care, and brought them unto Moses.

And on that day an incident took place which was destined to have important issues on the history of the great leader as well as on the people whom he led. "It came to pass on the morrow that Moses sat to judge the people; and the people stood by Moses from the morning unto the evening" (Exod. 18:13).

Moses' Habitual Practice
We get a sudden glimpse here into the kind of life which Moses at this time was leading. When the host encamped, and there was a day at liberty from the weariness of the march, he seems to have sat on a judgment seat, to which all the people came who had any disputes, or grievances, or matters about which they desired to obtain advice and Divine counsel. Despite all their murmurings they looked upon

him as the organ for the voice of God, and sought from his lips an authoritative declaration of the Divine will.

This blessed work of mediatorship was not borne by Moses as a Priest, for as yet the Priesthood was not constituted; but as a large-hearted, noble man, who was at leisure from himself, and had the ear of God. He was "for the people to God-ward."

We often wonder at Luther, who spent three hours each day in prayer and meditation; at Bishop Andrewes, spending the greater part of five hours each day in fellowship with God; at John Welsh, who thought that day ill spent which did not witness eight or ten hours of closet communion. It seems to us as if such prolonged praying must involve an endless monotony of vain repetitions. We forget that when men are sent to market with a host of commissions from their neighbors and friends, they must needs tarry longer than when they go only for themselves. It would be a very wholesome thing if the causes of others were to detain us more constantly before the Lord.

Moses' Assent

It cannot be God's will that any of His servants should wear away. He knows our frame too well to overtax its frail machinery. The bell never summons a servant to a duty concerning which God does not say to him, My grace is sufficient for thee; as thy day so shall thy strength be.

Sometimes God's workers make the mistake of burdening themselves with work which others could do as well as themselves, and indeed, would be the better for doing. This seems to have been the case with Moses.

Jethro's advice was therefore most timely, that he should provide out of all the people able men, with the three important qualifications, that they should fear God, love truth, and hate unjust gain. These were to deal with the small matters, while the greater ones were still brought to himself.

This policy was that which the apostles adopted when the business of the Church had so grown upon their hands as to engross too much of their time and energy. They could no longer combine the serving of tables with the ministry of the Word; and as they could not hesitate which side of their double office to abandon, they called in the help of Stephen and his colleagues "to serve tables," while they gave themselves to prayer and to the ministry of the Word.

We touch men most when we most touch God. The prophet and priest, the man of God, the teacher, these are among the choicest gifts of God to men. And if you are gifted specially in these directions, cultivate such endowments to the uttermost—they are rare enough—leaving other details to be cared for by others who may be cast in a more practical mold.

10

At the Foot of Sinai

Exodus 19:18

After a march of eighteen miles from the Red Sea, they came
out on a perfectly level plain of yellow sand, some two miles
long, and half a mile wide, nearly flat, and dotted over with
tamarisk bushes. The mountains which gather around this
plain have for the most part sloping sides, and form a kind of
natural amphitheatre.

Such was the chosen scene for the giving of the Law. There
the hosts of Israel remained stationary for long weeks; and
there, while clouds veiled the heights, and fire played from
peak to peak, and mysterious voices, resembling at times a
trumpet's notes, awoke unwonted echoes in the heart of the
hills, God met with His people and gave them His Law;
writing His name, not on tablets of stone merely, but on the
entire course of human history.

God's Object at Sinai

At the time of the Exodus the world was almost wholly given
to idolatry. The first objects of idolatrous worship were
probably simply the sun and moon and heavenly bodies or
other conspicuous objects of creative wisdom and power.
Afterwards the Deity was supposed to reside in men, and
even beasts. Of these, images were made and
worshipped—at first covered with drapery, but afterwards in
a state of nudity, and exerting the most demoralizing effect.

In dealing with this deluge of idolatry, God acted as with

the deluge of water that drowned the ancient world. He began with a single family, teaching them the sublime lessons concerning Himself; which when they had perfectly acquired, they were to make the common coin of the world.

God chose from the masses of heathendom one man, "called him alone," and led him to follow Him into a strange land. There, shut away from surrounding peoples, He began to teach him about Himself.

God welded the Hebrew people together into one, that they might be able to receive and retain as a part of their national life those great truths with which they were to be entrusted. So perfectly did God do this work, that while other nations have risen, reigned, and fallen, and their disintegration has been utter and final, the children of Abraham endure, like an imperishable rock, undestroyed by the chafe of the waves or the fret of the ages.

The Majesty of God
The natural scenery was sufficiently majestic; but it became more so as the incidents of the third day were unfolded. Was there not majesty in the thunders and lightnings; in the brooding cloud where clouds were almost unknown; in the flashing lightning dispelling the pitchy gloom; in the trumpet peal echoing through the hills?

It was amid such scenes that God spake. Could any combination of natural phenomena have given grander conceptions of the Majesty of the Divine Nature?

The Spirituality of God
What was their God like? Would He assume the form of anything that is in the heaven above, or in the earth beneath, or in the waters under the earth? Would it be in any, or in a combination of all, of these forms that they should see Him who had brought them out of Egypt? But on that memorable occasion, "when Moses brought forth the people out of the camp to meet God" (Exod. 19:17), they saw no likeness. He was there, for He spoke. But there was no outward form for the eye to discern.

The Holiness of God

This primal lesson was also taught in striking fashion by outward signs which impressed the sense. Bounds were erected to keep the beasts from grazing on the thin herbage of the lower slopes; whoever touched the Mount must die; all clothes were to be carefully washed against that third day; absolute purity was to be observed in heart and life; Moses alone was called up to the top of the Mount, where smoke and fire and lightning flash commingled, and the thunder peal vied with the trumpet blast; and when he had climbed thither, he was sent all the way down again for the express purpose of charging the people, and even the priests, not to break through upon the Lord to gaze, lest God should break forth upon them. All these significant acts converged to give outward and sensible manifestation of the Holiness of God.

The Royalty of God

In their triumphal ode of victory by the shores of the Red Sea, the people had confessed the right of Jehovah to reign over them for ever; but they were yet to learn that He was indeed absolute monarch. The Jewish state was a kingdom, and God was King. And the reality of His government appeared in the way in which Moses himself obeyed His behest. It was a sight never to be forgotten to see how their great leader Moses was absolutely subservient to the command issued from God's pavilion.

Every ordinance of the Law, every custom and provision for domestic and civil life, every item in the construction of the sanctuary and in the ordering of the priests, was due to the direct will of God, spoken from His mouth. God, and not Moses, was the Author of each proviso, the real Legislator, the real Lawgiver, the real King; Moses was but the mouthpiece, an intermediary to communicate God's decrees to His people. How clear was the testimony to the supremacy of the Most High! Such were some of the lessons taught at Sinai.

11

The Vision of God and Its Effect

Exodus 34:29

During long years the desire had been growing in the heart of Moses to see the face of God. "Show me now Thy way, that I may know Thee."

No invalid in the dark cold winter days so longs for the summer; no true heart so longs for its mate; no young bride just widowed so longs for the everlasting reunion of heaven, as do some saintly hearts for God.

But these longings are certain to be fulfilled, because God is faithful. There is no stronger argument for immortality than this; it must be, because all men forecast it. There is no stronger argument for retribution than this; it must be, because men's consciences demand it. There is no stronger argument for the Being of God than to say, It must be, because the heart of man craves infinite love; the mind of man infinite truth; the spirit of man infinite communion with spirit.

Obedience

We must learn to obey. This was the great characteristic of Moses. He was faithful in *all* God's house as a servant. God could always depend on him. He was a man after His own heart, who could fulfil all His will. And it was to him, rather than to the disobedient hearts of the people, that God revealed Himself.

Trust

"God called to Moses out of the midst of the cloud . . . and Moses went into the midst of the cloud" (Exod. 24:16-18). Thick banks of dense cloud, dark in their earthward aspect, though insufferably bright on their inner side, shut out the light of sun and the spectacles of earth, and shut him in with God. But he had not seen the vision, had he not been willing to pass through the cloud and to stand beneath the shadow of the Divine hand.

Courage

We must dare to be alone. When we read (Exod. 34:2, 3) those solemn words, "Be ready in the morning, and come up in the morning, and present thyself there to Me in the top of the mount: and no man shall come up with thee; neither let any man be seen throughout all the mount, neither let the flocks nor herds feed before the mount"—they seem to echo down to us in other but similar tones, "When thou prayest, enter into thy closet, and when thou hast shut thy door, pray to thy Father which is in secret" (Matt. 6:6).

Valuable as are the prolific opportunities for Christian culture and service which surround us, they will be disastrous indeed in their effect if they rob us of the time that we should otherwise spend with God, or give us a distaste for lonely heart-fellowship. Let the first moments of the day, when the heart is fresh, be given to God. Never see the face of man till you have seen the King. Dare to be much alone on the Mount.

Assurance

Perhaps Moses, as he entered the cloud, expected that the Almighty would pass before him, riding upon a cherub, flying upon the wings of the wind, girt with rainbow and storm, while the thunder rolled as drums in His march. But lo! he seemed to stand in a ravine, upon a ledge of rock, shadowed by a hand, while through that mountain rent passed the Divine procession; and a voice, still, sweet, penetrating, told that God was Love.

The answers to our prayers for spiritual vision may not always come as we expect. But, however they come, come they will. None of those who wait for Him shall be ashamed. He will satisfy desires which He has Himself implanted.

True Godliness

Such visions leave unmistakable traces. The face of Moses shone: and did not his heart and life shine also? Could it have been otherwise? Linen in which the housewife has laid rosemary and lavender will smell fragrantly; ordinary iron placed near a magnet becomes magnetic. And it is impossible for us to be much with God without becoming God-like.

Such traces are not perceived by those who present them. "Moses wist not that his face shone." He was glorious in all eyes but his own.

True Christian excellence is as unconscious of its beauty as Moses was; whenever it becomes self-conscious it loses its charm. Beware of the man who talks about his graces. There is such a thing as being proud of humility, and making capital out of our nothingness. The man who boasts of a shining face is a counterfeit and a cheat. The possessor of the genuine article never talks about it, never thinks about it; and would be almost overwhelmed to hear of any such thing being ascribed to him. The charm of a little child is its utter unconsciousness of self; and that is the charm in true God-likeness. It is like the bloom on a peach, the dew-jewels on the morning lawn, or the stillness of the surface of a mountain pool.

12

The Tabernacle

Exodus 25:9, 40

The heart of the Jewish people was the Tabernacle, around which their tents circled, and the movements of which determined the journeyings of the host. The Tabernacle also taught them some of the deepest thoughts about God, in a kind of picture language, which was best suited to their immature minds.

The Pattern of the Tabernacle
The tabernacle was patterned on the mount! Then clearly there must have been some visible phenomenon, some bright apparition, some glorious picture cast on the clouds or built on the old rocks. There may have been stakes and curtains, cherubs and lamps, gold and silver, altar and candlestick; but they would not bear the touch—they existed as a beautiful dream, like some mystery of cloud that stands for a moment in the heavens at sunset, and then is gone.

But it is almost inconceivable that God did not at the same time explain to Moses those wonderful conceptions of His own nature, and His relations to man, which were intended to be set forth in this material structure. In those days of hallowed intercourse, the Almighty Teacher must have impressed on the reverent and receptive mind of His pupil trains of holy thought which engrossed and delighted him.

God's Condescension

God said, "Let them make Me a sanctuary, that I may dwell among them" (Exod. 25:8).

Thus it was ordained that this large tent should be pitched among them, only differing from their own in its proportions and materials; but standing on the same level sand, struck and pitched at the same hour with theirs, and enduring the same vicissitudes of weather and travel. Did not this say, as plainly as words could, that the tabernacle of God was with men, and that He was willing to dwell with them and become their God? Did it not teach that Jehovah had become a pilgrim with the pilgrim host; no longer a God afar off, but a sharer in their national fortunes? And is not this the very lesson of the Incarnation?

God's Greatness

To this, too, a visible expression was to be given. The Tabernacle was the most superb building of its kind ever reared by man. It must have cost at least a quarter of a million sterling—an immense sum for that fugitive nation of slaves.

God's Unity

All around, the nations were under the spell of idolatry. But the Tabernacle, with all its differing parts, and materials, and accessories, was one. One ark; one incense altar; one altar of burnt offerings; one sacred purpose in every order and rite for the putting away of uncleanness. It stood, therefore, among men as perpetual protest against idolatry, and as an emphatic witness to the Unity of God. "Hear, O Israel; the Lord our God is one Lord" (Deut. 6:4). Such was the perpetual message that floated on the desert air from that unique structure.

God's Spirituality

On the mountain the lawgiver saw the robes of the King, but not the King; His glory, but not His person; His back part, but not His face; and the conception that God was a Spirit was conveyed to the people in that most striking form.

Enter the holy place; your eye is arrested by the heavy but magnificent curtain, wrought with cherubim, that cuts off six feet of the length of the entire structure. Pull that aside, and you pass into a chamber which is a perfect cube, a miniature of the New Jerusalem, whose length, and breadth, and height, are equal. In the Egyptian temple, this apartment would contain the crocodile or ibis; but here there was only a box, over which forms of exquisite beauty bent with outspread wings, and between them a light shone which was not borrowed from sun or stars. Could anything more significantly convey the idea that God was a Spirit?

God's Purity

The impression of this was produced by a series of comparisons. First, the Tabernacle stood within a courtyard fenced from public approach, the outer part could be trodden only by those men who had passed through certain rites of purification; and as to the inner, it could only be trodden once a year by the high priest, carefully cleansed by many rites, and clad in garments of special design, while the blood of slain animals, selected out of the herds for their freedom from any blemish or speck, was sprinkled around. All was done to impress upon the people the care with which they must approach God; and in this way impressions of His holiness were wrought into the national mind, which succeeding centuries have not been able to efface.

The Pattern Reproduced

There is a special interest to us all in this. We are not called to build again the Tabernacle, after that old pattern which has served its purpose, and fallen into disuse because superseded by the clearer revelations of the Gospel; yet there is an analogy which is full of instruction and inspiration in the life of every true believer, and deserves our attention for a moment.

As the Tabernacle dwelt in the mind of God before it was

reproduced on the desert sands, so does the life of each one exist, as a conception of that same infinite intelligence.

When a child is born into the world, with all its faculties shut up within it, as a flower in the bud, there is in the mind of God a perfect picture of what that life may become, an ideal to which it may be conformed.

So with the believer standing on the threshold of the Christian life, full of hope and purpose. For him also there is a perfect ideal stored in the Divine nature, of a life full of the blessedness of Beatitudes, and overflowing with the mighty works of the Gospels.

The main inquiry for us all as we enter on any fresh enterprise, or even pass over the threshold of each new day, should be—What is God's ideal, God's thought, God's pattern? And our one aim should be to understand it, and be sure that to fulfill it is to have lived well.

The Gradual Unfolding of God's Plan

Probably the account of the revelation of the successive parts of the Tabernacle is an exact transcript of the method by which the Divine design was unfolded to Moses' thought. Line upon line, precept upon precept—such is ever the Divine method.

We shall not be able to see far in front, nor the whole completed plan of our life; but as we complete one thing, another will be revealed, and then the next and the next. It may be that we shall have to fulfil the different portions of the Tabernacle of our life, without apparent connection with each other, "by divers portions and in divers manners," and we shall not understand the Divine purpose; but at the end of life we shall see that it was one complete and exquisite structure, of which no part was wanting.

The Tailoring of God's Plan

As the pattern was there on the Mount, there were the materials for its realization in the possession of the people below—the gold and silver and precious stones; the blue and purple and scarlet; the fine linen and goats' hair; the rams' skins and badgers' skins; the genius of the artificers; and the willingness of the people.

All things are added to the man who seeks first and only the kingdom of God.

Following Through

Again and again in the last chapter of Exodus we are told that all was done, "as the Lord commanded Moses." This was his supreme joy and satisfaction, that he had not added to or diminished from the Divine command; and so the work was finished. It would be well for us to cultivate the habit of immediate and entire subservience to the prompting of the Divine will, repeating it in the tiniest details as well as in the most difficult experiences.

Thus would the human life become harmonious with the Divine, the tabernacles of our lives would become the home of Him that inhabiteth eternity, and whose name is Holy; and there would be the settling down upon us of the Divine Shekinah, "the cloud by day and fire by night," through all our journeys, till we reach our Father's home.

13

A Bitter Disappointment

Numbers 14:25

It was a weary journey from Kibroth-hataavah to Hazeroth, and thence to Kadesh, probably the weariest of the entire route. Moses spoke of it afterwards as "that great and terrible wilderness" (Deut. 1:19). But at last the hosts reached Kadesh-barnea, on the very borders of the Land of Promise; within sight of the low hills, the flying buttresses, so to speak, of the verdant tableland, which first arrests the eye of the traveler coming up from the vast limestone plain of the desert.

Hope

As yet God had graciously veiled from him the weary journeys of the forty years that were to succeed. He had no idea of them. They had never entered into his calculations. From the way in which he spoke to the people, he evidently counted on a comparatively brief struggle, sharp, but short, through which they would pass to their possession. It never occurred to him that any one but himself would plan that campaign, even if Joshua led it; or that any other hand would settle the people in the land of their eager longings. These are the words he addressed to the people as they camped in sight of the rolling prairies of Canaan: "Ye are come unto the mountain of the Amorites, which the Lord our God doth give unto us. Behold the Lord thy God hath set the land before thee; go up and possess it, as the Lord of thy fathers hath

OLD TESTAMENT MEN OF FAITH

said unto thee; fear not, neither be discouraged" (Deut. 1:20, 21).

As he said these words, must there not have been, deep in his heart, a sigh of relief now that his task was almost done, and he might lay down his weighty responsibilities?

Is it not thus that we all picture to ourselves some blessed landscape, lying warm and sunny under the smile of heaven? Life is pretty hard just now: a march over a great and terrible wilderness; a stern fight; a bearing of burdens, for which we have only just got strength enough. But never mind, it cannot last—there must be respite; the long lane must have a turning; the wilderness march must have a Canaan; the lack of sympathy and tenderness must be swallowed up and forgotten in the embrace of a love which shall obliterate the memory of all, so that we shall awake as out of a brief, unpleasant dream. But suppose it be not so! What if He who loves us better than we love ourselves has marked our stations in a desert march, that leads right up to the mount from which we are to ascend to our Father's home!

Disappointment
The first mistake of the people was in desiring to spy out the land. Their self will was a profound mistake. Had not God promised to give them the land, and could they not trust His choice? Were not His eyes ever upon it, from the beginning to the end of the year? Why need they wish to spy it out? What about His promise to give it them? Why, then, need they be so anxious to see whether they could cope with its possessors? They had but, as Moses said, to go up and possess that which he had given.

Their second mistake was in receiving the discouraging report of the majority of the spies. Up to a certain point there was perfect agreement between them. "We came into the land whither thou sentest us, and surely it floweth with milk and honey, and this is the fruit of it." Then the ten said, "The people are strong, the cities are fenced and very great; and, moreover, we saw the children of Anak there. . . . We be not able to go up against the people, for they are stronger than we" (Deut. 1:28). But the two, Caleb and Joshua, whose names alone linger on our tongues as household words, replied, "If the Lord delight in us, then He will bring us into this land, and give it us" (Num. 14:8).

The difference between the two lay in this, that the ten looked at God through the difficulties, while the two looked at difficulties through God. And the people sided with the ten, and turned aside from the thought of God, to dwell long and sadly on the stupendous obstacles that menaced their occupation of the land.

Note, that they lost Canaan, not because of the graves of lust, but because of their unbelief.

Their next mistake was in the murmuring, which proposed to substitute a captain for their tried friend and God-given leader. "All the congregation lifted up their voice and cried; and the people wept that night: And all the children of Israel murmured against Moses and against Aaron, and said, Would God that we had died in the land of Egypt. . . . And they said one to another, Let us make a captain, and let us return into Egypt" (Num. 14:1-4).

Facing Disappointment

The dream of Moses for a speedy entrance into the land might even yet have been realized. If all the people were cut off, and he spared to be a second Abraham, the founder of the nation, it might be possible even yet for him to pass into the good land, and like Abraham settle there. And thus the trial came into his life. Satan tempts us, to reveal the evil in us; God to reveal the good. So God, knowing the hidden nobleness of His faithful servant, and eager that it should be revealed to all the world, suggested to him a proposal, that He should smite the people with pestilence, and disinherit them, and make of him a nation greater and mightier than they.

There are few grander passages in the whole Bible than that in which Moses puts away the testing suggestion as impossible. "If Thou shalt kill all this people as one man, then the nations which have heard the fame of Thee will speak, saying: Because the Lord was not able to bring this people into the land which He sware unto them, therefore He hath slain them in the wilderness" (Num. 14:15, 16).

In other words, Moses would not have the rest he longed for at the sacrifice of a ray of God's glory, or of the people with whom his life was linked, though they had sadly plagued and disowned him. And so he turned away from the open gate into Paradise, and again chose rather to suffer with the people in their afflictions than enjoy the pleasures of Canaan alone. Let us ponder the lesson; and when next a dear delight is within our reach, and it will be more for the glory of God and the good of others to turn from it, let us ask grace to take the rugged path of the wilderness, though it mean a lonely life for forty years, and a death on Pisgah.

14
How It Went Ill With Him

Numbers 20:11

It was but one act, one little act; but it blighted the fair flower of a noble life, and shut the one soul, whose faith had sustained the responsibilities of the Exodus with unflinching fortitude, from the reward which seemed so nearly within its grasp.

The wanderings of forty years were almost over. The congregation which had been scattered over the peninsula had converged towards the given meeting-place in Kadesh.

The demand of the people on the water supply at Kadesh was so great, that the streams were drained; whereupon there broke out again that spirit of murmuring and complaint which had cursed the former generation, and was now reproduced in their children. Oblivious to the unwavering care of all the preceding years, the people assembled themselves together against Moses, and against Aaron, though it was against Moses that they principally directed their reproach.

They professed to wish that they had died in the plague that Aaron's censer had stayed. They accused the brothers of malicious designs to effect the destruction of the whole assembly by thirst. Although the cloud of God brooded overhead, and the manna fell day by day, they cursed their abiding place as evil. They taunted Moses with the absence of figs, vines, and pomegranates. They demanded water. And this was the new generation of which he had cherished such high hopes, the new growth on the old stock! It could hardly

have been otherwise than that he should feel strongly pro-
voked.

However, he resumed his old position, prostrating himself
at the door of the tent of meeting until the growing light that
welled forth from the secret place indicated that the Divine
answer was near. Unlike the injunction on a similar occasion, which now lay back in the haze of years, Moses was
bidden, though he took the rod, not to use it; but to speak to
the rock with a certainty that the accents of his voice, smiting
on its flinty face, would have as much effect as ever the rod
had had previously, and would be followed by a rush of
crystal water. Yes, when God is with you, words are equivalent to rods; the gentlest whisper spoken in His name will
unlock the secrets of rocky chambers, and roll away great
stones, and splinter sepulchres where entombed life awaits a
summons.

Moses might have entered into these thoughts of God in
quieter and more tranquil moments; but just now he was
irritated, indignant, and hot with disappointment and
anger. When, therefore, the assembly was gathered together
in their thronging multitudes around him, he accosted them
as rebels. He spoke as if the gift of water depended on himself and Aaron. He betrayed his sense of the irksomeness of
their demand, and then vehemently smote the rock with his
rod twice. And as those blows reechoed through the still air,
they shivered forever the fabric woven by his dreams and
hopes.

The vision that had allured him through those long years
faded as light off Alpine snows at sunset; and angels were
sent to choose the site beneath the cliffs of Pisgah, where his
body should keep guard at the gate of the Land, in which he
had hoped to lie. What a warning is here, admonishing us
that we sometimes fail in our strongest point; and that a
noble career may be blasted by one small but significant and
forever lamentable failure; "The Lord said unto Moses and
Aaron, Because ye believed not in Me, to sanctify Me in the
eyes of the children of Israel, therefore ye shall not bring this

assembly into the land which I have given them" (Num. 20:12).

The people did not suffer through their leader's sin. The waters gushed from out the rock as plentifully as they would have done if the Divine injunctions had been precisely complied with. "The water came forth abundantly; and the congregation drank, and their cattle." Man's unbelief does not make the power of God of none effect: though we believe not, yet He remaineth faithful; He cannot deny Himself, or desert the people of His choice.

No doubt was possible as to the Divine command; and it had been distinctly infringed. He was not to strike, but to speak; and he had twice smitten the rock. In this way he had failed to sanctify God in the eyes of the people. He who ought to have set the example of implicit obedience to every jot and tittle, had inserted his own will and way as a substitute for God's. This could not be tolerated in one who was set to lead and teach the people.

They who disobey do not believe; and they who do not believe disobey. May the great High Priest, with His sharp, two-edged sword, pierce to our innermost heart, to cut away the least symptom of disobedience; then shall faith be strong, and through its gates we shall pass into the land of rest.

Moses drank very deeply of the bitter cup of disappointment. And it seems to have been his constant prayer that God would reverse or mitigate his sentence. "Let me go over, I pray Thee, and see the good land that is beyond Jordan, that goodly mountain, and Lebanon" (Deut. 3:25). No poet could have painted that land with more glowing colors. He dipped his brush in rainbow tints as he spoke of that good land— that land of brooks and fountains and depths; that land of wheat and barley, of vines and pomegranates and figs; that land of oil, olives, and honey. And no patriot ever yearned for fatherland as Moses to treat that blessed soil. With all the earnestness that he had used to plead for the people, he now pleaded for himself. But it was not to be. "The Lord was wroth, and said unto me, Let it suffice thee; speak no more unto Me of this matter." The sin was forgiven; but its consequences were allowed to work out to their sorrowful issue. There are experiences with us all in which God forgives our sin, but takes vengeance on our inventions. We reap as we have sown. We suffer where we have sinned.

15

The Death of Moses

Deuteronomy 34:5, 6

The thirty-second chapter of Deuteronomy is one of the sublimest human compositions on record. It was Moses' swan
song. It is the store from which later Scripture writers draw
plentifully. It has been called the Magna Charta of Prophecy.
It is worthy to be compared to one other song only, the Song
of the Lamb, with which it is combined by the harpers on the
margin of the glassy sea: "They sing the song of Moses, the
servant of God, and the song of the Lamb" (Rev. 15:3).

The repeated comparisons of God to a Rock; the lavish
kindness with which He had treated His people since He
first found them in a desert land; the comparison of the Eternal to a mother eagle in teaching its young to climb the unac-
customed steeps of air; the ingratitude with which His marvelous kindness had been requited; the dread fate to which
their rebellion must expose them; the mercy with which their
repentance would be greeted—all these are recorded in glowing, eloquent words, that stand for ever as a witness of how
stammering lips may speak when they have been touched
with the live altar coal. Or take the closing verses of the
Benediction on the tribes. The lonely glory of the God of
Jeshurun, who rides on the heavens to help and save His
people; the home which men may find in His eternal nature;
the underpinning everlasting arms; the irresistible might
with which He thrusts out the enemy from before the forward march of the soul He loves; the safe though isolated

dwelling of Israel; the fertility of the soil and the generosity
of the clouds; the blessedness of having Jehovah as the shield
of help and the sword of excellency—all these features of the
blessed life are delineated by the master hand of one who
dipped his brush in the colors mixed by his own experience.

What glimpses we get of the inner life of this noble man!
All that he wrought on earth was the outcome of the secret
abiding of his soul in God. God was his home, his help, his
stay. He was nothing: God was all. And all that he accomplished on the earth was due to that Mighty One indwelling,
fulfilling, and working out through him, as his organ and
instrument, His own consummate plans.

Thus Moses drew his life work to a close. Behind him, a
long and glorious life, before, the ministry and worship of
the heavenly sanctuary. Here, the shekinah; there, the un-
veiled face. Here, the tent and pilgrim march; there the everlasting rest. Here, the promised land, beheld from afar, but
not entered; there, the goodly land beyond Jordan entered
and possessed. What though it was a wrench to pass away,
with the crowning stone not placed on the structure of his
life; to depart and be with God was far better!

The Bible is the book of life. Its pages teem with biog-
raphy; they contain but scant memorials of death. The only
death they describe at length is that of Him who in dying
slew death. The very minuteness of the description there
shows how unique and all-important it was. Men make more
of death than of life as a gauge of character. A few pious
sentences spoken then will go far to efface the memory of
years of inconsistency. God makes most of life.

The records of Scripture find little room for dying tes-
timonies, words, or experiences; while they abound in
stories of the exploits and words of those who have stormed
and suffered and wrought in life's arena. This may explain
why, contrary to human custom and expectation, the death
of the great Lawgiver is described with such brief simplicity.

We are told that *He* buried him; as if the Almighty would
not delegate the sacred office to any inferior or human hand.

As we trust God to supply the needs of the body in life, so let us trust Him for its burial in death. He marks where the dust of each of His children mingles with its mother earth. When a grave is opened, His eye rests on it; and though no foot may ever tread its soil, no hand keep it decked with flowers, He never forgets it; and none will be overlooked when the archangel blows his trumpet over land and sea.

BOOK IV: DAVID

1
Taken From the Sheepfolds

I Samuel 16:1, 13

The story of David opens with a dramatic contrast between the fresh hope of his young life and the rejection of the self-willed King Saul. In the selection of every man for high office in the service of God and man, there are two sides—the Divine and the human: the heavenly summons, and the earthly answer to its ringing notes elaborated in history.

The Earthly Side
Once in the prophecy by Isaiah and twice in the Book of Revelation, our Lord is called the "Root of David." "The Lion of the tribe of Judah, the Root of David, hath prevailed to open the book and to loose its seven seals" (Rev. 5:5). And before the curtain of the Ages fell, "I am the root and the offspring of David, and the bright and morning star."

The idea suggested is of an old root, deep hidden in the earth, which sends up its green scions and sturdy stems. David's character may be considered as an emanation from the Son of God before He took the nature of man, and an anticipation of what He was to be and do in the fulness of time. Jesus was the Son of David, yet He was his progenitor. Thus we return to the ancient puzzle, that Jesus of Nazareth is at once David's Lord and Son (Mark 12:35-37).

There are four great words about the choice of David, the last of which strikes deeply into the heart of the great mystery.

The Lord hath sought Him a man (I Sam. 13:14). No one can know the day or hour when God passes by, seeking for chosen vessels and goodly pearls. When least expecting it, we are being scrutinized, in daily commonplaces, to see if we shall be faithful in more momentous issues. Let us be always on the alert, our loins girt, our lamps burning, our nets mended and cleansed.

I have found David My servant (Psa. 89:20). There is ecstasy in the voice, like the thrice repeated *found* of Luke 15. Which was the moment of that blessed discovery? Was it one dawn when the young shepherd led his flock to pasture; or one morning when he rescued a trembling lamb from lion or bear; or one afternoon when the first conception of the Shepherd Psalm stirred in his heart; or one night when he heard the heavens declaring the glory of God? He chose David to be His servant (Psa. 78:70). The people chose Saul; but God chose David. This made him strong. He was conscious that the purpose of God lay beneath him. We are immovable when we touch the bedrock of God's choice, and hear Him say, "He is a chosen vessel unto Me, to bear My name" (Acts 9:15).

The Lord hath appointed him to be Prince (I Sam. 13:14). Appointments are not solely due to patronage or won by industry; they are of God. *He* bringeth low and lifteth up. David emerged as a sun from a wrack of clouds, because God willed it. Fit yourself for God's service; be faithful: He will presently appoint thee; promotion comes from above.

I have provided Me a King (I Sam. 16:1). That answers everything. The Divine provision meets every need, silences every anxiety. Let us not yield to anxious forebodings for the future of the Church, or of our land. God has provided against all contingencies. He has His prepared instrument and at the precise moment at which it will tell with the greatest effect, it will be produced and launched on the air.

Consider the formative influences of David's young life. The family dwelt on the ancestral property to which Boaz had brought the Rose of Moab. Perhaps it was somewhat de-

cayed; the conditions under which Jesse brought up his large
family probably severely taxed the endurance and industry
of them all. David says nothing of his father, but twice
speaks of his mother as "the handmaid of the Lord." From
her he derived his poetic gift, his sensitive nature, his deeply
religious character. To his mother he was David the beloved,
and probably she first heard the psalms which have charmed
and soothed the world. He honored them both with dutiful
care.

Nature was his nurse, his companion, his teacher.
Bethlehem is situated six miles to the south of Jerusalem, two
thousand feet above the level of the Mediterranean. On the
gentle slopes of the hills the fig, olive, and vine grow
luxuriantly; and in the valleys are the rich cornfields which
gave the place its name, the House of Bread. The moorlands
around Bethlehem, however, are wild, gaunt, strong—
character breeding. There David first imbibed that knowledge of natural scenery and of pastoral pursuits which colored all his afterlife and poetry.

Such were the schools of his youth. But pre-eminently his
spirit lay open to the Spirit of God, which brooded over his
young life, teaching, quickening, and ennobling him, opening to him the books of nature and revelation, and pervading
his heart with trust.

He had not the splendid physique of his brother Eliab,
who so impressed the aged prophet. But he was strong and
athletic. His feet were nimble as a gazelle's; he could leap a
wall; a bow of steel could be easily broken by his young
arms; and a stone from his sling would hit the mark with
precision. Too slight to wear a man's armor, and yet able to
rend a lion or bear. His face glowing with health. The beauty
of his fair complexion in strong contrast to the darker visages
of his companions. The sensitiveness of the poet's soul,
combined with daring, resource, and power to command.
His dress, a coarse and simple tunic; his equipment, the
wallet sling, the rod and staff.

His soul is reflected in the Psalms that must be attributed

to this period of his life, so free from the pressure of sorrow, anxiety and strife, as the eighth, nineteenth, twenty-third, and twenty-ninth. So full of wonder that Jehovah should care for man, and yet so sure that He was his shepherd; so deeply stirred by the aspect of the heavens, and yet convinced that the words of God were equally Divine; so afraid of secret faults and presumptuous sins; so anxious to join the universal chorus of praise, ascending from the orchestra of nature, but yet so certain that there were yearnings and faculties within his soul, in which it could not participate. Ah, guileless, blessed boy! Thy God loves thee, and thou shalt teach us many a lesson as we turn again the pages of thy wonderful career.

The Heavenly Summons

The life of David is remarkable. Few have had so varied a career—shepherd and monarch; poet and soldier; champion and outlaw; beloved and persecuted; vanquishing the Philistines and accompanying them into battle. In all he seemed possessed of a special power with God and man, which could not be accounted for until we read, *"The Spirit of the Lord came mightily on David from that day forward"* (v. 13).

It began like any ordinary day. No angel trumpet heralded it. With the first glimmer of light the boy was on his way to pasture lands. As the morning hours sped onwards, many duties would engross his watchful soul—strengthening the weak, healing that which was sick, binding up that which was broken, and seeking that which was lost; his song may have filled the listening air. "A cunning player on the harp was he." A messenger suddenly broke upon this pastoral scene with the tidings of Samuel's arrival; the prophet had refused to eat of the hastily prepared banquet until the shepherd boy had joined the guests. His father sent to summon him with all speed. How the young eyes must have flashed with pleasure to feel that the family circle in great Samuel's eyes was not complete till he had come! He therefore left his sheep with the messenger, and started at full speed.

We must not suppose that now, for the first time, the Spirit of God wrought in David's heart. Scripture always distinguishes between the regenerating and the anointing grace of the Holy Spirit. From his earliest days, David had probably been the subject of his quickening and renewing work; but he had probably never experienced that special unction of the Holy One symbolized in the anointing oil, and indispensable for all successful spiritual work. How often have we met with the children of God who had no special power in witness bearing, nor freedom in speech, nor ability to grapple with the hearts and consciences of men. They needed what would be to them as electricity to the wire; the Spirit of God has been *in* but not *on* them. We have seen such awake and claim the Divine anointing; and suddenly they have begun to speak with new tongues, and men have not been able to resist their reasonings of sin, righteousness, and judgment to come. This blessed anointing for service cannot be ours, except there has been a previous gracious work on the heart, the new life of God. There must be humility, fidelity, cleansing and a close walk with God. The descending flame must fall upon a consecrated life. All these had been wrought in David; he was prepared for this special unction. It may be, reader, that in the obscurity of your life, you are being prepared for a similar experience. Be careful to obey God's least prompting, whether to do or suffer; that you be prepared for the golden moment.

When David reached the village, there were his father and his seven brothers, probably waiting for him to go together to the public banquet. An unusual restraint lay upon the rough tongues and harsh behavior with which Eliab and the rest were wont to treat him. No sooner had he entered, than the Lord said to Samuel, "Arise, anoint him; for this is he!" Then Samuel took the horn of oil and poured its contents on the head of the astonished lad.

It is likely that the bystanders did not realize the significance of that act; but David probably understood. The oil was symbolical, the visible sign that the Spirit of God had come mightily on the shepherd lad. For Jesus there was a dove. For the disciples there was a flame on each bowed head. These outward symbols have passed from general use. We must believe that we have received when we have fulfilled the conditions of humility and the faith that claims (Gal. 3:14).

From that memorable day David returned to his sheep; and as the months went slowly by, he must have greatly wondered when he would have an opportunity of using his new-found force. He had to learn that we are sometimes strengthened with all might to patience and longsuffering as the prelude to heroic deeds; we have to wrestle with the lion in the hills that we may be prepared to meet Goliath in the valley.

2

Summoned to the Palace

I Samuel 16:18, 19

After his anointing, David returned to his sheep. When Saul, advised by his courtiers, sent for him to charm away his melancholy, this was the specific indication he gave to Jesse, his father, "Send me David, thy son, which is with the sheep." It says much for the boy's character that he should have returned to the fold, faithfully fulfilling the routine of daily duty, and waiting for God to do what Samuel had spoken to him of. So Jesus left the temple, where a radiant glimpse had been afforded of doing His Father's business, to be subject to His parents in the carpenter's shop. One of Saul's young men said, "Behold, I have seen a son of Jesse the Bethlehemite, that is cunning in playing, and a mighty man of valor, and a man of war, and prudent in speech, and a comely person, and the Lord is with him" (v. 18). These five characteristics enable us to form a graphic conception of the young hero.

The Minstrel
He had the poetic temperament, and he had beside the power of translating into speech and song. His psalms commemorate as long as man shall live, the story of the green meadow land where his flocks grazed at noon; the little stream of whose limpid waters they drank; the smooth paths selected for their feet; the rocky defiles where they were in danger of lion and bear. We might add to these his marvelous power in depicting the sacred hush of dawn, the thun-

derstorms that broke over Palestine, rolling peal after peal, from the great Mediterranean, over the cedars of Lebanon to the far-distant wilderness of Kadesh, followed by torrents of rain, and these by clear shining in peace (Psa. 23, 19, 8, 29).

The Psalm began with David. Its lyric beauty and tender grace; its rhythmic measure; its exuberant hallelujahs and plaintive lamentations; its inimitable expression of the changeful play of light and shade over the soul; its blending of nature and godliness; its references to the life of men and the world, as regarded from the standpoint of God—these elements in the Psalter which have endeared it to holy souls in every age owe their origin to the poetic, heaven-touched soul of the sweet singer of Israel.

The Young Warrior

There was abundant opportunity for the education of his prowess. The Philistines' frontier was not far away. Many a skirmish had the men of Bethlehem with the border warriors, who would sweep down upon the produce of their vineyards and cornfields. In these David acquired the character of a man of valor and a mighty man of war. It may be that sometimes he had to stand alone against a handful of sheep-stealers. He needed to be on the alert against the wild beasts that prowled among the hills of Judah hungry, deadly. For these he had no fear. He smote them, and delivered the trembling lambs from their mouth. He caught them by their beard and slew them. A proud young Samson, laughing in the fulness of his manly strength.

But he would have been the last to attribute his exploits to his sinewy strength. By faith he had learned to avail himself of the might of God. "It is God that girdeth me with strength." Through faith he subdued kingdoms, stopped the mouths of lions, escaped the edge of the sword, waxed mighty in war, turned to flight armies of aliens.

The One Prudent in Speech

The sagacity of David will appear as our story proceeds. He

was as prudent to advise and scheme as he was swift to execute. He had understanding of the times, of human hearts, of wise policy; and he knew just how and when to act. Frank to his friends, generous to his foes, constant in his attachments, calm in danger, patient in trouble, chivalrous and knightly, he had every element of a born leader of men, and was equally at home in the counsels of the state and the decisions of the battlefield. And this was no doubt due to the repose of his spirit in God. The sad mistakes he made may be traced to his yielding to impulse and passion, to his forgetfulness of drawing near unto God, and inquiring of Him before taking any important step.

The One Charming in Presence
He was David the beloved. Wherever he moved, he cast the spell of his personal magnetism. Saul yielded to it, and thawed; the servants of the royal household loved him; Michal loved him; the soul of Jonathan was knit with his soul; the women of Israel forgot their loyalty to Saul, as they sounded the praises of the young hero. So he passed through life, beloved of God and man, the soil of his soul was capable of bearing crops to enrich the world.

The One Accompanied by God
He had no hesitation in describing himself as "thy servant," liable to hidden and presumptuous faults, from which he desired to be delivered. He thought of God as his Rock, Redeemer, Shepherd, and Host in the house of life, his Comforter in every darksome glen. God's Word restored his soul, rejoiced his heart, enlightened his eyes. He set the Lord always before him; because He was at his right hand, he could not be moved; and therefore his heart was glad.

3

Borne Through the Battle

I Samuel 17

The Philistines had marched up the valley Elah, encamping on its western slope; Saul pitched his camp on the other side. That valley was to witness an encounter which brought into fullest contrast the principles on which God's warriors are to contend—not only with flesh and blood, but against the principalities and powers of darkness. Three figures stand out sharply defined.

First, the Philistine Champion. He was nine feet six inches in height; he was heavily armed, protected by an immense shield borne by another in front of him, so as to leave his arms and hands free; he wielded a ponderous spear, while sword and javelin were girt to his side; he was apt at braggadocio and defied the armies of the living God.

Second, Saul. The king of Israel took his first step away from God when he permitted himself to be betrayed into undue haste and offered the burnt offering at Michmase. He took further steps in the outburst of indignation against Jonathan for violating his regulation about abstinence from food. But the final break took place when he disobeyed the distinct command of Jehovah and spared Agag and the choice of the spoil. Then he rejected the word of the Lord, and God gave him up to his own evil heart. From that moment his course was always downward. From the disobedient heart God withdraws His keeping power; and as it is no longer tenanted by the Spirit of the Most High, it becomes

at once the prey and habitation of unclean spirits. Such
was Saul's heart.

He was forsaken by the Spirit of God; troubled by an evil
spirit from the Lord; and discordant in heart and life. Faith
was impossible for it is the health bloom of the soul. When,
therefore, Goliath stalked through the valley of Elah, and
defied the armies of Israel, Saul was greatly afraid. Even now
the formula of his former faith and fervor came easily to his
lips, as he assured the young shepherd that the Lord would
certainly be with him; but he dared not adventure himself in
conflict with what he reckoned were utterly overwhelming
odds. He was near daunting David with his materialism and
unbelief: "Thou art not able to go against this Philistine to
fight with him; for thou art but a youth, and he a man of war
from his youth" (v. 33).

Third, David. He was but a youth. No sword was in his
hand; he carried a staff, probably his shepherd's crook; no
armor had he save the breastplate of righteousness and the
helmet of salvation; no weapon, but a sling. But he was in
possession of a mystic spiritual power: the living God was a
reality to him. His countrymen were not simply servants to
Saul; they were the army of the living God. He had no doubt
that the Lord would vindicate His glorious name, and deliver
into his hands this uncircumcised Philistine.

Solitary Faith

As day after day he considered the heavens and earth, they
appeared as one vast tent, the material dwelling place of the
eternal Spirit. God was as real to him as Jesse, or his
brothers, or Saul, or Goliath. God's presence he bore with
him, undisturbed by the shout of the soldiers and the searching questions addressed to him by Saul.

This is the secret. There is no short cut to the life of faith,
which is the all-vital condition of a holy and victorious life.
We must have meditation and fellowship with God. That our
souls should have their mountains of fellowship, their valleys beneath the shadow of a great rock, their nights when

darkness has veiled the material and opened the view of the eternal, is as indispensable as food. Thus alone can God's presence become the fixed possession of the soul, enabling it to say, "Thou art near, O God."

Lonely Conflict
The story of the lion and the bear had been extracted from David by a desire to magnify Jehovah. Possibly there had been many conflicts so that his faith had become strengthened by use, as he was being prepared for this supreme conflict. What we are in solitude, we shall be in public. Do not for a moment suppose, O self-indulgent disciple, that a great occasion will dower thee with heroism of which thou betrayest no trace in secret hours. The crisis will only reveal the true quality and temper of the soul. Lonely hours are fullest of temptation; it is in these we must conquer if we would be victorious when the eyes of some great assembly are fastened upon us.

The Test of Daily Life
There are some who think that the loftiest spiritual life is incompatible with daily toil and the friction of the home. "Emancipate us from these," they cry, "give us nothing to do except to nurse our souls to noble deeds." It was not thus with David. When Jesse bade David take his three elder sons rations there was ready acquiescence: "he rose up early in the morning, and took, and went, as Jesse had commanded him." And before he left his flock he was careful to entrust it with a keeper. We must always watch not to neglect one duty for another.

Bearing Rebuke Meekly
Reaching the camp, he found the troops forming in battle array, and ran to the front. He had already saluted his brothers when he was arrested by the braggart Goliath across the valley, and saw Israel turn to flee. He learned that even Saul shared the general panic and had issued rewards for a

champion. He gathered confirmation, evincing the open-eyed wonder of his soul "any man's heart should fail."

Eliab had no patience with the words and bearing of his young brother. Something should be said to thrust him back into his right place. "Why art thou come down? With whom," he said, with a sneer, "hast thou left those few sheep in the wilderness?" (v. 28). Ah, what venom in those words! David, however, ruled his spirit and answered softly. "Surely," said he, "my father's wish to learn of your welfare was cause enough to bring me here." The victory over Goliath was won! To have lost his temper would have broken the alliance of his soul with God, but to meet evil with good and maintain unbroken composure, not only showed the beauty of his spirit's armor, but cemented his alliance with God.

To bear with meekness the spiteful attacks of malice and envy; not to be overcome by evil, but to overcome evil with good; to suffer wrong; to possess one's soul patience; to keep the mouth with a bridle; to pass unruffled through a very cyclone of unkindliness and misrepresentation—this is possible only to those in whose breasts the dove-like Spirit has found an abiding place. These are they who bear themselves as heroes in the fight. Those who are gentlest under provocation are strongest. Meekness is an attribute of might.

Withstanding Carnal Reasonings

Saul was very eager for David to adopt his armor, though he dared not don it himself: "Don't be rash; don't expect a miracle; trust God, and go; but be wise. Adopt ordinary precautions."

It was a critical hour. Had David turned aside to act on these suggestions, he would have forfeited the Divine alliance conditioned by his faith. There is no sin in using means: but they must come second, not first; they must be such as God suggests. It is a sore temptation to adopt them and hope that God will bless them, instead of waiting before Him to know what He could have done. But an unseen hand withdrew David from temptation. He had already yielded to Saul's advice so far as to have donned his armor. Then he turned to Saul and said, "I cannot go with these"; and he put them off. It was now the Lord alone; and he was able to accost the giant with the words, "The Lord saveth not with sword and spear."

His faith had been put to the severest tests and was approved. The furnace of trial had shown it to be of heavenly temper. Goliath shall know that there is a God in Israel.

Open Faith

The two armies waited expectant; every eye was suddenly attracted by the slight young figure which emerged from the ranks of Israel and descended the slope. For a little David was hid from view, then to the amazement of the Philistines, he sprang up on the further bank, and rapidly moved towards their huge champion. When Goliath realized that the youth was daring to accept his challenge, he arose to meet David, cursing and threatening him that his blood should encrimson the mountain sward. "Then said David to the Philistine, Thou comest to me with a sword, and with a spear, and with a javelin; but I come to thee in the name of the Lord of Hosts, the God of the armies of Israel, whom thou hast defied."

The Talisman of Victory. "The name of the Lord of Hosts." Throughout the Scriptures, a name is a revelation of character. It catches up some moral or physical peculiarity or special gift. The name of God stands for those Divine attributes and qualities which make Him what He is. The special quality that David extracted is indicated in the words, the Lord of Hosts. God was Captain of the embattled hosts of Israel. But there was probably something of this sort in David's thought: he conceived of angels and worlds, of the armies of heaven and the elements of matter, of winds and waves, of life and death, as a vast ordered army, obedient to the commands of their Captain, Jehovah of Hosts.

To come in the name of the Lord of Hosts implied his own identification by faith with this sacred name. An Englishman in a foreign land occupies a very different position, and speaks in a very different tone, according to whether he assumes a private capacity as an ordinary traveler, or acts as ambassador of his country. In the former case he speaks in his own name, and receives what respect and obedience it can obtain. In the latter he is conscious of being identified with Great Britain; England speaks through his lips; the might of England is ready to enforce his demands; and every power England wields is pledged to avenge any indignity to him.

It were well to lay aside everything that might hinder our union with the Divine nature, to become so absolutely identified with God that His name might be our strong tower, our battle cry, our secret of victory. Oh to be able to approach each wrong doer, each confederacy of evil, each assault of darkness, each tribe of savages, each drink-sodden district, each congregation of the unsaved and impenitent, with the words, "I come in the name of the Lord of Hosts!"

Pure Motives

David's one ambition was to take away the reproach from Israel, and to let all the earth know that there was a God in Israel. We must be wary here. It is so easy to confuse issues, to suppose that we are contending for the glory of God, when we are really combating for our church, our cause, our prejudices or opinions. To fall into this sin, though unconsciously, is to forfeit the right to use His sacred name. How constantly we need to expose our hearts to the Holy Spirit, that He may wholly cleanse them, and fill them with an all-consuming devotion to the glory of God!

Acknowledging God's Sovereignty

David said that the whole matter was God's; the overthrow of Goliath was not in his province at all. "The battle is the Lord's . . . This day will the Lord deliver thee into mine hand . . . The Lord saveth, and He will give you into our hand." And David's attitude has been that of every man who has wrought great exploits in the behalf of righteousness. We are not called to work for Him, but to let Him work through us. Of Him and through Him and to Him are all things. The battle is not ours, but His. His skill must direct us; His might empower us; His uplifted hands bring us victory.

Avoiding Worldly Counsel
It must have been a hard thing for a youth to oppose his opinion to Saul's, so solicitous for his welfare. David withstood the siren song, and remained unaffected by the blandishments of royal favor.

Using the Name
Those who use the name are willing to stand alone. The lad asked no comradeship, sympathy or succor; the Lord of Hosts was with him, the God of Jacob was his refuge.

They are deliberate. He was free from nervous trepidation which often unfits us to play our part. Our hearts will throb, our movements become so fitful and unsteady. Calmly he went down the slope and selected the pebbles. His mind was kept in perfect peace, because it was stayed on God. He did not go by haste or flight, because the Lord went before him.

They are fearless. When the moment came for the conflict, there was no fear of the result; no tremor in the voice that answered the rough taunt; no falter in the arm that wielded the sling; no lack of precision in the aim that drove the stone to the one part of the Philistine's body that was unprotected and vulnerable.

They are more than conquerors. The stone sank into the giant's forehead; he fell stunned to the earth. There was no time to lose; before he could recover or his comrades overcome their stupefied amazement, his head had been hewn from his body by his own sword. When the Philistines saw that their champion was dead they fled. The spoils of victory lay with the victor. David took the head of the Philistine as a trophy.

The man who knows God is strong to do exploits. All the

might of God awaits the disposal of our faith. As a child by touching a button may set in motion a mighty steamship, so a stripling who has learned to reckon on God may bring the forces of Deity to bear on men and things on the world's battlefield. This is the victory that overcomes the world, the flesh, and the devil—even our faith.

4

Imperiled in the Palace

I Samuel 18:1; 20:21-37; Psalm 59:9, 17

There is nothing in the annals of human affection nobler than
the bond of love between two pure and noble men.

Jonathan's Love

David was in all probability profoundly influenced by the
character of Jonathan. "When David had made an end of
speaking unto Saul, the soul of Jonathan was knit with the
soul of David, and Jonathan loved him as his own soul." That
night a royal messenger may have summoned David to
Jonathan's pavilion, on entering which he was greeted with
the warm embrace of a brotherly affection which was never
to wane. The boy soldier must have shrunk back as unworthy, but such consideration was swept away before the
rush of Jonathan's affection as he stripped himself of robe
and apparel, of sword and bow and girdle, and gave them all
to David. "Then Jonathan and David made a covenant, because he loved him as his own soul" (v. 1).

Consider the qualities of this friend. Jehovah chose him for
the molding of the character of His beloved; be prepared to
surrender to His care the choice of your most intimate associates, the companion who shall strengthen you when
weak, and develop latent unknown qualities.

He was every inch a man; he was withal very sensitive and
tender. Jonathan had a marvelous power of affection. He was
distinctly religious: he discerns the hand of the Lord, and in

their last interview, "Jonathan came to David there, and strengthened his hand in God." He must have God and be in God, who would give the consolations of God to his brother.

Consider the conflict of Jonathan's life. He was devoted to his father; Jonathan clung to him as if he hoped that by his own allegiance to God he might reverse the effects of his father's failure, and still hold the kingdom for their race. His hopes, however, were destined to disappointment, for he saw his father drifting further down the strong tide that bore him out from God.

When he woke up to find how truly he loved David, a new difficulty entered his life. His love for David made him eager to promote reconciliation between his father and his friend. Repeated failure proved the fruitlessness of his dream and then the thought must have suggested itself to him: Why not extricate yourself from this sinking ship while there is time? Why not join your fortunes with God's choice? The kingdom of the future is growing up around him—identify yourself with it, though it be against your father.

The temptation was masterful, but it fell blunt at his feet. Stronger than the ties of human love were those of duty, sonship, loyalty to God's anointed king; and in some supreme moment he turned his back on the appeal of his heart, and elected to stand beside his father. From that choice he never flinched. It was one of the grandest exhibitions of the triumph of principle over passion, of duty over inclination, that the annals of history record. Conflicts like these await us all—when the appointment of God says one thing, and the choice of the heart says another; may God's grace enable you to follow as straight a course as Jonathan.

Saul's Hate
As the victorious army returned home from the valley of Elah, the whole land went forth in greeting. To the song of victory there came this refrain strikingly discordant to the soul of the king: "Saul hath slain his thousands, And David his ten thousands" (I Sam. 21:11). In that hour jealousy

awoke in Saul's heart, the pitted speck in the fruit of his character, destined to rot and ruin all. Happy had he been if he had trodden the hell spark beneath his feet, but "Saul eyed David from that day and forward."

But Saul was more than jealous. He set himself to thwart God's purpose. He supposed that if only he could take David's life, God's purpose would miscarry. Saul's murderous passion sought to fulfill itself in many ways. On the following day he twice hurled his javelin at the minstrel, but the weapon only sped harmlessly past. Next, Saul gave him an important military commission in the vain hope that worldly prominence might lead him to some traitorous deed. But David behaved himself wisely in all his ways, so that the king stood in awe of him. Then he offered the young soldier his eldest daughter in marriage, and withdrew the offer as the nuptials approached, but all his efforts failed to arouse even a transient impulse for revenge. Again, by the lure of his second daughter, Michal, as prize to be won by the evidence of one hundred Philistines having been slain, he sought to involve his rival in frays out of which only a miracle could bring him unhurt. But David returned unscathed with double the number required; and the love of the people grew.

Thwarted, the God-forsaken monarch, driven by fury, spake to Jonathan and to all his servants that they should rid him of David but that plot failed, for Jonathan loved him. Jonathan indeed stood in the breach to turn away his father's anger, and elicited from him the promise that his friend should not be put to death. But his pleadings had only a temporary effect; for shortly after the javelin again quivered past the young minstrel he fled to his young wife and home. And Saul, intent on murder, "sent messengers unto David's house, to watch and slay him in the morning."

Michal's quick wit saved her husband's life. She let him down through the window, and he escaped; while an image placed in the bed led Saul's emissaries to suppose that he was sick. When shortly after, the king proposed to snatch his prey from the sacred college and from Samuel, three sets of messengers were rendered powerless by the Divine afflatus, and an arrest was put on Saul himself, who was prostrated before the mighty impression of God's Spirit, and lay helpless on the earth (I Sam. 19:24). That must have been a marvelous experience for David. By faith he knew that he was hidden beneath an invisible wing, as a stream of electricity poured over a heap of jewels protects them from the hand of the plunderer; so did the presence of God environ and protect both Samuel and David. And thus God will still do for each of His persecuted ones. "In the secret of His tabernacle shall He hide them, He shall set them up upon a rock."

David's Composure
This hunted man provides a lesson. Saul is his inveterate foe; traps and snares are laid for him on all sides. Yet all the while his heart is tranquil—yea, it actually breaks forth into praise. What was the secret of his serenity?

It lay, first, in the conviction of what God was. God was his strength—that was God within him; God was his high tower—that was God without and around him. He was God-possessed and God-encompassed. There was no demand for which He was not sufficient, no peril which He could not keep at bay. What a blessed conception! You are too weak for some great task which has been entrusted to your care. "O Lord," you cry, "wherewith shall I save Israel?" Then the Spirit of God reveals God as strength to become the principle of a new and heaven-born energy superior to every difficulty. O weakest of the weak, remember Jesus Christ, and take Him to be the strength of thy life; be strong, yea be strong, in the grace that is in Christ Jesus.

Or turn to the other conception. See those fugitive soldiers, hotly pursued by their enemies; on yonder cliff is perched a fortress. Breathlessly they scale the ascent, rush across the drawbridge, let down the portcullis, and fling themselves on the sward, and know that they are safe. God is all that to the soul which has learned to put Him between itself and everything. Add the further conception with which the Psalm closes, that God is the fount of mercy: when we dare to believe that there is mercy in Saul's hate in the clouds that veil our sky in the sharpest, bitterest experiences—when we can sing with David: "I will sing of Thy strength; Yea, I will sing aloud of Thy mercy in the morning, For Thou hast been my high tower, and a refuge in the day of my distress."

It lay, next, in his attitude toward God. "O my strength, I will wait on Thee." The word is used in the Hebrew of the shepherd, the watchman, the sentry. Is this our habitual attitude? Too many direct their prayer, but do not look up the ladder for the descending angels, laden with the heavenly answer. We pray, but we do not wait; we ask, but we do not expect to receive; we knock, but we are gone before the door is opened.

This lesson is for us to learn—to reckon on God; to believe that He cannot deceive our trust; to be sure that none that wait on Him can be ashamed; to appropriate by faith; to know that we have the petitions we desired, though we have no sense of possession—this is waiting upon God: this will keep us calm and change our waiting into song.

The Message of the Arrows

The feast of the new moon, when Saul invited the chief men to a banquet, was opportune for testing the real sentiments of Saul. David suggested that he should absent himself, visiting his father's home at Bethlehem instead, and be back by the third day. In the meantime, Jonathan was to watch narrowly his father's behavior. This scheme was arranged within the palace; it seemed wiser to continue in some secluded spot, where only the living things of the woods could behold the tears, and hear the ingenious plan of Jonathan in which directions to the little lad would express the secret which would either lift David to peace and safety, or thrust him into despair.

The arrows taught much. A noble friend was standing in the breach. Jonathan was a jewel of the first water; daring, strong, yet tender, true to his friend; and tenacious of principle. It was no child's play that he undertook and probably he was quite prepared for the outburst that followed his manly protest for his absent friend. On the first feast day, Saul noticed David's absence; second, he turned sharply on Jonathan and asked the reason. Jonathan's instant answer about David's desire to see his family brought an outburst of ungovernable rage. Jonathan made one vain attempt to reason with the furious monarch; he might as well have tried to arrest the swelling of Jordan. In passion, the king cast his spear at him to smite him. Then Jonathan knew that they must prepare for the worst; and left the table in anger, grieved for his friend.

Never be ashamed to own a friend. Do not count him your friend whose name you are ashamed to mention, and with whose lot you blush to be identified: but when you have entered into an alliance with another soul, dare to stand up for him at all cost. There is something still nobler, when one dares in any company to avow his loyalty to the Lord Jesus. Let us never flinch, but as we trust that He will confess our name before His Father and the angels, let us not be ashamed of His.

Never be ashamed to speak up for the cause of truth. Jonathan took the noble course: his father was before him, with his claims on his respect—the king, with the power of life and death; but he dared not hold his peace. Had it been simply a question of his own position or respect of mere courtesy, he would have been the first to put his hand upon his mouth. But it was a question of truth, righteousness, justice; and if he were to be still, he would forfeit the respect of his own conscience.

But it may be asked, is it not unseemly to obtrude opinions among those who are older and more learned than ourselves? Yes; but there is all the difference in the world between opinions and those great basic principles of truth, morality and right. And when you stand up for these, you do not seek to exalt your own goodness, or win an advantage; but simply to lift the standard from being trampled in the mud.

There was imminent danger. "Jonathan knew that it was determined of his father to put David to death" (v. 38). As the lad ran, Jonathan shot an arrow beyond him: "And as soon as the lad was gone, David arose and fell to the ground, and bowed himself and they kissed one another, and wept until David exceeded" (v. 41). David knew that "the Lord had sent him away" (v. 22).

There are things we never leave behind. David had an inalienable possession in the love of his friend, in the devotion of the people, in the memory of God's goodness and delivering care, in the Divine presence, in the Psalms which he had already made for himself. There are threads woven into the fabric of our life which can never be extracted.

There is a divine purpose determining our course. To the lad there was but royal caprice in the flight of the arrow; how little did he divine the purpose of his master. There is no chance in a good man's life—behind the arrow's flight there is the loving purpose of our Heavenly Father.

The going forth is necessary to secure greater happiness than we leave. Had David lingered in the palace, his life would have been forfeited, and he would have missed glory in after years. This was the way to the throne. This mountain pass was the path to the happy valley. Follow the arrow's flight then—beyond the warm circle to the icy north; beyond the known to the unknown. Like Abraham, go into the land which God will show thee; let David's assurance be yours: "Thou wilt show me the path of life."

Human love must suffer separation. The friends met only once more before Jonathan's death. Jonathan seems overcast that their happy intercourse would never again be renewed. "Go in peace," Jonathan said, finally, as though he could no longer bear the awful anguish of that parting, "The Lord shall be between me and thee, and between my seed and thy seed, for ever." Then David departed to become a fugitive while Jonathan returned sadly to the palace, to one who had outraged his tenderest sensibilities.

There are hours that leave scars on hearts; but Christ comes to us in these dark moments: "Let not your heart be troubled . . . trust in Me." There is no comfort like this, to believe that He is ordering each detail, that love is prompting each action of His hand, to utterly trust Him—this bridges the yawning gulf of separation.

5

Almost Gone

I Samuel 21; 22; Psalm 56; 34

It is not easy to walk with God. The air that beats around the Himalaya heights of Divine fellowship is rare, and hard to breathe; human feet tire after a little: and faith, hard put to it, is inclined to give up the effort of keeping step with the Divine pace. So David found it; and there came a terrible lapse, the steps and consequences of which, together with his recovery, must engage us for a space.

The Steps of David's Decline
The first sign was his remark to Jonathan that there was but a step between himself and death (I Sam. 20:3). His faith was beginning to falter; for nothing could have been more definite than the Divine assurances that he was to be king. He looked at God through the mist of circumstances, instead of looking at circumstances through the golden haze of God's very present help. Next, he adopted a subterfuge, which was not worthy of him nor of his mighty Friend. This was a further descent from the high place of heavenly fellowship and testimony. God is light, and light is truth; and those who walk with Him must put on the armor of light.

Late in the afternoon the king's son-in-law arrived with a handful of followers at Nob, a peaceful secluded spot. Its inhabitants were engaged in the service of the sanctuary, four score and six persons with their wives, their children, their oxen, asses and sheep. Into that holy spot hardly a ripple came from the storms that swept the outer world. The path to the simple sanctuary was only trodden by occasional visitors; the presence of two or three additional strangers overbalanced the slender fare; there were not five loaves of common bread to spare.

It was necessary to answer the questions, and allay the suspicions of the priest; while making excuses and enlisting his willing cooperation in the matter of provisions and arms, a chill struck his heart as he saw the dark visage of Doeg, the Edomite, "the chiefest of the herdmen that belonged to Saul." The whole story would be mercilessly retailed to the vengeful monarch. Uneasiness for his unsuspecting host and fear for himself filled his heart; and as soon as the Sabbath was over, with all haste he struck across the hills to the valley of Elah, where he had achieved the great victory of his life. Ten miles beyond lay the proud Philistine city of Gath, which at that time had sent its champion forth in all pride. What worse fate could await him at Gath, than that which threatened him each hour he lingered within Judah! He resolved to make the plunge.

To his dismay, he was instantly recognized and regarded with hatred as having slain his ten thousands. David became aware of the evil impression and saw the peril of imprisonment or execution. He saved himself by the unworthy subterfuge of counterfeiting the behavior of a madman, drumming on the city gate, and allowing his spittle to fall down upon his beard. His device succeeded; Achish dismissed him with the humorous remark that he had already madmen enough around him. This certainly was one of the least dignified episodes in David's varied life, very unworthy of God's anointed; and the shame was that there would have been no need for it, if he had not departed from the living God.

At first sight we are startled with the apparent discrepancy between the scenes just described and the 56th Psalm, but closer inspection will reveal many resemblances between the singer's circumstances and his touching words; and we are reminded that beneath much which is unworthy there may burn a true devotion, an eager yearning after God, a soul of good amid things evil.

The major part of this exquisite psalm consists of two stanzas, which culminate in the same refrain; the remainder is full of hope and praise, when his heart is fixed, trusting the Lord. He sees the mark of his footprints to the edge of the precipice, and recognizes the Divine power and grace which has delivered his feet from falling. He regains the sunny uplands so shamefully renounced in his flight to Nob, from Nob to Gath, from Gath to feigned insanity. Henceforth he will walk before God in the light of life. Truth, purity, joy, shall be the vesture of his soul.

The Consequences to Ahimelech

A child of God may be restored, yet the consequences of his sin may involve sufferings to many innocent lives. So it was in this instance. When Saul was endeavoring to excite sympathy by enumerating the supposed wrongs he had suffered at the hand of David, Doeg ingratiated himself in the royal favor by narrating what he had seen at Nob. He carefully withheld the innocence of the priest, and made it appear that he and his house were accomplices with David, perhaps bent on helping David to gain supreme power. In vain Ahimelech persisted in the avowal of his unconsciousness of the quarrel between Saul and his son-in-law—before night fell the entire priestly community was exterminated. One survivor, Abiathar, escaped, carrying the ephod; and one day, to his horror, David beheld the disheveled, blood-smeared form of the priest as he sped up the valley to find shelter with the outlaw band in the Cave of Adullam.

Children of God beware! Sin is bitter to the conscience of the sinner, and its consequences upon others. Let us walk circumspectly, prayerfully, exercising our consciences repeatedly to see if there be any swerving from strict integrity; lest seeds be scattered beyond recovery, to bear bitter har-

vests in the lives of those who are involved in the consequences of our deeds.

The Cave of Adullam

Leaving Gath, David hastily recrossed the frontier. His life,
however, was in great jeopardy and he did not risk involving
his relatives by seeking shelter at Bethlehem. There was no
alternative but to adopt the life of a fugitive amid the familiar
hills of Judah. Two miles up the valley of Elah from Gath
there is a labyrinth of hills deeply honeycombed with caves;
one of these, near the ancient city of Adullam afforded David
shelter. It is a dark vault, the entrance of which is a low
window in the perpendicular face of the cliff; and its position
made it possible for him to cross from one country to another, as occasion required. Thither fled his whole family,
dreading, no doubt, the violence of Saul's hatred; and thither
also came every one that was in distress, and in debt, and
discontented, and he became captain over them. David's fi-
lial love traversed the entire distance from Adullam to Moab
to secure an asylum for his father and mother, who were
probably too aged to stand the hardships and dangers of his
fugitive life.

No doubt the Holy Ghost desires us to trace an analogy
between David's history and that of the Lord Jesus. The parallel is as minute as it is instructive.

A Rejected King on the Throne

Saul by disobedience had forfeited his right to reign and the
sentence of deposition was awaiting execution. Similarly,
the dark fallen spirit, Satan, was once anointed, set on the
holy mountain of God, and perfect till unrighteousness was
found in him. Not improbably he derives the title which our
Lord gave him of "prince of this world" from his original
appointment as God's representative; but in his fall he forfeited his glorious position, and man was created as his substitute. Meanwhile, Satan still holds the throne of the world.

He has cast his javelin at the King after God's own heart in the temptation and in Gethsemane. All through the present age he has been doing his worst to exterminate the hidden Kingdom of Jesus, but all his attempts must fail. As Saul fell on the field of Gilboa, so the prince of darkness shall be finally cast into the bottomless pit.

David's Kingdom Hidden

It was a true kingdom, though in mystery, veiled in the darkness of Adullam's Cave. Such was the experience of David: and also of that Divine King, forsakenness on the Cross, and rejected in the grave; whose person and kingdom are now hidden from the world. The day is not far distant when the Lord shall be manifested with His saints, and take His great power and reign. The army constituted from such unpromising materials shall follow Him on white horses in radiant array. Meanwhile His kingdom is "in mystery."

David Separated

Driven without the camp of Israel, with the feasts, the counsels, the home politics and foreign wars, they had no immediate connection. The lot of an exile, the path of the wanderer was meted out to David; his way to the throne lay through multiplied difficulties and sorrows; and there must have been a perpetual sadness and loneliness in his soul.

The King of men is still outside human politics and society. Those who desire to be His subjects, and to share the glories of those coming days when He shall have dominion must go out to Him without the camp, willing to forsake all.

Awaiting God's Time

Whatever provocation Saul gave, he never retaliated. However easy the opportunity of advantage, he was prepared to wait God's time, to receive supreme power in God's way. It is thus through the centuries that our Saviour is waiting. Now is the time of the *patience* of Jesus Christ; here is the patience of the saints.

The Cave and its Inmates

The tidings of David's retreat in the cave spread swiftly; and those pressed by poverty and bitterness of soul began to flock around him. The young leader soon found himself head of four hundred men, a motley crew! For the few loyal to him, there were multitudes full of their own grievances. Their tempers were probably turbulent and fierce, requiring statesmanship to reduce them to discipline and order so that they became the nucleus of the greatest army of their time. We must not think of David as a bandit; but rather as a frontier guard to defend the land against the Amalekites and Philistines, who were perpetually raiding it at the time of harvest. He became the defender of his people, though exiled from them. He and his men were described as a wall to the sheep masters and agriculturists "both by night and day" (I Sam. 25:16).

Turn from David to Him, who, though cast out from this world is ever gathering the poor and outcast, the leper and sinner, the blind and brokenhearted, those who are in debt, and discontented, and making them into soldiers.

Did these wild, rough soldiers love David for alleviating their distress? Much more should we love Him: He has paid our debts with His precious blood; relieved us from our creditors; clothed us in His perfect beauty; allayed our sorrows; stilled our souls. Did David and his followers grow with the years in a fellowship of sharing common dangers? What an incentive to us to seek a fellowship with our blessed Lord that shall grow closer for every day of trial we share with Him!

The Cave and its Song

Many allusions connect the thirty-fourth Psalm with the Cave of Adullam. There the little host needed the encamping angel; there the young lions roared in search of food; there also God's care was perpetually requisitioned to keep fugitives lest they should be broken by falling down the crags (vv. 7, 10, 20). The soul which is living a separated life, with sin judged, forsaken, and forgiven, behind it, may count on these four:

Deliverance—even in the midst of difficulties and perplexities which have been caused by its own misdeeds (vv. 4, 7, 17, 19).

Enlightenment—for what the dawn is to the weary watcher, that God will be to the soul if only the face is turned towards His (v. 5).

Perfect Provision—it shall lack nothing it really needs (v. 10).

The Sense of God's nighness—nearer than the nearest (v. 18).

If, in that cave, with so many to distract, every hour, David was able to realize the presence of God, how much more possible it must be for us! Once that is realized, all the conditions of the best life are fulfilled. What makes the difference between the grey of winter and the beauty of the spring? Is it not that the sun is nigh, and nature assimilates its glorious color?

So backslider! broken heart! contrite spirit! do not look back on past failure nor dread recurring sin; but look up to the face of Jesus. Dwell in the secret place of the Most High. Enter with boldness the Holiest, to remain there. Ask the Holy Spirit to enable you to realize the constant presence of God. Say many a time each day, even when you do not feel it, "Thou art nigh; Thou art here." Make your home in the sense of God's nearness. Oh, taste the sweetness of such a life. It was thus that Jesus thought of His Father; and it is thus that you will realize the happiest, strongest experiences possible to the saints. "The Lord is nigh unto them that are of a broken heart, and saveth such as be of a contrite spirit."

6
Singing in Sorrow
I Samuel 23; Psalm 27

David's lifelong habit of waiting upon God for direction and guidance is instructive and stimulating. Notice that the successive steps of his career were taken after waiting upon God. The advice he gives to us all in the Psalm which dates from this period was the outcome of his own deepest experience: "Wait on the Lord: Be strong, and let thine heart take courage; Yea, wait thou on the Lord" (v. 14).

The Psalmist's Desire
Several items of internal evidence connect Psalm 27 with this period of David's life. His fortunes were as dark as the cave, therefore he spoke of God as his light; he was in daily peril, therefore God would be his salvation. Jehovah was more really his stronghold than even that fortress of rock. Evildoers might come on him to eat up his flesh, but they would stumble and fall, as Goliath had done in that very ravine; hosts might encamp against him, war might rise, but in this would he be confident. He would be hid in the covert of God's tent, or be set upon a rock inaccessible to his foes. True, he had no longer the old home in Bethlehem; in that sense his father and mother had forsaken him (v. 10). But God would be father and mother both. Further references to his extreme need and anguish to the false witnesses who breathed out cruelty—Doeg's treachery—combine to associate this lovely and pathetic psalm with the cave. Such a

cry must frequently have broken from his heart in those sad and dark days.

David mentions the Lord's house, tabernacle, and temple, the desire for an abiding place in the house of the Lord—the wish of his shepherd days, of his cave experiences, and of his exile when fleeing from Absalom—of Divine fellowship which would supply a constant flow of direction in all the dark and tortuous pathways of his history. What fresh meaning invests his words when read under this light! He desired to abide with God face to face, that whenever the Divine summons was heard, though in whispers "Seek ye My face," he might be near enough to hear it, and reply, "Thy face, Lord, will I seek" (v. 8).

His Habitual Practice

When the trembling Abiathar had told his story, David addressed to him words which have a sweet application when placed in the lips of Christ. Our outcast King, driven beyond the camp, receives each fugitive: "Abide thou with Me," He says; "fear not! for he that seeketh My life seeketh thy life: with Me thou shalt be in safeguard." Abiathar brought with him, rescued from the sack of the little town, the sacred ephod, within which were the sacred Urim and Thummim. The words signify "Light and Perfection." It is not certain what they refer to. The most probable explanation is the following: The High Priest's inner garment was a white linen tunic; over this he wore a blue robe, and above this the ephod of white twined linen, inwrought with blue, purple, scarlet, and gold. To this was affixed the breastplate, in which were twelve precious stones, corresponding to the twelve tribes of Israel. In this breastplate were probably either one or two resplendent diamonds, through which God manifested His will. If to any question reverently put to Him by the Priest, the answer was "no," the light in these precious stones dimmed; if it was "yes," they flashed with splendor.

It was a great gain to have this method of communication.

Gad was with him, as the representative of the prophetic
office; now Abiathar and the ephod represented the most
precious prerogative of the priesthood. By these, especially
the latter, he was able at any moment to know the will of
God. This was the holy practice of his life: to wait on God,
quelling the fever of his soul, and compelling the crowd of
impetuous thoughts to be in abeyance until time had been
given for the clear disclosure of the Divine plan. Like a
traveler in a strange country who is utterly dependent on his
guide, so David lifted up his soul for the supreme direction
God only can give.

Our Guidance Today

When Israel came up out of Egypt, they were led across the
desert by the pillar of cloud and fire. After they were settled
in their own land, the Urim and Thummim took its place.
After a while, this fell into disuse, and the prophets spake as
they were moved by the Holy Ghost. These, even in the early
church played a very important part in the ordering of God's
people in His way. But the prophets were silenced as the
apostolic age came to a close. What is our oracle of appeal?
Are pious souls without the means of inquiring of the Lord,
and receiving His clear direction on difficult questions? Not
so; for the ascended Lord foretold that he who overcame
should receive a *white stone,* and the word *white* means resplendent, lustrous. It probably refers to those stones in the
High Priest's breastplate, that dimmed or flashed with the
Divine oracles. On them the Holy Name, Jehovah, was in-
scribed and similarly it is said that on the white stone, which
each believer should receive who had overcome in the spiritual conflict against sin and the world, a new name should be
written, unknown save to him that received it (Rev. 2:17). In
other words, each child of God has his own Urim and
Thummim stone, which is a conscience void of offense, a
heart cleansed in the blood of Christ, a spiritual nature filled
by the Holy Spirit of God.

When we are in doubt, when voices urge this course or the

other, when prudence utters one advice and faith another, then let us be still in God's presence; let us study His Word; let us lift up our faces, eager only to know what the Lord shall determine—and before long a distinct impression will be made, the unmistakable forthtelling of His counsel. It is not wise, in the earlier stages of Christian life, to depend on this alone; but to wait for the corroboration of circumstances. But those who have had many dealings with God know well the value of secret fellowship with Him, to ascertain His will.

Hymns of the Hunted

The church owes many of her sweetest hymns to the profound anguish which wrung the hearts of her noblest children. Many of David's psalms date from those dark days when he was hunted as a partridge upon the mountains. His path may be tracked through the Psalter, as well as in the sacred narrative. This gifted singer elicited the music concealed in the least congenial haunts and these wild desolations are now immortal, contributing chords to the complete music of the soul. We will, for a little, trace the parallel lines of David's history and song.

Keilah

While sheltering in the forest of Hareth, tidings came, "Behold, the Philistines are fighting against Keilah, and they rob the threshing floors" (I Sam. 23:1). The labors of the year were being carried off, and the cattle. There was probably a covert appeal for help; Saul was too far away to be available for rapid action; David was alert, near at hand. The appeal ratified by the Divine voice, he went down into the plains, met the marauders, smote them with great slaughter, and brought back all the spoil to the rejoicing townsfolk, who gladly lodged and entertained him and his men. It was a brief spell of sunshine. To be again in a town that had "gates and bars" was as welcome as the comforts of civilization are after the privations of the Tartar steppes. And this gleam of comfort probably elicited from the minstrel chieftain Psalm

31, "Blessed be the Lord, for He hath showed me His marvelous loving kindness in a strong city."

Ziph

His stay in Keilah was brought to a summary close by the tidings that Saul was preparing an expedition to take him. These tidings were confirmed through the ephod and the further information was communicated that the cowardly and ungrateful townsfolk save themselves by surrendering their deliverer. Then David and his six hundred departed out of Keilah and went whithersoever they could go. The leader, with the more intrepid and devoted followers, made his way to the neighborhood of Ziph, about three miles south of Hebron. This was about the lowest ebb in David's fortunes. The king was searching for him every day to seek his life. He knew, so Jonathan told his friend in a hurried interview in the wood, that David would be king over Israel. But this did not abate his determination to take his life if he could. What a desperate condition his soul had reached!

In addition to this relentless hate, there was the meditated treachery of the Ziphites, who sought to curry favor with the king by betraying David's lurking place. David moved further south where a conical hill gives a far extended view of the surrounding country. But to the spot the men of Ziph conducted the king; the little band found the hill on which they gathered surrounded by the royal troops, and their escape impossible. At this juncture a breathless messenger burst in on Saul with the words, "Haste thee, and come; for the Philistines have made a raid on the land." Then David drew a long sigh of relief, and sang Psalm 54, "Save me, O God, by Thy name, and judge me by Thy might."

Engedi

From Maon the heat of the pursuit was over, and David removed eastward to the Dead Sea. On the western shore there is a little piece of level ground, covered with tropical vegetation, fenced in by giant cliffs jutting out into the dark waters of the lake, its beauty maintained by a tepid stream which issues from the limestone rock four hundred feet above. This was David's next resort—Engedi, the haunt of the wild goat—where deep caverns in the steep cliffs, and the abundance of water supply furnished two of the important items. Here the Psalmist sets his experiences to music in two priceless songs. Psalm 57, "Be merciful unto me, O God, for my soul taketh refuge in Thee"; and Psalm 142, "I cry with my voice unto the Lord, with my voice unto the Lord, do I make supplication."

Wilderness experiences also gave rise to other psalms. Among these are Psalms 11, 13, 17, 22, 25, 44.

Men are as lions. "My soul is among lions, I lie among them that are set on fire." His soul takes refuge in God, in the shadow of His wings; as he had often seen the eaglets do beneath the broad pinion of the parent bird. God is his Rock, he hides in Him as his fugitive band in the deep sides of the cave. It shall happen to His enemies as so often happened to hunters in those very wilds, when they fell down the crumbling sides of pits dug to trap the creatures of the forest. At night he shelters in God; with his psaltery he awakes the dawn.

He does not spare his epithets for those that misrepresented and maligned him. But of Saul he says nothing, unless there is a veiled allusion to him in the plural, with which he describes the violent men that sought after his life. There is a plaintive allusion to happy days, past forever, but there are no words of reproach, no repayment of hate with hate. In this there is an anticipation of the teaching and temper of Jesus.

His conscience was void of offense toward God and man. If challenged as to sinlessness he would have acknowledged that he was constantly in need of the propitiating sacrifices. But, in respect to Saul, he protested his absolute innocence; and turned confidently to God, with clean hands and a pure heart.

Of all sources of pain, there is none that stings so sharply as the malevolence of our fellows. This is what David suffered from most of all. To his sensitive spirit it was torture; that though he was innocent, though willing to pray on their behalf, yet his calumniators pursued him with unrelenting malice—"Their teeth are spears and arrows, and their tongue a sharp sword." But his appeal was to God, the Righteous One, who would shelter him during trial, and ultimately bring out his righteousness as the light.

If any are unjustly maligned, let them rest in the Lord and wait patiently. Some time may elapse, but presently God will arise, and lift the poor out of the dust, "to inherit the throne of glory."

7

Waiting for the Lord

I Samuel 24; 26; Psalm 62; 7

As David reviewed the innumerable evils that had encompassed him, he attributed his deliverance to God only. During all these long and sad experiences his attitude was, "I waited patiently for the Lord." There is a clear distinction between waiting *on* the Lord and waiting *for* the Lord: we wait *on* the Lord by prayer and supplication, looking for the indication of His will; we wait *for* the Lord by patience and submission, looking for the interposition of His hand. How perfectly David had learned this lesson!

The Basis of Waiting for God

There must be a promise to justify us, or some definite committal of God on which we can rest as the unmistakable revelation of His purpose. In the wood of Ziph, Jonathan had given this to his friend like a messenger from God. The weary heart had drunk it in as the parched land drinks water! "Fear not," he had said, "for the hand of Saul my father shall not find thee; and thou shalt be king over Israel, and I shall be next unto thee" (I Sam. 23:17).

Besides this, David was conscious of faculty and God-given ability to grasp the helm of the kingdom, and guide the sorely tossed bark into calmer waters. He became convinced that God had a great purpose in his life and settled it in his own mind that he would wait patiently for the Lord to do as He had said. Whenever the moment came for him to sit on the throne it should be from first to last the Divine gift, and the Divine performance.

Engedi

One afternoon when Saul with three thousand men was in hot pursuit of David amid the wild and tangled rocks of Engedi, a strange incident put him completely in David's power. It was a time of breathless heat; every living thing, except perhaps the little lizards, had crept away into shelter. David and his men were in the inmost recesses of an immense cavern. Into that very cave Saul came. His men had gone forward; the intense silence threw him off his guard; he lingered a little in the entrance. These caves are dark as midnight, and keen eyes cannot see five paces inward; but one within, looking toward the entrance, can observe with perfect distinctness all that takes place in that direction. How little did the king realize the intense interest with which he was being watched by six hundred pairs of eyes, and the peril! The whole band was thrilled with excitement. Now was the opportunity to end their wanderings and hardships by one thrust of the spear. They whispered "Seize your opportunity! God Himself has brought him here that you should avenge your wrongs."

With great difficulty David restrained them, curbed his own passion, and contented himself with creeping near and cutting off the king's robe to prove to him afterwards how completely he had been in his power. But even after Saul had gone forth and David's men crowded around full of sudden remonstrance, he was struck with remorse, and he said to them, "The Lord forbid that I should do this thing unto my lord, the Lord's anointed" (I Sam. 24:6).

Hachilah

Previously at this spot David had been nearly trapped. This time the tables were turned. Once more Saul was in pursuit of his rival, "having three thousand chosen men of Israel with him" (I Sam. 26:2). Having ascertained the exact situation of the royal camp, David went to inspect it from an overhanging cliff. On the outskirts the wagons made a rude barricade, within these were the soldiers' quarters, and in the innermost circle Saul and Abner were posted; but the watches were badly kept, and no precaution was taken against a sudden attack.

A sudden inspiration seized David, and he proposed to Abishai and Ahimelech, the Hittite, that they should visit the camp by night. Abishai gladly volunteered to accompany him, and guided by the clear moonlight they crept down the hill, crossed the ravine, picked their way through the wagons and the sleeping soldiers, stood for a moment whispering over the prostrate form of the king, bore off his spear and water bottle from Saul's head, and then "gat them away, and no man saw it, nor knew it; neither did any awake, because a deep sleep from the Lord was fallen upon them."

Thus, again, Saul had been in his power; but he had restrained himself. Abishai could not understand his secret. To him it seemed a most natural and lawful act for David to take the life of a man who was so infatuated for his destruction; surely he could have no objection against Abishai doing it. In that whispered colloquy over the sleeping monarch, Abishai had suggested that God had delivered his enemy into his chieftain's hand, and had offered to smite him with a stroke so deadly that there would be neither sigh nor groan to awaken Abner or his body guard. But David would not have it.

"No," he said, "no one can smite the Lord's anointed and be guiltless. When his appointed death hour comes, God will take him either by natural process or amid battle. But my hand shall not curtail his days. I will wait God's time" (I Sam. 26:9, 10).

On these occasions David acted with the magnanimity that became a hero and a saint. He would take no mean advantage of his adversary nor retaliate. He refused argument that opportunity meant permission. He quieted the impetuous

fever of his soul and elected to await the slow unfolding of
the Divine purpose.

Waiting for God Restrains Crime

Bitter indeed had David's remorse been if he had put forth
his hand against Saul's life. It would have robbed his harp of
all its music. True, months were still to pass, full of anxiety
and suspense, before coronation shouts rang, but they were
forgotten as snow dissolves in the river, and then there was
nothing to regret. Be still, O heart! wait for God; this will
keep thee from acts and words which would shadow thy
whole after life.

Waiting for God Inspires Courage

What an intrepid spirit this was that dared to cry after the
king and hold up the skirt of his robe; that challenged two
brave men of his army to a feat from which one of them
shrank! Ah! the man who is living in the Divine purpose has
quenchless courage. He knows that no weapon formed
against him shall prosper, and that every tongue against him
shall be condemned. He fears nothing, except to do wrong
and to grieve God.

Waiting for God Gives Great Rest

Out of such experiences as these David wrote the 37th Psalm
which, though it belongs to a later period, forever embalms
the conclusions of this. Mellow wisdom gathers up the
maxims wrought out in the fires of early manhood. "Fret not
thyself because of evildoers: neither be thou envious against
them that work unrighteousness: For they shall soon be cut
down like the grass, and wither as the green herb."

The exhortations of this exquisite psalm, to trust in the
Lord, to delight in the Lord, to roll the way of life on the
Lord, to rest in the Lord and wait patiently for Him, and
especially the repeated injunction not to fret, are all bathed in
new meaning. Live on the Divine purpose. Be not eager for

thyself, but only that God's work be done. He will take care of thy interests, if thou carest for His. Calm thyself; rest thee; sit still and trust—God is working out the plan of thy life; in His own time, the best time, He shall give thee the desires of thine heart.

Waiting for God Induces Penitence in Others

When David gave such unmistakable evidences of his self-restraint, loyalty and surviving affection; when he so clearly established his innocence; when he appealed with such reverence from the misrepresentations of earth to the decisions of the Divine Judge—the miserable monarch wept and confessed that he had "played the fool, and erred exceedingly." Saul recognized David's nobility; the old chivalrous nature which had so captivated the nation in earlier days flashed out with an expiring flicker; and he went so far as to admit that David would be king. Nothing but such forbearance on David's part could have brought him so near repentance.

Thus we may win men still. We win most when we appear to have yielded most; and gain advantages by refusing to take them wrongfully. The man who can wait for God is a man of power, and others will bend beneath his scepter. To be under authority to God is to have soldiers under us who do our bidding.

The Blessing in Time of Slander

It is surprising to find Saul in search of David, after the incidents described. There seemed so entire a reconciliation between them, and yet after so short a space Saul is again on the war path. These capricious changes may have been due to the malady from which he was suffering; but a more satisfactory explanation has been suggested which casts fresh light on the seventh Psalm. It is headed *Shiggaion of David, which he sang unto the Lord.* That is, it is an irregular ode, expressing by sudden changes the emotion of its author. We have often to sing these Shiggaion meters; our songs are frequently broken with groans; but we do well still to sing with such tunefulness as we may. Happy are they who can find themes for singing to the Lord in every sad and bitter experience!

8

Crowned at Last!

II Samuel 1:4

Two whole days had passed since the slaughter of Amalek and it appeared as though David were awaiting some sign to determine his future course. What should he do next? Build again the ruined city? Or was there something else in the Divine program of his life? What tidings were there of Saul, of the beloved Jonathan, and of his comrades?

On the third day a young man rushed into the camp, his clothes rent and earth upon his head. He made straight for David, and fell at his feet. His tidings were told, each word stabbing David to the quick. Israel had fled before the foe; large numbers were fallen on the battlefield; Saul and Jonathan were dead also. That moment David knew that the thundercloud so long over his head had broken, the expectations of years were being realized; but he had no thought for the marvelous change in his fortunes. His generous soul poured out a flood of the noblest tears man ever shed, for Saul and for Jonathan, for the people of the Lord, and for Israel.

David's Treatment of Saul's Memory

David seems to have been as one stunned till the evening, and then he aroused himself to show respect to Saul.

He gave short shrift to the Amalekite. On his own showing he had slain the Lord's anointed and the regicide should pay the extreme penalty for the deed confessed.

He next poured out his grief in the song of the bow, which at first was sung by Judah, and has since passed into the literature of the world as an unrivaled model of a funeral dirge. The Dead March in *Saul* is a familiar strain in every national mourning. It was originally called the Song of the Bow (v. 18), because of reference to that weapon.

Israel's loss is brought out in Philistia's exultant welcome of their returning warriors; in the curse on the mountains polluted with gore and in the exploits which the heroes wrought before they fell. Then the psalmist in pathetic reminiscence of friendship with the departed forgets all he had suffered at the hands of Saul; his love refuses to consider anything but what had been brave and fair and noble in his liege lord. "Lovely and pleasant," he inscribes on the memorial cenotaph.

For Jonathan there must be a special stanza; every memory of whom was very pleasant, like sweet music. "Thy love to me was wonderful, passing the love of women."

He sent a message of thanks. The indignity with which the Philistines had treated the royal bodies had been amply expiated by the devotion of the men of Jabesh-Gilead. They had not forgotten that Saul's first act as king had been to deliver them from a horrible fate; and had taken the bodies of Saul and his three sons from Bethshan to their own city, where they had been reverently buried. As soon as David heard this he sent to Jabesh-Gilead, thanking them for their devotion and promising to requite the kindness.

In all this David evinced great magnanimity. There was no thought of his own interests, escaping from himself in his devotion and care for another. It is the secret of all self-oblivion. Live in another's life, especially in Christ, and you will be freed from the constant obtrusion and tyranny of self.

David's Attitude Toward the Kingdom

How completely his soul had come back to its equipoise in God! It was for God to give him the kingdom, and therefore he refused to take one step toward the throne apart from the direct Divine impulse. So many reasons might have been alleged for immediate action. The kingdom was overrun by Philistines—for the next five years there was no settled government among the northern tribes. It must have been difficult to restrain himself from gathering the forces of Israel and flinging himself on the foe. He was God's designated king, and it would have been natural for him to step up to the empty throne. But David, refusing the judgment of his eyes, inquired of the Lord, "Shall I go up into any of the cities of Judah?" And when the Divine oracle directed him to Hebron, he settled quietly with his followers among the villages in its vicinity, waiting till the men of Judah came, and owned him king. Then for the second time he was anointed.

Anointed first by Samuel in his father's house, he was now anointed king over his own people; just as the Lord Jesus was anointed first by Jordan, and again as the representative of His people, when He ascended for them into the presence of the Father.

At each great crisis of our life, especially some new and enlarged sphere of service, we should seek a fresh anointing to fulfill its fresh demands. There should be successive anointings in our life history as our opportunities widen out in ever-increasing circles. When leaving for college and again when stepping forth to the first cure of souls; when standing at the altar to become a wife, and again when bending over the cradle of the first babe; when summoned to public office in church or State—each new step should be characterized by a definite waiting on God, that there may be a recharging of the spirit with His might.

David's Reign in Hebron

For seven years and six months David was king in Hebron over Judah. He was in the prime of life, thirty years of age, and seems to have given himself to the enjoyment of the quiet sanctities of home. Sandwiched between two references to the long war between his house and that of Saul is the record of his wives and his children (3:2-5).

Throughout those years he preserved the spirit of waiting expectancy. In this he reminds us of our Lord, who sits at His Father's side, till His foes are made the footstool of His feet. Similarly, David sat on the throne of Judah, in the city of Hebron—which means *fellowship*—waiting until God had removed all obstacles, and smoothed the pathway to the supreme dignity which He had promised.

He maintained an almost passive policy; what fighting was necessary, was left to Joab. The overtures for the transference of the kingdom of Israel were finally made by Abner himself, who for years had known that he was fighting against God; and who at last told the puppet king whom he had set up, that what God had sworn to David, he was resolved to effect—namely, to translate the kingdom from the house of Saul to David. The negotiations with Israel and Benjamin were carried out by Abner who went finally to speak in the ears of David all that seemed good to Israel and to Benjamin. It was Abner who proposed to David to gather all Israel unto him, addressing him as lord and king, and bidding him prepare to rule over all that his soul desired (3:17-21). Throughout these transactions, David quietly received what was offered; and only asserted himself with intensity and passion on two occasions, to clear himself of complicity in crime, and to show his abhorrence of those who had perpetrated them.

It was a noble spectacle when the king followed the bier of Abner, and wept at his grave. He forgot his persistent foe, and remembered only a prince and a great man; and he wove a chaplet of elegiacs to lay on his grave, as he had done for Saul's. All the people took notice of it, and it pleased them. Then followed the dastardly assassination of the puppet king, Ishbosheth. As soon as they bore the tidings to David he turned to the Lord and solemnly swore that he would require at their hands the blood of the murdered man.

Then came all Israel and offered him the crown of the entire kingdom. They remembered his kinship with them as their bone and flesh; recalled when he led their armies; and reminded him of the Divine promise that he should be shepherd and prince. Then David became their constitutional king and was solemnly anointed for the third time—as the Son of Man shall be one day acknowledged king over the world and shall reign without a rival.

It is to this period that we must attribute Psalm 18, which touches the high-water mark of rapturous thankfulness and adoration. Every precious name for God is laid under contribution; the figure of his coming to rescue his servant in a thunderstorm is unparalleled in sublimity. There is throughout an appreciation of the tenderness and love of God's dealings.

9

Enthroned in Jerusalem

II Samuel 5; 6; 21:15; 23:8

It must have been an imposing assembly that came to crown
David king. For three days they remained, keeping high festival. The Philistines, however, were watching with profound dissatisfaction. So long as David was leaving them free
to raid the northern tribes they were not disposed to inter-
fere; but when they heard that they had anointed David king
over all Israel, all the Philistines went down to seek David.
They probably waited until Israel had dispersed to their
homes, and then poured over into Judah in such vast numbers, cutting off the northern tribes, that he was forced to
retire with his men to the celebrated fortress cave of Adullam
(2 Sam. 5:17 and 23:13, 14).

A Sudden Reversal of Fortune

It is probable that David took refuge in God. These were days
when he walked very closely with his Almighty Friend, and
he did not waver his confidence that God would perfect what
concerned him. Such sudden reversals come to us all—to
wean us from confidence in men and things; to force us to
root ourselves in God alone. It was salutary that David be
reminded at this crisis of his history that he was as dependent on God as ever, and that He who had given could as
easily take back His gifts. Child of mortality in the hour of
most radiant triumphs, thou must understand that thy place
and power are thine only as His gift, and as a trusteeship for

His glory. Be not surprised then if He makes thy throne tremble now and again, and that thou mayest remember that it rests only on His will, the forth-putting of His might. This contrast presents a striking analogy to our Lord, who after His anointing at Jordan, was driven by the Spirit into the wilderness to be tempted of the devil. It is the law of the spiritual life. The bright light of popularity is too strong for the development of the Divine life. Solitude, temptation, conflict—these are the flames that burn the Divine colors into our characters, the blessings made available for the poor, the brokenhearted, the prisoners, the captives, the blind.

Gleams of Light

The misty gloom was lit by some notable incidents, prodigies of valor were performed around the person of their Prince, whom his followers delighted to call the Light of Israel, albeit for the hour obscured by clinging mists (II Samuel 21:17).

What marvels may be wrought by the inspiration of a single life! We revert to that hour when, by that very spot, an unknown youth stepped forth from the affrighted hosts of Israel to face the dreaded Goliath. Now after some fifteen years there were scores of men, animated by his spirit, inspired by his faith, who pushed him gently back, and told him that they must bear the brunt of the conflict, since his life, which was the fountain source of all their energy, must be carefully withheld from needless peril.

Thus the lives of great men light up other lives. They mold their contemporaries. The inspiration of a Wesley's career raises a great army of preachers. The enthusiasm of a Carey, a Livingstone, a Paton stirs multitudes of hearts with missionary zeal. Those who had been the disciples of Jesus became His apostles and martyrs. His own life of self-sacrifice for men has become the beacon fire that has summoned myriads from the lowland valley of selfishness to the surrender, the self-denial, the anguish of the cross.

The Water of Bethlehem!

Adullam was not far from Bethlehem. Often David had led his father's flocks to pasture where he was now sheltering; and the familiar scenes recalled Jesse, his mother, and his boyhood home. Over yonder, almost within sight, a garrison of Philistines held Bethlehem. Suddenly longing swept across him to taste the water of the well of Bethlehem; he gave expression to the wish, not suspecting that his stalwarts would be foolhardy enough to attempt to gratify his whim. However, he miscalculated; he had not gauged the warmth of their affection.

Three of his mightiest warriors stole secretly out of the cave down the valley, through the host of the Philistines, drew water from the well, and before they had been missed, placed the brimming vessel in David's hands. It was the priceless expression of a love that was stronger than death. He could not drink it—the blood it might have cost! He arose and poured it out as a libation to God, as though the gift were fit only to be made to Him; saying, "My God, forbid it me that I should do this, shall I drink of the blood of these men that have put their lives in jeopardy?" We have another example in this graphic episode of David's marvelous self-control.

It were well if all young men and women, and others also, would ask themselves whether certain gratifications, in which they have indulged, are not purchased at too dear a cost. Could they quaff the cup of pleasure if they realized that it was presented at the cost of scores of souls whose virtue was being sacrificed behind the scenes? Could they drink of the intoxicating cup if they realized that the drinking customs of society were annually costing the happiness and eternal welfare of myriads?

How often we sigh for the waters of the well of Bethlehem! We dwell longingly on never-to-be-forgotten memories. Oh to see again that face; to feel that gentle hand; to hear that voice! Oh for that fresh vision of life, that devotion to the

Saviour, that new love! Oh to drink of water of the well of Bethlehem! They are vain regrets; there are no mighties strong enough to fetch back the past. But the quest of the soul may yet be satisfied by Him who said, "He that drinketh of this water shall thirst again; but he that drinketh of the water that I shall give him, shall never thirst: but it shall be in him a spring of water, rising up to everlasting life."

The Overthrow of the Philistines

In this hour David inquired of the Lord, saying, "Shall I go up against the Philistines? Wilt Thou deliver them into mine hand?" (II Sam. 5:19). In reply, he received the Divine assurance of victory; and when the battle commenced, it seemed to him as if the Lord were sweeping them before Him like a winter flood. "The Lord," said he, "hath broken forth upon mine enemies" (v. 20).

Again the Philistines came up to assert supremacy, and again David waited on the Lord. It was well that he did so; because the plan of campaign was not as before. Those that rely on God must be careful to be in constant touch with Him. The aid given yesterday in one form, will be given tomorrow in another.

The movement in the mulberry trees, which indicated advance on the foe, suggests invisible angelic squadrons passing onward to the battle. "The Lord is gone out before thee to smite the host of the Philistines." Then David broke on their ranks and pursued them down into the maritime plain.

Sometimes we have to march, sometimes to halt; now we are called to action, again to suffering. We must admit no stereotyped methods. Let there be living faith in God; the perception of the new departure which the Spirit of God is intending and the willingness to follow, though it be at the sacrifice of all the older prejudices. Then shall we know what God can do in our lives.

Jerusalem, The Holy City

One of the first acts of the new king was to secure a suitable capital for his kingdom. And his choice of Jerusalem was a masterpiece of policy and statesmanship. Surely it was more; it was the result of the direct guidance of the Spirit of God. It was highly desirable that the capital should be accessible to the whole country, and should possess the features that rendered it fit to become the heart and brain of the national life. It must be capable of being strongly fortified, to preserve the sacred treasures of the kingdom inviolate. It must combine features of strength and beauty to arouse the national pride and devotion. It must be hallowed by sacred associations to become the religious center of the people's holiest life. All these features blended in Jerusalem, and commended it to David's Divinely-guided judgment.

The Capture
Making a levy of all Israel, David went up to Jerusalem in person. The Jebusites ridiculed the attempt to dislodge them, but through Jacob's prowess the city speedily fell into David's hands; and he dwelt in the stronghold, afterwards known as Zion, or the City of David.

David's first act was to extend the fortification. This first success laid the foundation of David's greatness. "He waxed greater and greater; for the Lord, the God of hosts, was with him." Indeed, neighboring nations hastened to seek his alliance (I Chron. 9:7-9; II Sam. 5:11).

A Fair Dawn
It has been suggested that we owe Psalm 101 to this hour in David's life. He finds himself suddenly called to conduct the internal administration of a great nation; the new needs were demanding new expression. Departments of law and justice, of finance, and of military organization, were rapidly becoming localized at the capital. The palace and court were every day thronged with those who sought promotion to offices of trust. No mistake should be made in these early selections, and the country should be reassured as to the character of the men whom the king was to entrust with its concerns. For

these purposes this psalm may have been prepared.

The royal psalmist declares that he will behave himself wisely with a perfect heart. He will hate the work of those that turn aside. He describes those who shall be his chosen counselors and ministers. He will listen to no slanders; if he discovers deceit or misrepresentation, he pledges himself to dismiss him instantly. His energies should be devoted to cutting off all iniquity from the city and the land, while his eyes should be upon all the faithful, *they* should dwell with him, and he would choose as his attendants those who walked in a perfect way.

It was a fair ideal. These early days of the new kingdom were fitly described as a morning without clouds, the righteous ruler, ruling men in the fear of God, and thrusting away the ungodly as thorns stood clear-cut before him. If only he had obeyed and followed without swerving, what years of anguish would have been saved!

The Ark on Mount Zion

As soon as David had acquired a capital, he was eager to make it the religious as well as the political center of the national life. He resolved to place in a temporary structure by his palace, the almost forgotten Ark; which, since its return from the Philistines, had found a temporary resting place some eleven miles southwest of Jerusalem in the house of Abinadab.

In all probability David felt unable to remove the Tabernacle at Gibeah—because the priests maintained the burnt offering continually upon the altar. But David's purpose would be sufficiently served by the presence of the Ark in the new city. He sent abroad everywhere to gather priests, Levites and people, to bring again the sacred emblem.

The Mistake of the Cart

It was a great procession that wended its way to the little town. In addition to a vast host of priests and Levites, and people, there were thirty thousand chosen soldiers, to protect the assembly.

Probably to this occasion we owe Psalm 132, in which the royal singer records the determination that whenever he should be established in his kingdom, one of his earliest acts would be to find out a tabernacle for the mighty one of Jacob.

But one fatal mistake marred the day and postponed the nation's high hope. It was strictly ordained in the law of Moses, that Levites alone, specially consecrated to the task, should bear the Ark upon their shoulders, not touching it with their hands, lest they should die (Num. 4:15; 7:9), enforcing the sanctity of the service of the Most High. This command had, however, fallen into disuse with much else; and it was arranged that the Ark should be carried on a new cart driven by the two sons of Abinadab. The Philistines had used such a cart ignorantly; but for Israel to set aside the repeated injunction of the Levitical law could not be condoned, lest the entire Levitical code should be treated as a dead letter.

The oxen started amid a blast of song and trumpet, and all went well until the oxen stumbled and the ark shook violently. Then Uzzah, the younger son of Abinadab, put out his hand to steady it and instantly fell dead. The effect was terrific; panic spread through the awed crowd. David was greatly dismayed, afraid of God that day. So he directed that the Ark should be deposited in the vicinity, and there it remained for three months. The terrified crowds returned to Jerusalem. How important it was at this juncture to insist on literal obedience to the ancient code! If man's caprice set its injunctions at defiance, the entire system might have fallen into disuse.

The Shoulders of Living Men

"The Lord blessed the home of Obededom" (II Sam. 6:11). Meanwhile David searched into the Divine directions for the conveyance of the sacred emblem. Again a vast concourse was gathered. This time, however, the children of the Levites bare the Ark upon their shoulders, with the staves. Then the white-robed choirs, the sweet strains of the bands, the measured march of the thousands, the stately procession of the elders, the shoutings of the crowds—together made up such a welcome as was worthy of the occasion. David, responsive as a musical instrument to a master hand, clad in a linen ephod, danced before the Lord. So they brought in the Ark of the Lord, and set it in its place. The one cloud that marred the gladness of the day was the biting speech of Michal, who had no sympathy with her husband's religion. Perhaps she was jealous at David's independence of her and her father's house—hence the venom in her speech to the man whom she had loved and whose life she had once saved.

Three Majestic Psalms
Upon this occasion three of the greatest psalms were composed: 15, 68 and 24. Psalm 15 was evidently composed with direct reference to the death of Uzzah, and in answer to the question, "Lord who shall sojourn in Thy tabernacle—Who shall dwell in Thy holy hill?" Psalm 68 was chanted as a processional hymn. It begins with the ancient formula in the desert mark: "Let God arise, let His enemies be scattered."

But Psalm 24 is perhaps the master ode of the three. It begins with a marvelous conception, when we consider the narrowness of ordinary Jewish exclusiveness: "The earth is the Lord's, and the fulness thereof: the world, and they that dwell therein." The first half of the psalm answers the question as to who may stand before God (vv. 3-6). They must be clean in hands, and pure in heart; no mere external ceremonial will meet the case. The requirement of this holy God is the righteousness which He alone can give to those who seek His face. The second half declares God's willingness to abide with man upon the earth.

10
Building the Kingdom

II Samuel 7, 8; I Chronicles 18-20; II Chronicles 6:8

With the assistance of Hiram of Tyre, a palace of cedar had been erected for David on Mount Zion. It was a great contrast to the temporary structure for the Ark. One day the impulse came to David to realize a purpose long in his heart. Calling Nathan the prophet, now mentioned for the first time, he announced his intention of building a house for God. The prophet cordially assented to the proposal; but in the night, when he was more able to ascertain the thought of God, the word of the Lord bade him stay the king from taking further steps in that direction.

The next day he broke the news to David with the utmost gentleness. Indeed, in the account it is difficult to detect the direct negative. The king was hardly sensible of disappointment amid the rush of overwhelming gladness which Nathan's words aroused. "Wilt thou build a house for God?—He will build thee an house."

A Noble Purpose
It was a great thought that came to David. It was in part suggested by the exigencies of the situation. An immense body of men were gathering around the Ark for whom it was necessary to find suitable headquarters; and this no doubt partly urged David towards the fulfillment of his purpose. But there was a deeper reason; to show his love for God, to establish some monument of his reverence, devotion, and lasting gratitude.

It is thus, especially in young life, that great conceptions visit the soul, ideals of surpassing beauty, resolves of service for God and man and all life is set to a higher key. "I will do this great thing for God," the young heart says to itself, altogether heedless of sacrifice, tears, blood. The bugle notes of lofty purpose ring out gladly, summoning the soul to noble exploit. Young people, never surrender your ideal, nor act unworthily of it, nor disobey the heavenly vision. Above all, when you come to the house of cedar, be more than ever careful to remember the purpose that visited you as you kept your father's sheep.

Unrealized Ideals

There is no definite "no" spoken by God's gentle lips. He presses His promises and blessings upon us, and leads us forward in love. Like David, we are lovingly carried forward from sentence to sentence in life's long speech of Divine care and bounty; and often we find that our purpose is not destined to work out just as we thought. The picture is always *to be* painted; the book is always *to be* written; the immortal song *to be* sung.

Late-Coming Explanations

What we know not now, we shall know hereafter. Years after David said to Solomon his son, "The word of the Lord came to me, saying, Thou hast shed blood abundantly, and hast made great wars, thou shalt not build a house unto My name" (1 Chron. 22:8). The bloodstained hand might not raise the temple of peace. As the years passed, the reason for God's refusal grew clear. Meanwhile, David possessed his soul in patience and said to himself: God has a reason, though I cannot understand it.

Some day we shall understand that God has a reason in every "no." He would reveal it to us if we could bear it: but it is better not to pry into the mystery of His providence. He fences our questions, saying, "If I will that he tarry, what is that to thee!" But the time will come, probably in this life—

certainly in the next—when from the eminence of the years
we shall descry why He led us as He did.

Eventual Blessings

Solomon completes the story: "The Lord said unto David my
father, Whereas it was in thine heart to build an house for
My name, thou didst well that it was in thine heart" (II
Chron. 6:8). David was a better man because he had given
expression to the noble purpose. Its gleam left a permanent
glow on his life. The rejected candidate to the mission field
stands upon a higher platform than those who were never
touched by the glow of missionary enthusiasm. For a woman
to have loved passionately, even though dark waters en-
gulfed her love, leaves her richer, deeper, than if she had
never loved, nor been loved in return. "Thou didst well that
it was in thine heart."

God will credit us with what we would have been if we
might. He that has the missionary's heart, though tied to an
office stool, is reckoned as one of that noble band; the
woman at Zarephath, who did nothing more than share her
last meal with the prophet, shall have a prophet's reward; the
soul that thrills with the loftiest impulses, which the cares of
dependent relatives stay in fulfillment, will be surprised one
day to find itself credited with the harvest which would have
been reaped, had those seed germs been cast on more pro-
pitious soil. In the glory David will find himself credited
with the building of the temple on Mount Zion.

Doing the Next Thing

The energy which David would have expended in building
the temple wrought itself out in gathering the materials for it.
"I have prepared with all my might for the house of my
God . . ." (I Chron. 29:2, etc.). If you cannot have what you
hoped, do not allow your energies to run to waste; but arise
and help others to achieve. If you may not build, you may
gather materials for him that shall.

Somehow God makes up to us. He stooped over David's

life in blessing. The promise made through Nathan was threefold: (1) That David's house should reign forever; (2) that David's seed should build the temple; (3) that the kingdom of Israel should be made sure. The glowing words could only be realized in Him whom Peter declares David foresaw. There is only One whose reign can be permanent, who can build the true temple of God (Acts 2:30). But how great the honor that He should be David's Son!

Then David the king went in and sat before the Lord, and he said, "Who am I, O Lord God. . ." (II Sam. 7:18). We have no words to characterize the exuberant outflow of his soul in that transcendent hour. There was no complaint that the purpose of his heart was thwarted. Does God withhold the less, and not give the greater? Does He refuse the offer we make, and not bestow some heavenly gift that enriches for evermore? Dare to trust Him: let His assurances comfort thee. Claim that He should do as He said, and know that not one good thing shall fail: "For brass He will bring gold: the Lord shall be unto thee an everlasting light, and thy God thy glory."

A Great Kingdom

The time of rest was broken in upon by a succession of fierce wars. One after another the surrounding nations gathered together, singly or in confederacies, against David. "The nations raged; the kingdoms were moved." But David smote and subdued them. The border of Israel was carried to the line of the Euphrates, so that the ancient promise made by God to Abraham was fulfilled: "Unto thy seed have I given this land, from the river of Egypt unto the great river, the river Euphrates" (Gen. 15:18).

These years of war gave birth to some of the grandest of the psalms, among which may be numbered 2, 20, 21, 60, 110.

While the foes are in sight, the hero king is permitted a vision into the unseen. The day of his foe's attack is that in which he receives new assurance of sonship, and is bidden to claim the nations for his inheritance. He hears the chime of the Divine promise above the tumult of his fear: "Thou shalt break them with a rod of iron; Thou shalt dash them in pieces like a potter's vessel." His people pray that the Lord may send him help and he replies, "I know that the Lord saveth His anointed; He will answer him from His holy heaven with the saving strength of His right hand." He knows that the Most High will destroy his enemies.

Catching the contagion of his faith, they triumph in God's salvation, and in His name set up their banners. They believe that God, as a Man of War, is going forth with their hosts, and will tread down their adversaries. They are characterized by the willingness of their service—no mercenaries are pressed into their ranks: they gladly gather around the standard. They are clad not in mail, but in the fine linen of the priests; "the beauties of holiness," a phrase which suggests that the warfare was conducted by religious men, as an act of worship to God. They are numerous as the dewdrops that bespangle the morning grass.

What an exquisite conception of David's ideal for his soldiers, and of the knightly chivalry, of the purity, truth, and righteousness, in which all the soldiers of the Messiah should be arrayed!

The armies of the alien cannot stand the onset of those heaven-accoutered soldiers. Kings of armies flee apace. They are bowed down and fallen in bittered, hopeless defeat. In the time of God's anger they are swallowed up in His wrath; their dead bodies strew the battlefield. As the triumphant army returns singers and minstrels, Benjamin and Judah, Zebulun and Naphtali, join in the mighty anthem: "God is unto us a God of deliverances."

All this has a further reference. In David we have a type of the Messiah. For, of a truth, against the Holy Servant Jesus, whom God has anointed, both the Gentiles and the peoples of Israel have gathered together. Men have refused His sway, and do refuse it; but God hath sworn, and will not repent, that to Him every knee shall bow, and every tongue confess: and it is more sure than that tomorrow's sun will rise that, before long, great voices shall be heard in heaven, saying, "The kingdoms of the world are become the kingdoms of our Lord, and of His Christ: and He shall reign for ever and ever" (Rev. 11:15-18).

11

Chastened for Sin

II Samuel 11-19

The Sin of David's Life
The chronicler omits this terrible blot on David's life, but the older record sets down each item without excuse. Myriads in the same dark labyrinth of sin, have discovered the glimmer of light by which the soul may pass back into the day. "Thy sins, which are many, are forgiven thee; go in peace."

The Circumstances
For seventeen years David had enjoyed prosperity and adulation. This was fraught with peril. The rigors of the Alps are less to be dreaded than the heat of the enervating plains of the Campagna. In direct violation of the law of Moses, David took unto him more concubines and wives, sowing to himself the inevitable harvest of quarreling and crime, besides fostering in himself sensual indulgence. He had also yielded to indolence, allowing Joab and his brave soldiers to do the fighting around Rabbah, while he tarried at Jerusalem.

One afternoon the king was lounging on his palace roof. In that hour there came a truant thought, to satisfy whose hunger he descended into the home of a poor man and took his one ewe lamb, although his own folds were filled with flocks. The Scripture record lays the burden of the sin on the king alone, before whose absolute power Bath-sheba may have felt herself obliged to yield. One brief spell of passionate indulgence, and then!—his character blasted irretrievably; his peace vanished; the foundations of his kingdom imperiled; the Lord displeased; and great occasion given to his enemies to blaspheme! Let us beware of our light, unguarded hours. Middle life has no immunity from temptations and perils which beset the young. One false step may ruin a reputation built up by years of spiritual vigor.

The results could not be hidden; instant steps must be taken to veil the sin—Uriah must come home! He came, but he refused to go to his home while the great war was still in process. There was no alternative but that he should die; if a child was to be born, Uriah's lips should not disown it. He bore to Joab, all unwitting, the letter which was his own death warrant. Uriah was set in the forefront to die. Bathsheba lamented for her dead husband, and within seven days was taken into David's house. A great relief this—the child would be born under the cover of lawful wedlock! There was one fatal flaw, however, "The thing that David had done displeased the Lord" (II Sam. 11:27). David and the world were to hear more of it. But oh, the bitter sorrow, that he who had spoken of walking with a perfect heart in Divine fellowship, with all the splendid record of his life, should have fallen thus! The psalmist, the king, the lover of God, all trampled in the mire by one dark, passionate outburst. Oh to wear the white flower of a blameless life to the end!

Delayed Repentance

The better the man, the dearer the price he pays for sinful pleasure. For twelve whole months the royal sinner wrapped his sin in his bosom and refused to confess. But in Psalm 32 he tells us how he felt. His bones waxed old; he was parched with fever heat, day and night God's hand lay heavily upon him.

Nathan's advent must have been a positive relief. He told what seemed to be a real story of highhanded wrong; and David's anger was greatly kindled. Then as lightning on a dark night suddenly reveals to the traveler the precipice, the awful sentence, "Thou art the man!" revealed David to himself and brought him to his knees. Nathan reminded him of the past, specially the unstinted goodness of God. A sunny background made recent events look the darker. "Thou hast despised His word; thou hast slain Uriah; thou hast taken his wife. The child shall die; thy wives shall be treated as thou hast dealt with his; out of thine own house evil shall rise against thee." "I have sinned against the Lord," was David's confession, followed by a flood of tears—and instantly his scorched heart found relief. Oh, blessed showers that visit parched souls!

When Nathan had gone, he beat out that brief confession into Psalm 51, that all the world might use it. The one sin and the many transgressions; the evil done against God; the in-bred evil; the ache of the broken bones; the unclean heart; the loss of joy; the fear of forfeiting the Holy Spirit; the broken and contrite heart—thus the surcharged waters of the inner lake broke forth turbid and dark. Ah, those cries for God's mercies! Nothing less could erase the dark legend from the book of remembrance, or rub out the stains from his robe, or make the leprous flesh whole. To be clean; to be whiter than snow; to sing aloud once more; to be infilled with a steadfast spirit; to point transgressors to the Father— these were the petitions that sin-weary heart laid upon the altar, sweeter than burnt offering or incense. Immediately on his acknowledgment of sin, Nathan said, "The Lord hath put away thy sin." "I said, I will confess my transgressions unto the Lord, and Thou forgavest the iniquity of my sin."

Penitent soul! Believe in the instantaneous forgiveness of sins. Confession is interrupted with the outbreak of the Father's love, which while it hates sin, yearns over the prodigal.

Sin is dark, dangerous, damnable: but it cannot staunch the love of God that dates from eternity. The only thing that can really hurt the soul is to keep its confession pent within itself. If it dares to cry, "Be merciful to me, the sinner, for the sake of the blood that was shed," it instantly becomes white as snow on Alpine peaks.

The Stripes of God and Men

Sin may be forgiven and yet a long train of sad consequences ensue. The law of cause and effect will follow on though God's mercy to His repentant children will be shown in converting the results of their sin into the fires of their purification; in setting alleviation against their afflictions; and in finally staying further evil. All these facts stand out upon the pages which tell the story of God's chastisement, alleviations, and deliverances.

He will forgive, but He may have to use the rod; He may restore to His favor, and yet permit us to drink bitter waters. Be patient and submissive; thou wilt come forth a white soul, and men shall learn through thy experiences the goodness and severity of God.

God's Chastisements

Bath-sheba's little child was very sick and the father fasted and lay on the earth. He suffered more in seeing the anguish of the babe than if ten times its pain had been inflicted on himself. It cuts to the quick when the innocent suffer for our crimes. On the seventh day the child died.

Two years after, one of his sons treated his sister as David had treated Uriah's wife. A man never sees the worst of himself until it reappears in his child. In Ammon's sin David beheld his own unbridled passions; and in his murder by Absalom David encountered again his own blood-guiltiness. Absalom's fratricide would never have taken place if David had punished Ammon. But how could he allot that penalty to his son's impurity which he had evaded for himself? Nor could he punish Absalom for murder, when he had eluded the murderer's fate.

When Absalom's rebellion broke out, it received the immediate adherence of David's most trusted counselor. What swept Ahithophel into that great conspiracy? The reason is given in the genealogical tables, which show that he was the grandfather of Bath-sheba, and that his son Eliam was the comrade of Uriah.

It is thought that at this time David was smitten with some severe form of disease. Psalms 41 and 55 are supposed to record his sufferings; they tell his depression, the visitors that surrounded his bed, and the comments they passed on the sick man.

The most terrible blow of all was the rebellion of Absalom. His beautiful figure; ready wit; apparent sympathy with the anxieties and disappointments of the people; his sumptuous splendor—all these had for four years been undermining David's throne, and stealing away the hearts of the people: so when he erected his standard at Hebron and was proclaimed king it was evident that the people had lost their former reverence and love for David—perhaps the story of his sin had alienated them, and they hurried to pay their homage at the shrine of the new prince.

We need not recount the successive steps of those stormy days. The panic-stricken flight of the king; the barefoot ascent of Olivet; the anguish that wept; the shameful cursing of Shimei; the apparent treachery of Mephibosheth; the humiliation of David's wives; the gathering of all Israel together unto Absalom—such were the strokes of the Father's rod that fell fast upon His child. They appeared to emanate from the malignity of man; but David knew that the cup held to his lips had been mixed by heaven, and was not the punishment of a Judge, but the chastisement of a Father.

Outside the story of Christ, there is nothing more beautiful than David's behavior through this tangle of thorns. "Carry back the Ark of God," he said to Zadok; "He may bring me again to see both it and His habitation; but if not, behold, here am I, let Him do to me as seemeth good unto Him." And when Shimei called him a man of blood, David said to Abishai, "The Lord hath permitted him to curse, and who shall say, Wherefore hast thou done so?" Thus when Judas brought the bitter cup to Christ, the Master said, "It is the cup My Father hath given Me to drink." Let us never forget the lesson. Pain and sorrow may be devised against us, but if God permits such things to reach us, by the time that they have passed through the thin wire of His sieve they have become His will for us; and we may look up into His face and know that we are not the sport of chance, or wild misfortune, but are being trained as sons.

God's Alleviations

They came in many ways. The bitter hour of trial revealed a love on the part of his adherents of which the old king may have become a little oblivious.

Ahithophel's defection cut him to the quick. He tells the story in the psalms. He winced to think that the friend in whom he trusted had lifted up his heel against him; but then Hushai came to meet him with grief, and was willing as his friend to plead in the council chamber of Absalom.

Shimei might curse him; but Ittai the stranger, a man of Gath, with all his men, sware allegiance for life or death.

Zadok and Abiathar are there with the Ark in common sorrow for their master; Ziba meets him with summer fruits and loaves of bread; Shobi, and Machir, and Barzillai make provision for his hungry and thirsty followers; his people tell him that he must not enter the battle, because his life is priceless, and worth ten thousand of theirs. It was as though God stooped over that stricken soul, and as the blows of the rod cut furrows in the sufferer's back, the balm of Gilead was poured into the gaping wounds. Voices spoke gently; pitiful compassion rained tender assurances; and the bright-harnessed angels of God's protection encamped about his path and his lying down.

Thus he came to sing some of his sweetest songs, and among them Psalm 3, 4, 61, 62, 143. The two former are his morning and evening hymns, when his cedar palace was exchanged for the blue canopy of the sky. He has many adversaries, who say, "There is no help for him in God"; but he reckons that he is well guarded.

He is not afraid of ten thousands of the people; he lies down in peace and awakes in safety, because the Lord sustains him. The Lord hath set him apart for Himself, and the light of His face will put more gladness into his heart than the treasures of the kingdom which he seemed to have forfeited for ever. Then in the drought-smitten land his soul thirsts to see the power and glory of God, as in the sanctuary; and already he realizes satisfaction. To long for God is to find Him; to thirst after Him is to feel water flowing over the parched lips. With these came a clear prevision of the issue of the terrible strife: "The king shall rejoice in God: Every one that sweareth by Him shall glory: But the mouth of them that speak lies shall be stopped."

God's Deliverance

The raw troops of Absalom were unable to stand the shock of David's veterans, and fled. Absalom himself was dispatched by the ruthless Joab. The Pendulum of the people's loyalty swang back to its old allegiance; even the men of Judah having so readily followed Absalom, repented; Shimei cringed at his feet; Mephibosheth established his unfaltering loyalty. Barzillai was bound to the royal house for ever. All seemed ending well.

One unfortunate occurrence delayed the peaceful conclusion: Sheba sounded the trumpet of sedition, and the ten tribes immediately seceded, and another formidable revolt yawned at David's feet; and it was only put down by incredible exertions on the part of Joab. The death of Sheba was the last episode in this rebellion.

Many were the afflictions of God's servant, but out of them all he was delivered. When he had learned the lesson, the rod was stayed. He had been chastened with the stripes of God and men: but God did not take away His mercy from him as from Saul: his house, his throne and kingdom, in spite of many conflicting forces, being made sure. Thus always—the chastisements, but amid all the love of God, carrying out His redemptive purpose, never hasting, never resting, never forgetting, but making all things work together till the evil is eliminated, and the soul purged. Then the afterglow of blessing, the calm ending of the life in a serene sundown.

12

Seeing the Temple at Sunset

I Chronicles 22-29

A period of ten years of comparative repose was granted David between the revolts of Absalom and Sheba and his death. It is probable that David walked softly and humbly with God, concentrating on the erection of the Temple.

The Site
This was indicated in the following manner. He conceived the design of numbering Israel and Judah. The chronicler says that Satan moved him to it, while the older record attributes the suggestion to the anger of the Lord. It is not impossible to reconcile these two statements, since the Old Testament writers so frequently attribute to God's agency what we would refer to His permissive Providence.

The sin of numbering the people probably lay in its motive. David was animated by a spirit of pride; he was eager to make a fine show among the surrounding nations. There was a tendency to exchange waiting on God for trust in human prowess. In spite of the remonstrances of Joab and others, the king persisted.

When the enumeration was nearly complete, David's heart smote him, and he said unto the Lord: "I have sinned greatly in that I have done." He saw how far he had swerved from the idea of the theocracy, in which God's sovereignty alone determined the nation's policy. He had substituted his own whim for the Divine edict. He might be forgiven, but must submit to one of three modes of chastisement. It was wise to choose to fall into the hands of God; but the plague, sweeping through the country, came like a destroying army to the holy city, and it seemed as if the angel of the Lord were hovering, sword in hand, to begin his terrible commission. Then David cried unto the Lord, pleading that His judgments might be stayed. And the angel of the Lord stayed by the threshing floor of Araunah—there on Mount Moriah, where centuries before the angel had stayed the uplifted knife of Abraham, God said, "It is enough; stay thine hand." That spot became the site of the temple.

The Builder
The last year of David's life, and the fortieth of his reign, was embittered by a final revolt. It stirred the old lionheart, and he aroused himself with a flash of his former energy for the erection of the Divine will communicated to him years before. Not many hours passed before Solomon had been anointed king in Gihon, by Zadok and Nathan.

It was probably about this time that David gave Solomon the charge to build the house for God. He recapitulated the steps by which he had been led: he then enumerated the treasures he had accumulated, and the preparatory works which had been set on foot. At the close of this solemn charge, he added instructions to direct Solomon in his behavior towards Joab and Shimei for the peace of the realm.

The Pattern
David's choice must be ratified in a popular assembly, gathered at the royal command (I Chron. 28:1). What an august spectacle must that have been when for the last time the aged king stood face to face with the men who had helped to make Israel great, many of whom had followed him from comparative obscurity! He recited the circumstances of his desire to build the temple, and the substitution of Solomon

for himself. Then turning to the stripling that stood beside him, he bade him be strong and carry out the Divine purpose.

Next followed the pattern of all the house, communicated to David by the Spirit of God, and an inventory of the treasures from which each article was to be constructed. To David's imagination the splendid temple stood forth in every part complete. His contribution had been most munificent; and he turned to the vast concourse, asking princes and people to fill their hands with gifts. The response was splendid. It is probable that never before or since has such a contribution been made at one time for religious purposes; but, better than all, the gifts were made willingly and gladly.

With a full heart David blessed the Lord before all the congregation. His lips were touched with the olden fire; his thoughts expanded beneath the warmth of his imagination, and rose to heaven; he ascribed to Jehovah the universal kingdom, and recognized that all which had been contributed that day had been first received. Standing upon the threshold of the other world, his days seemed as a shadow in which there was no abiding; and then the king and father pleaded for Solomon, that he might keep the Divine statutes and build the house. Lastly, he turned to the people, and bade them join in ascriptions of praise, and there went forth such a shout of jubilation, of blessing and praise, that the welkin rang again; while a great religious festival crowned the proceedings.

It was a worthy conclusion to a great life! How long after David lingered, we cannot tell. One record says simply that "David slept with his fathers, and was buried in the city of David"; another, that "he died in a good old age, full of days, riches, and honor." But perhaps the noblest is that uttered by the Holy Spirit, through Paul, "David, after he had served his own generation according to the will of God, fell on sleep and saw corruption."

Like a tired infant's, those aged eyes closed in the last sleep, and the spirit joined the mighty dead. His sepulchre remained to the day of Pentecost, for Peter refers to it; but the man whom God had raised up was drinking of the river of His pleasures, and became satisfied as he awoke in His likeness. The fairest dreams of his Lord that had ever visited his soul fell short of the reality; and upon his aged face must have rested in death a look of glad surprise, as though the half had not been told.

BOOK V: ELIJAH

1

The Source of Elijah's Strength

I Kings 17

This chapter begins with the conjunction "And": it is, therefore, an addition to what has gone before; and it is *God's* addition.

That "And" is ominous enough to His foes; but it is full of hope and promise to His friends.

Things were dark enough. After the death of Solomon, his kingdom split into two parts—the southern under Rehoboam his son; the northern under Jeroboam, who was desperately eager to keep his hold on his people; but he feared to lose it, if they continued to go, two or three times in the year, to the annual feasts at Jerusalem. He resolved, therefore, to set up the worship of Jehovah in his own territories; and erected two temples, one at Dan, in the extreme north, the other at Bethel, in the extreme south. And in each of these he placed a golden calf; that the God of Israel might be worshiped "under the form of a calf that eateth hay."

After many revolutions, and much bloodshed, the kingdom passed into the hands of a military adventurer, Omri. The son of this man was Ahab, of whom it is said, "he did more to provoke the Lord God of Israel to anger than all the kings of Israel that were before him" (I Kings 16:33).

When the young and beautiful Jezebel left the palaces of Tyre, to become the consort of the newly crowned king of Israel, it was no doubt regarded as a splendid match. But, like many a splendid match, it was fraught with misery and disaster. No one can disobey God's plain words against intermarriage with the ungodly without suffering for it at last.

As she left her palace home, Jezebel would be vehemently urged by the priests to do her utmost to introduce into Israel the hideous and cruel rites of her hereditary religion. Shrines and temples began to rise in all parts of the land in honor of these false deities; while the altars of Jehovah were ruthlessly broken down.

But God is never at a loss. The land may be overrun with sin; the lamps of witness may seem all extinguished; the whole force of the popular current may run counter to His truth; and the plot may threaten to be within a hair's breadth of entire success; but, all the time, He will be preparing a weak man in some obscure highland village; and in the moment of greatest need will send him forth, as His all-sufficient answer to the worst plottings of His foes.

An Inhabitant of Gilead

Gilead lay east of the Jordan; it was wild and rugged; its hills were covered with shaggy forests; its valleys were the haunt of fierce wild beasts. The inhabitants of Gilead partook of the character of their country—wild, lawless, and unkempt. They dwelt in rude stone villages; and subsisted by keeping flocks of sheep.

Elijah grew up like the other lads of his age, a shepherd on those wild hills. As he grew to manhood, his erect figure, his shaggy locks, his cloak of camel's hair, his muscular, sinewy strength distinguished him from the dwellers in lowland valleys; but we must not look to these things for the secret of his strength.

Deeply taught in Scripture, Elijah yearned, with passionate desire, that his people should give God His meed of honor. And when the dread tidings came of what was transpiring across the Jordan; how Jezebel had thrown down God's altars, and slain His prophets, and replaced them by the impious rites of her Tyrian deities—his blood ran liquid fire; his indignation burst all bounds; he was "very jealous for the Lord God of hosts."

But the question was, How should he act? What could he do, a wild, untutored child of the desert? There was only one thing he could do—the resource of all much-tried souls—he could pray; and he did: "he prayed earnestly" (James 5:17). And in his prayer he seems to have been led back to a denunciation made, years before, by Moses to the people—that if they turned aside, and served other gods and worshiped them, the Lord's wrath would be kindled against them; and He would shut up the heaven, that there should be no rain (Deut. 11:17). And so he set himself to pray that the terrible threat might be literally fulfilled. "He prayed earnestly that it might not rain."

A terrible prayer indeed! Granted; and yet, was it not more terrible for the people to forget and ignore the God of their fathers, and to give themselves up to the licentious orgies of Baal and Astarte? Remember, too, what a wrong construction might be put upon the utter silence of God Himself. "These things hast thou done, and I kept silence; thou thoughtest that I was altogether such an one as thyself: but I will reprove thee, and set them in order before thine eyes."

Physical suffering is a smaller calamity than moral delinquency. And the love of God does not shrink from inflicting such suffering, if, as a result, the plague of sin may be cut out as a cancer, and stayed. It may be, reader, that this is why there is so much sorrow in thy life. Thou art suffering a terrible drought, before which all the springs of thy prosperity are drying up. This is not a chance; it is the work of One who loves thee too well to permit thee to forsake Himself without making one effort to arrest and change thee.

As Elijah prayed, the conviction was wrought into his mind that it should be even as he prayed; and that he should go to acquaint Ahab with the fact. Whatever might be the hazard to himself, both king and people must be made to connect their calamities with the true cause.

This interview needed no ordinary moral strength. It was no child's play for the untutored child of the desert to go on such an errand to that splendid court! Yet he went and came unhurt, in the panoply of a might which seemed invulnerable.

What was the secret of that strength? If it can be shown that it was due to something inherent in Elijah, and peculiar to himself; some special quality of soul, to which ordinary men can lay no claim—then we may as well close our enquiries, and turn away from the inaccessible heights that mock us. But if it can be shown, as I think it can, that this splendid life was lived, not by its inherent qualities, but by sources of strength which are within the reach of the humblest child of God who reads these lines, then every line of it is an inspiration, beckoning us to its own glorious level.

Elijah's strength did not lie in himself or his surroundings. He was of humble extraction. He is expressly said to have been "a man of like passions" with ourselves. When the natural soil of his nature shows itself, it is not richer than that of the majority of men; and, if anything, it is the reverse.

Elijah gives us three indications of the source of his strength. *"As Jehovah liveth."* To all beside, Jehovah might seem dead; but to him, He was the one supreme reality of life. The man who has heard Jesus say, "I am He that liveth," will also hear Him say, "Fear not! be strong, yea, be strong."

"Before whom I stand." He was standing in the presence of Ahab; but he was conscious of the presence of a greater than any earthly monarch, even the presence of Jehovah. Let us cultivate this habitual recognition of the presence of God; it will lift us above all other fear.

The word "Elijah" may be rendered—Jehovah is my God; but there is another possible translation—*Jehovah is my strength.* This gives the key to his life. God was the strength of his life; of whom should he be afraid? What a revelation is given us in this name! Oh that it were true of each of us! Yet, why should it not be? Let us from henceforth cease from our own strength, which, at the best, is weakness; and let us appropriate God's by daily, hourly faith.

2

Beside the Drying Brook

I Kings 17

We are studying the life of a man of like passions with ourselves—weak where we are weak, failing where we would fail; but who stood singlehanded against his people, and stemmed the tide of idolatry and sin, and turned a nation back to God. And he did it by the use of resources which are within reach of us all.

This man, by whom God threshed the mountains, was only a worm at the best. Faith made him all he became; and faith will do as much for us. All power is in God; and it hath pleased Him to store it all in the risen Saviour, as in some vast reservoir; and those stores are brought into human hearts by the Holy Ghost. Oh for Elijah's receptiveness, that we might be able, therefore, to do exploits for God and truth!

But, before this can happen, we must pass through the same education as he. You must go to Cherith and Zarephath before you can stand on Carmel. Even the faith you have must be pruned, and educated, and matured, that it may become strong enough to subdue kingdoms, work righteousness, and turn to flight armies of aliens.

Notice, then, the steps in God's education of His servants.

One Step at a Time
This is an elementary lesson; but it is hard to learn. No doubt Elijah found it so. Before he left Thisbe for Samaria, to deliver the message that burdened his soul, he would naturally inquire, what he should do when he had delivered it. How

would he be received? What would be the outcome? If he had asked those questions of God, and waited for a reply before he left his highland home, he would never have gone at all. Our Father only shows us one step at a time—and that, the next; and He bids us take it in faith.

Directly God's servant took the step to which he was led, and delivered the message, then "the word of the Lord came to him, saying: Get thee hence, hide thyself by the brook Cherith" (vv. 2, 3).

I like that phrase, "the word of the Lord came to him." He did not need to go to search for it; it *came* to him. And so it will come to you. It may come through the Word of God; or through a distinct impression made on your heart by the Holy Ghost; or through circumstances: but it will find you out, and tell you what you are to do.

The Value of the Hidden Life

"Get thee hence, and turn thee eastward, and hide thyself by the brook Cherith." The man who is to take a high place before his fellows, must take a low place before his God; and there is no better manner of bringing a man down, than by dropping him suddenly out of a sphere to which he was beginning to think himself essential and compelling him to consider in the sequestered vale of some Cherith how mixed are his motives, and how insignificant his strength.

Every saintly soul that would wield great power with men must win it in some hidden Cherith. The acquisition of spiritual power is impossible, unless we can hide ourselves from men and from ourselves in some deep gorge, where we may absorb the power of the eternal God; as vegetation through long ages absorbed those qualities of sunshine, which it now gives back through burning coal.

Not one of us therefore can dispense with some Cherith, where we may taste the sweets and imbibe the power of a life hidden with Christ, and in Christ by the power of the Holy Ghost. Sometimes a human spirit, intent on its quest, may even find its Cherith in a crowd; of such a one God is its all-sufficient abode, and the secret place of the Most High its most holy place.

Trusting God Absolutely

We yield at first a timid obedience to a command which seems to involve manifest impossibilities; but when we find that God is even better than His word, our faith groweth exceedingly, and we advance to further feats of faith and service. This is how God trains His young eaglets to fly. At last nothing is impossible. This is the key to Elijah's experience.

One evening, as we may imagine, Elijah reached the narrow gorge, down which the brook bounded with musical babble toward the Jordan. All along the streamlet's course the moss would make a carpet of richer hue and softer texture than could be found in the palaces of kings. And, yonder, came the young ravens—"the young ravens that lack and suffer hunger," bringing bread and flesh. What a lesson was this of God's power to provide for His child! In after days Elijah would often recur to it, as dating a new epoch in his life. "I can never doubt God again. I am thankful that He shut me off from all other supplies, and threw me back on Himself. I am sure that He will never fail me, whatsoever the circumstances of strait or trial through which He may call me to pass."

There is strong emphasis on the word *there*. "I have commanded the ravens to feed thee *there*" (v. 4). Elijah might have preferred many hiding-places to Cherith; but that was the only place to which the ravens would bring his supplies; and, as long as he was there, God was pledged to provide for him. Our supreme thought should be: "Am I where God wants me to be?" If so, God will work a direct miracle, sooner than suffer us to perish for lack. The manna always accompanies the pillar of cloud. If we do His will on earth, He will give us daily bread.

Sitting by Drying Brooks

"It came to pass after a while that the brook dried up" (v. 9). Our wildest fancy can but inadequately realize the condition to which the Land of Promise was reduced by the first few months of drought. There was no rain to revive vegetation, or replenish the supplies of water. There was no dew, to sprinkle the parched, cracked earth with refreshing tears. And so Cherith began to sing less cheerily. Its voice grew fainter and fainter; till its bed became a course of stones, baking in the scorching heat. It dried up.

What did Elijah think? Did he think that God had forgotten him? Did he begin to make plans for himself? This would have been human; but we will hope that he waited quietly for God, quieting himself as a weaned child, as he sang, "My soul, wait thou only upon God; for my expectation is from Him."

Many of us have had to sit by drying brooks; perhaps some are sitting by them now—the drying brook of popularity, the drying brook of health, the drying brook of money, the drying brook of friendship, which for long has been diminishing, and threatens soon to cease. Ah, it is hard to sit beside a drying brook—much harder than to face the prophets of Baal on Carmel.

Why does God let them dry? He wants to teach us not to trust in His gifts but in Himself. He wants to loosen our roots ere He removes us to some other sphere of service and education. He wants to put in stronger contrast the river of throne-water that never dries. Let us learn these lessons, and turn from our failing Cheriths to our unfailing Saviour. All sufficiency resides in Him—unexhausted by the flight of the ages; undiminished by the thirst of saints. "He that drinketh of this water shall thirst again: but he that drinketh of the water that I shall give him shall never thirst; but it shall be in him a well of water, springing up into everlasting life" (John 4:14).

3

Ordered to Zarephath

I Kings 17

A friend of mine, spending a few days in the neighborhood of our English lakes, came upon the most beautiful shrubs he had ever seen. Arrested by their extraordinary luxuriance, he inquired the cause; and learned that it was due to a judicious system of transplanting, constantly pursued. Whatever may be the effect of such a process in nature, it is certainly true that our heavenly Father employs similar methods to secure the highest results in us. He is constantly transplanting us. And though these changes threaten at times to hinder all steady progress in the Divine life, yet, if they are rightly borne, they result in the most exquisite manifestations of Christian character and experience.

Another illustration of the same truth is given by the prophet Jeremiah, when he says, "Moab hath been at ease from his youth; and he hath settled on his lees; and hath not been emptied from vessel to vessel; neither hath he gone into captivity: therefore his taste remained in him, and his scent is not changed" (Jer. 48:11). Grape juice, when first expressed is impure and thick; it is left in vessels for a time till fermentation has done its work, and a thick sediment, called lees, has been precipitated to the bottom. When this is done, the liquid is carefully drawn off into another vessel, so that all the precipitated sediment is left behind. This emptying process is repeated again and again, till the offensive odor that came from the *"must"* has passed away, and the liquid has become clear and beautiful.

Will not this cast light upon God's dealings with Elijah? Once he stood in the vessel, "Home"; then emptied into the vessel "Jezreel"; then into the vessel, "Cherith"; and now into the fourth vessel, "Zarephath": and all that he might not settle upon his lees, but might be urged towards a goal of moral greatness. Take heart, ye who are compelled to be constantly on the move—pitching the tent tonight, and summoned by the moving cloud and the trumpet call to strike it tomorrow. Believe only that your circumstances are those most suited to develop your character. They have been selected out of all possible combinations of events and conditions, in order to effect in you the highest finish of usefulness and beauty; they would have been the ones selected by you, if all the wide range of omniscient knowledge had been within your reach.

Waiting

"It came to pass, after awhile, that the brook dried up, because there had been no rain in the land" (v. 7). Week after week, with unfaltering and steadfast spirit, Elijah watched that dwindling brook; often tempted to stagger through unbelief, but refusing to allow his circumstances to come between himself and God. The birds fled; the wild creatures of field and forest came no more to drink; the brook was dry. Only then, to his patient and unwavering spirit "the word of the Lord came, saying, Arise, get thee to Zarephath" (v. 9).

Most of us would have got anxious and worn with planning long before that. We are all too full of our own schemes, and plans, and contrivings. We sketch out our program and rush into it; and only when we are met by insuperable obstacles do we begin to reflect whether it was God's will, or to appeal to Him.

Would that we were content to wait for God to unveil His plan, so that our life might be simply the working out of His thought, the exemplification of His ideal!

Obedience

"So he arose and went to Zarephath," as before he had gone to Cherith, and as presently he would go to show himself to Ahab.

This is the turning point in many Christian lives. We catch sight of God's ideal; we vow to be only His; we dedicate ourselves upon the altar. Then there comes a command clear and unmistakable. We must leave some beloved Cherith, and go to some unwelcome Zarephath; we must speak some word, take some step, cut off some habit: and we shrink from it—the cost is too great. But, directly we refuse obedience, the light dies off the landscape of our lives, and dark clouds fling their shadows far and near.

We do not win salvation by our obedience. But, being saved, we must obey. Our Saviour adjures us, by the love we bear to Himself, to keep His commandments. And He does so because He wants us to taste His rarest gifts; and because He knows that in the keeping of His commandments there is great reward.

Trials

"Zarephath" means a smelting furnace. It lay outside the Land of Canaan. Many things might have made it distasteful to the prophet. It belonged to the land from which Jezebel had brought her impious tribe. It was impossible to reach it save by a weary journey of 100 miles. And then to be sustained by a widow woman belonging to a heathen people! Surely it was a smelting furnace for cleansing out any alloy of pride, or self-reliance, or independence which might be lurking in the recesses of his heart.

And there was much of the refining fire in the character of his reception. When he reached the straggling town it was probably toward nightfall; and at the city gate a widow woman was gathering a few sticks to prepare the evening meal. The widow may have had some premonition of his coming. There would seem to be some suggestion of this in the words, *"I have commanded* a widow woman to sustain thee." There must have been something in her which could not be found in the many widows of the land of Israel (Luke 4:25, 26).

She was not, therefore, surprised at the prophet's request, and silently went to fetch a cup of cold water (Matt. 10:42). Encouraged by her willingness, Elijah asked her to bring with her a morsel of bread. It was a modest request; but it unlocked the silent agony of her soul. She had not a cake, but a handful of meal in a barrel, and a little oil in a cruse; and she was about to make one last repast for herself and her son and, having eaten it, they had no alternative but to lie down together and die.

It is thus that God leads His people still. He will not suffer us to be tempted beyond that which we are able to bear. But it is written, "Everything that may abide the fire, ye shall make it go through the fire, and it shall be clean" (Num. 31:23). If, then, there is aught in you that can bear the ordeal, be sure you will be put into the furnace. You will be put into it by the hand of Love; and kept in it only till patience has done her perfect work.

God's Bounty

Circumstances were certainly very depressing; but what are they to a man whose inner self is occupied with the presence and power of God? God had said that he should be fed, and by that widow; and so it should be, though the earth and heaven should pass away. And so with heroic faith Elijah said: "Fear not; go and do as thou hast said: for thus saith the Lord God of Israel, The barrel of meal shall not waste, neither shall the cruse of oil fail, until the day that the Lord sendeth rain upon the earth" (v. 14).

Our only need is to inquire if we are at that point in God's pattern where He would have us be. If we are, though it seem impossible for us to be maintained, the thing impossible shall be done. We shall be sustained by a miracle, if no ordinary means will suffice.

4

The Spirit and Power of Elijah

I Kings 17

Who that have traveled in Switzerland can forget the early mornings, when they have been summoned from sleep to await the dawn? A strange light spreads outward from the eastern sky; at last one of the loftiest Alps is smitten with the roseate flush of dawn; then another, and another, till the whole sisterhood of peaks is transfigured with burning splendor. But during all this time, the valleys below are veiled in darkness. And it is only after hours have passed away that the blessed sunlight penetrates to the scattered chalets, sparkles in the brooks, casts shadows from the stones and flowers.

This will illustrate the difference between the dispensation which closed with the first advent of our Lord, and that in which it is our happiness to live. Each has been blessed with the ministry of the Holy Ghost; but it is in this age alone that He has been poured forth, on sons and daughters, on servants and handmaidens (Acts 2:17). In the previous age He was bestowed, in His especial grace and fulness, only on the *elite* of the household of faith. Now the humblest and weakest may be bathed in His divine and sacred influence; but in Elijah's time, those only who were Alpine in their character knew what His eternal fulness meant.

Elijah was one of these men filled with the Holy Ghost. Elisha's one desire was that he should be heir to the Spirit which was so manifestly upon his master (II Kings 2:9). And years after, when the angel of God spake to Zacharias in the Temple, he could find no better illustration of the presence of the Holy Ghost in his promised child, than by saying, "He shall go before Him in the spirit and power of Elias" (Luke 1:15-17).

The glorious ministry of Elijah was therefore due, not to any inherent qualities in himself, but to the extraordinary indwelling of the Holy Ghost—given to him as to other holy men of God, in the old time—through faith. If then we could but have that same Spirit in an equal measure we should be able to repeat his marvelous deeds. So the question for us all is, whether the Holy Ghost is working with and through us in power; if He be, then, though our nature be paltry and weak, He shall effect through us the same mighty deeds as through men vastly our superiors in mental and moral force. Nay, we may even glory in our infirmities, that this Divine power may rest upon us more conspicuously, and that the glory may be more evidently God's.

This is surely what we want. And this is what we may have.

But there are three conditions with which we must comply, if we would receive and keep this blessed gift.

Emptying

God cannot fill us if we are already filled. It took ten days to drain the Apostles but the emptying process was an indispensable preliminary to the Day of Pentecost. For Elijah, this process went on beside the drying brook, and during the long and dreary march to Zarephath, and throughout his sojourn there. It took apparently three years and six months but it was well spent; for in proportion as he became emptied of self, and self-sufficiency, and self-dependence, he became filled with the Spirit of Power: so that Carmel itself, with all its heroic deeds, was gloriously possible to him.

Are we prepared for God to empty us of all that is in any wise contrary to His will? If not, let us ask Him to work in us to will His own good pleasure. But if we are willing, let us present our emptied nature to the Son of God, that He may fill us with the fulness of the Spirit.

We should not seek to know the presence of the Holy Ghost by any signs pointing to Himself. He reveals not Himself, but Christ. He glorifies Him (John 16:14). And the surest symptoms that He is within are—sensitiveness as to sin, tenderness of conscience, and the growing preciousness of Jesus, the fragrance of His name, sympathy with His purposes.

Faithfulness

This is so indispensable, that repeated emphasis must be laid upon it. Christ reiterated His appeals for the keeping of His commands, in almost every sentence of His closing discourses with His disciples (John 14:15, 21, 23, 24). He gives the secret of His own abiding in His Father's love in these striking words: "As the Father gave Me commandment, even so I do. If ye keep My commandments, ye shall abide in My love; even as I have kept My Father's commandments, and abide in His love" (John 15:10). Instant and implicit obedience to the teaching of the Word, and to the inner prompting of the Holy Spirit, is an absolute condition of keeping, or increasing, the store of sacred influence. If only every believer who reads these lines would resolve from this hour to imitate Elijah, who went and did according to the word of the Lord (I Kings 17:5 and 10)—not with the thought of merit, but beneath the inspiration of love; not in the weightier matters only, but in the crossings of the *t's*, and the dottings of the *i's*—they would find at once that there would open before them a life of almost inconceivable glory. It is from the heights of unwavering obedience that we catch sight of the wide and open sea of blessedness. The exact obedience of Elias is the inviolable condition of receiving and keeping "the Spirit and Power of Elias."

Depending on God

Elijah, the widow, and her son, lived on their daily replenished stores; but it was on God's Word that Elijah fed during those long and slow-moving days. And sitting with the widow and her son, he would make that Word the topic of his constant talk; so that she was compelled to refer to it in these significant terms: "I know that the word of the Lord in thy mouth is truth" (I Kings 17:24).

This is the further absolute condition of becoming and remaining filled with the Holy Ghost. The Spirit works with and through the Word. What the wire is to the electric spark; what the corn-grain is to the spirit of life—that the Word of God is to the Spirit of God. If then we neglect the reverent study of Scripture, we cut ourselves off from the very vehicle through which God's Spirit enters human spirits.

We may note, in closing, the remarkable admission of the widow: "I know that thou art a man of God" (I Kings 17:24). We talk of the man of letters, the man of honor, the man of mark; but how infinitely better to be known as a man of God. And how splendid the tribute, when we are so addressed by those with whom we have been wont to live! When a man is filled with the Holy Ghost, the more he is known, the more clearly he is proved to be a man of God.

And the power of the indwelling Spirit evinced itself, in Elijah's case, in the marvelous effect produced on that widow and her child. The widow was convinced of sin, and led to the truth of God. The son was brought back from death into a resurrection life. And such results shall accrue in your experience, if you will only seek to be filled with the fulness of God. "He that believeth in Me, the works that I do shall he do also; and greater works than these shall he do; because I go unto my Father" (John 14:12).

5

The Test of the Home Life

I Kings 17

Many a man might bear himself as a hero and saint in the solitudes of Cherith, or on the heights of Carmel, and yet wretchedly fail in the home life of Zarephath. It is one thing to commune with God in the solitudes of nature, and to perform splendid acts of devotion and zeal for Him in the presence of thousands; but it is quite another to walk with Him day by day in the midst of a home, with its many calls for the constant forgetfulness of self.

If our religion is what it should be, it will resemble the law of gravitation; which not only controls the planets in their spheres, but guides the course of each dust grain. Everything will come beneath its sway—each look, each word, each trivial act. "My grace is sufficient for thee," is the one answer of Jesus Christ to all inquiries; the one reply to all excuses and complaints about trying circumstances.

In our last chapter, we saw something of the power and Spirit with which Elijah was filled and endued. But we are now to follow him into a home, and see how he bears the test of home life; and we shall learn to admire and love him the more.

Contentment

The fare in the widow's home was frugal enough; and there was only sufficient of it for their daily needs. Human nature, which was as strong in the prophet as in the rest of us, would have preferred to be able to count sacks of meal and barrels of oil.

If God were to give us the choice between seeing our provision and keeping it ourselves, or not seeing it and leaving Him to deal it out, day by day, most of us would be almost sure to choose the former alternative. But we should be far wiser to say, "I am content to trust Thee, Father, the living God, who givest us all things richly to enjoy. Keep Thou the stores under Thine own hand, they will give me less anxiety; they will not lead me into temptation; they will not expose me to be jealous of others less favored than myself."

And those who live thus are better off, because the responsibility of maintaining them rests wholly upon God. If God guarantees, as He does, our support, does it much matter whether we can see the sources from which He will obtain it? It might gratify our curiosity, but it would not make them more sure.

Gentleness Under Provocation

We do not know how long the mother hung over her dying child. He may have been struck down like the little fellow who cried, "My head! My head!" and faded in one summer's afternoon; or he may have lingered beneath the spell of a wearying illness, which not only wore out his life, but overtaxed his mother's nerves so that she spoke unadvisedly and cruelly to the man who had brought deliverance to her home: "Art thou come to call my sin to remembrance, and to slay my son?"

A remark, so uncalled-for and unjust, might well have stung the prophet to the quick, or prompted a bitter reply, had his goodness been anything less than inspired by the Holy Ghost. But "The fruit of the Spirit is love, joy, peace, longsuffering, *gentleness*." Elijah simply said, "Give me thy son." If there were a momentary uprising of indignation, it was immediately quelled by the Dove which had come to brood in his heart.

If the Holy Spirit is really filling the heart, there will come

over the rudest, the least refined, the most selfish, a marvelous change; there will be a gentleness in speech, in the very
tones of the voice; a tender thoughtfulness in the smallest
actions; a peace passing understanding on the face; and
these shall be the evident seal of the Holy Ghost, the mint-
mark of heaven. Are they evident in ourselves?

The Power of a Holy Life

Somewhere in the background of this woman's life there was
a dark deed, which stood out before her mind as her sin—
"my sin" (I Kings 17:18). It may have been connected with
the birth of that very son. It had probably been committed
long years before, and had then filled her with a keen agony
of mind. But of later years, the keen sense of remorse had
become dulled; sometimes she even lost all recollection of her
sin for weeks and months together.

It is remarkable how different is the mental stimulus which
is required by different castes of mind, to awaken dormant
memories. But in the case of the woman of Zarephath it was
Elijah's holy life, combined with her own terrible sorrow.
Beneath the spell of these two voices her memory gave up its
dead, and her conscience was quickened into vigorous life.
"Art thou come unto me to call my sin to remembrance?"

Oh to live in the power of the Holy Ghost! Our looks
would sometimes then convict the stoutest sinners of sin; as
it is recorded of Finney, whose grieved face brought conviction to a young woman, and through her to a whole factory of
operatives. Our holy walk would be a standing rebuke; our
words would then be sharp two-edged swords, piercing to
the dividing of the joints and marrow, of soul and spirit.

The Secret of Giving Life

It is a characteristic of those who are filled with the Holy
Ghost, that they carry with them everywhere the spirit of
life, even resurrection-life. But mark the conditions under
which alone we shall be able to fulfil this glorious function.

Lonely wrestlings. "He took him out of her bosom, and

carried him up into a loft, where he abode, and laid him upon his own bed. And he cried unto the Lord" (vv. 19, 20). We are not specific enough in prayer; and we do not spend enough time in intercession, dwelling with holy ardor on each beloved name, and on each heart-rending case. What wonder that we achieve so little!

Humility. "He measured himself upon the child" (v. 21). How wonderful that so great a man should spend so much time and thought on that slender frame, and be content to bring himself into direct contact with that which might be thought to defile! It is a touching spectacle; but we must imitate it in some measure.

Perseverance. "He measured himself three times, and cried unto the Lord" (v. 21). He was not soon daunted. It is thus that God tests the genuineness of our desire. These deferred answers lead us to lengths of holy boldness and pertinacity of which we should not otherwise have dreamed, but from which we shall never go back.

And his supplications met with the favor of God. "The Lord heard the voice of Elijah; and the soul of the child came into him again, and he revived" (v. 22). And as the prophet presented him to the grateful and rejoicing mother, he must have been beyond all things gratified with her simple testimony to the reality and power of the life which the Holy Ghost had begotten within him: "Now by this I know that thou art a man of God, and that the word of the Lord in thy mouth is truth" (v. 24).

6

The Plan of Campaign

I Kings 18

After many days the word of the Lord again summoned Elijah to be on the move. Months, and even years, had passed in the retirement of Zarephath; the widow and her son had become bound to him by the most sacred ties; the humble home, with its loft and barrel of meal and cruse of oil, was hallowed with delightful memories of the unfailing carefulness of God.

When Elijah left Zarephath, it is more than probable that his mind was utterly destitute of any fixed plan of action. He knew that he must show himself to Ahab; and that rain was not far away: for these were his definite marching orders—"Go, show thyself unto Ahab; and I will send rain upon the earth" (v. 1). But more than that he knew not.

The plan of this great campaign for God against Baal, for truth against error, may have been suddenly revealed to Elijah on his journey from Zarephath to find Ahab. But it is quite as likely that it was revealed in pieces, like the separate bits of a children's puzzle—handed out, one by one, from the parent to the child, who might be confused to do with more than one at a time. This is so often God's way; and they who trust Him utterly are quite pleased to have it so. There is even a novelty and beauty in life, when every step is unforeseen and unexpected, and opens up new vistas of loveliness in God's management and in Himself.

If we seek to think ourselves into Elijah's attitude of heart and mind, as he left the shelter of Zarephath, and began to pass through the incidents that culminated in Carmel, it seems to have been threefold. And surely it is of surpassing interest to learn how such a man felt, as he approached the sublime crisis of his life.

Inspired by God

"Let it be known that Thou art God in Israel" (v. 36). He neither knew nor cared to know what would become of himself; but his soul was on fire with a holy jealousy for the glory of God. He could not bear to think of those wrecked altars or martyred prophets. He could not bear to think that his people were beginning to imagine that the God of Abraham, of Isaac, and of Israel had abdicated in favor of these false deities brought newly in. And when he was compelled to face these things, his spirit was stirred to its depths with indignation and sorrow.

Well would it be if each one of us were similarly inspired! We are very eager for the success of *our* work, *our* church, *our* sect. We are wholly occupied with the interests of our own tiny pools, oblivious of the great sea of divine glory lying near by, in perpetual sunshine. Is it strange that we have so small a measure of success? But in this, also, God is willing to lift our daily experience to the level of our loftiest ideals. Only trust Him to do it; ask and expect Him to fill you with the fire of that zeal which burnt in the heart of Elijah. It was not more natural to him than it is to any one of us. It was simply one of the fruits of the indwelling of the Holy Ghost.

Only a Servant

"Let it be known that Thou art God in Israel; *and that I am Thy servant.*" It was not for the slave in olden times to originate, or scheme, or plan; but to be pliant to the least expression of the master's will. And this was the attitude of Elijah's spirit—surrendered, yielded, emptied; plastic to the hands that reach down out of heaven molding men.

This attitude is the true one for us all. Are we not too fond of doing things for God, instead of letting God do what He chooses through us? We often miss doing what He sorely wants to do, because we insist on carrying out some little whim of our own. This is the blight on much of the activity of Christian people at the present time. They are not satisfied to be as the Apostle Paul was, "the slave of Jesus Christ" (Rom. 1:1, marg.).

Working Out God's Plan

"Let it be known this day that Thou art God in Israel; and that I am Thy servant; and *that I have done all these things according to Thy word.*" When once a man feels that he is working out God's plan, and that God is working out His plan through him, he is invincible. God's plan is His purpose; and God's purpose shall be accomplished, though earth and heaven pass away. And this was doubtless one element in Elijah's splendid strength.

There are many ways of learning God's plan. Sometimes it is revealed *in circumstances*—not always pleasant; but ever acceptable, because revealing our Father's will. Sometimes God's plan is revealed *by strong impressions of duty*, which increase in proportion as they are prayed over, and are tested by the Word of God.

There are many voices by which God can speak His will to the truly surrendered spirit. If there is any confusion as to what it is, it is due to one of these two causes: either the will is not fully yielded to do God's will, so soon as known or the time of perfect knowledge has not arrived, and we must be content quietly to wait for the salvation of God. It is a true rule for us all, to do nothing, so long as we are in any uncertainty; but to examine ourselves, and to act so soon as we know.

The plan, as Elijah unfolded it to Ahab, was eminently adapted to the circumstances of the case. All Israel was to be gathered by royal summons to Carmel, a noble site for a national meeting ground. Special care was to be taken for to secure the presence of the representatives of the systems that had dared to rival the worship of Jehovah; "the prophets of Baal four hundred and fifty, and the prophets of the Asherah four hundred, which eat at Jezebel's table" (v. 19). A test was then to be imposed on these rival systems, which the adherents of Baal could not possibly refuse; for he was the Sun-god, and this was a trial by fire.

Elijah knew that the altar of Baal would remain smokeless. He was equally sure that Jehovah would answer his faith by fire, as He had done again and again in the glorious past. He felt convinced also that the people, unable to escape the evidence of their senses, would for ever disavow the accursed systems of Phoenicia, and would return once more to the worship of the God of their fathers.

It is probable that, in the case of Ahab, only so much of this plan was disclosed as was necessary to secure the gathering of the people. It is not likely that he would have been so pliant, unless allured by the bait of rain. "So Ahab sent unto all the children of Israel, and gathered the prophets together unto Mount Carmel" (v. 20).

We do not know how this was done; but doubtless the royal word would be passed through the country by a system of messengers. But in any case this summoning of the people must have taken a few days. And it is by that interval of waiting that we are for a moment arrested. It was like the momentary pause before long lines of armed men are launched at each other in the shock of battle.

In my opinion, Elijah spent those memorable days of waiting on Carmel itself; sheltering himself and the lad in some wild cave at night, and by day going carefully over the scene of the approaching conflict. How mournfully would he bend over the stones of that altar, which was broken down! How eagerly would he search out the original twelve stones, strewn recklessly afar, and covered by wild undergrowth. How constantly would he stay himself upon his God, and gird himself for the coming conflict by effectual fervent prayer. Would he not learn the way down to Kishon's brook beneath, and visit the perennial spring, from which he would fill the barrels again and yet again.

It is a sublime spectacle—this yielded, surrendered man, awaiting on Carmel, in steadfast faith, the gathering of the people, and the unfolding of the purpose of God. He had no fear about the issue; and as the days rolled by, his soul rose in higher and ever higher joy. He expected soon to see a nation at the feet of God.

And he was all this, not because he was of a different make to ourselves; but because he had got into the blessed habit of dealing with God at first hand, as a Living Reality, in whose presence it was his privilege and glory always to stand.

7

Conflict on Mount Carmel

I Kings 18

It is early morning upon Mount Carmel. We are standing on the highest point, looking northwards to where Hermon rears its snow-capped head to heaven. Around us on the left lies the Mediterranean Sea. Immediately at Carmel's base winds Kishon's ancient brook, and beyond it stretches the plain of Esdraelon, the garden of Palestine, but now sere and barren with three years' drought. Away there in the distance is the city of Jezreel, with the royal palace and the idol distinctly visible.

From all sides the crowds are making their way towards this spot, which, from the remotest times, has been associated with worship. No work is being done anywhere and the whole thought of young and old is concentrated on that mighty convocation to which Ahab has summoned them.

But our thought turns from the natural panorama. And we fix our thought with intense interest on that one man, who, with flashing eye and compressed lip, awaits the quiet hush which will presently fall upon that mighty concourse. One man against a nation! See, with what malignant glances his every movement is watched by the priests. If they may have their way, he will never touch yonder plain again.

But do not fear for Elijah—he needs no sympathy! He is consciously standing in the presence of One to whom the nations of men are as grasshoppers. All heaven is at his back. He is only a man of like passions with ourselves, but he is full of faith and spiritual power. This very day, by faith you

shall see him subdue a kingdom; work righteousness; escape
the edge of the sword; wax valiant in the fight; and turn to
flight armies of the aliens.

A Remonstrance

"Elijah came unto all the people and said, How long halt ye
between two opinions? If Jehovah be God, follow Him; but if
Baal, then follow him." He did not doubt for a moment that
Jehovah was God. But he wanted to show the people the
absurdity of their position which was illogical. But the time
had come for the nation to be arrested in its attempt to
mingle the worship of Jehovah and of Baal; and compelled to
choose between the two issues that presented themselves.

A Challenge

"The God that answereth by fire, let Him be God." It was a
fair proposal; because Baal was the lord of the sun. The vo-
taries of Baal could not therefore refuse. And every Israelite
could recall many an occasion in the glorious past when
Jehovah had answered by fire. It was the emblem of Jehovah,
and the sign of His acceptance of His people's service.

When Elijah, therefore, proposed that each side should
offer a bullock, and await an answer by fire, he secured the
immediate acquiescence of the people.

That proposal was made in the perfect assurance that God
would not fail him. Was it to be supposed for a moment that
God would push His servant into the front of the battle, and
then leave him? Granted that a miracle must be wrought ere
the sun set: there was no difficulty about that to a man who
lived in the secret place of the Most High. Miracles are only
the results of the higher laws of His presence chamber.

Be sure that you are in God's plan; then forward in God's
name!—the very elements shall obey you, and fire shall leap
from heaven at your command.

Withering Sarcasm

For the first time in their existence, the false priests were
unable to insert the secret spark of fire among the faggots

that lay upon their altar. They were compelled, therefore, to rely on a direct appeal to their patron deity. Round and round the altar they went in the mystic choric dance, and all the while repeating the monotonous chant, "Baal, hear us! Hear us, Baal!" But there was no voice, nor any that answered.

Elijah could ill conceal his delight in their defeat. He could afford to mock them, by suggesting a cause for the indifference of their god: "Cry aloud, for he is a god; either he is talking, or he is pursuing, or he is in a journey, or peradventure he sleepeth, and must be awakened."

Thus three more hours passed by.

An Invitation

His time had come at last; and his first act was to invite the people nearer. He knew what his faith and prayer had won from God; but he wanted the answer of fire to be beyond dispute. As he sought, with reverent care, those scattered stones; and built them together so that the twelve stood as one—meet symbol of the unity of the ideal Israel in the sight of God—the keen glances of the people, in his close proximity, could see that there was no inserted torch or secret spark.

Do we not want a few more, who, amid the scatterings of the present day, can still discern the true unity of the Church, the body of Christ? We may never see that unity visibly manifested until we see the Bride, the Lamb's wife, descend out of heaven from God, having the glory of God. But nevertheless we can enter into God's ideal of it as a spiritual unity, existing unbroken in His thought, and unaffected by the divisions of our times. Is it not clear that, during this age, the Church of Christ was never meant to be a visible corporate body, but to be a great spiritual reality, consisting of all faithful and loyal spirits, in all communions, who, holding the Head, are necessarily one with each other?

A Command

His faith was exuberant. He was so sure of God, that he

dared to heap difficulties in His way, knowing that there is no real difficulty for infinite power. Oh, matchless faith! which can laugh at impossibilities, and can even heap them one upon another, to have the pleasure of seeing God vanquish them.

The altar was reared; the wood laid in order; the bullock cut in pieces: but to prevent any possibility of fraud, and to make the coming miracle still more wonderful, Elijah said, "Fill four barrels with water, and pour it on the sacrifice and on the wood." This they did three times, till the wood was drenched, and the water filled the trench, making it impossible for a spark to travel across.

Alas, few of us have faith like this! We are not so sure of God that we dare to pile difficulties in His way. We all try our best to make it easy for Him to help us. Yet what this man had, we too may have, by prayer and fasting.

A Prayer

Such a prayer! It was quiet and assured, confident of an answer. Its chief burden was that God should vindicate Himself that day, in showing Himself to be God indeed, and in turning the people's heart back to Himself.

Whenever we can so lose ourselves in prayer as to forget personal interest, and to plead for the glory of God, we have reached a vantage from which we can win anything from Him.

Is it strange that "the fire of the Lord fell, and consumed the burnt sacrifice, and the wood, and the stones, and the dust, and licked up the water that was in the trench?" (v. 38). It could not have been otherwise! And let us not think that this is an old-world tale, never to be repeated. If there were the same need, and if any one of us exercised the same faith, we might again see fire descending. Our God is a consuming fire; and when once the unity of His people is recognized, and His presence is sought, He will descend, overcoming all obstacles, and converting a drenched and dripping sacrifice into food on which He Himself can feed.

8
Rain at Last!

I Kings 18

Ahab must have stood by Elijah in the Kishon gorge as sentence was executed against the priests of Baal; not daring to resist the outburst of popular indignation, or to attempt to shield the men whom he had himself encouraged and introduced. When the last priest had bitten the dust, Elijah turned to the king, and said, "Get thee up, eat and drink; for there is a sound of abundance of rain" (v. 41).

What a contrast between these two men! "Ahab went up to eat and drink. And Elijah went up to the top of Carmel; and he cast himself down upon the earth, and put his face between his knees" (v. 42). I think I can see them ascending those heights together: no sympathy; no common joy; no reciprocated thanksgiving. The king turns straight off to his tents; while the servant of God climbs steadily up to the highest part of the mountain, from which a marvelous view could be obtained of the broad expanse of the Mediterranean, which slept under the growing stillness of the coming night.

There are certain characteristics in Elijah's prayer, which we must notice as we pass; because they should form part of all true prayer.

God's Promise

It was based on the promise of God. When Elijah was summoned from Zarephath to resume his public work, his marching orders were capped by the specific promise of rain:

"Go, show thyself unto Ahab; and I will send rain on the earth." To natural reason this might have seemed to render prayer unnecessary. Would not God fulfil His promise, and send the rain, altogether irrespective of further prayer?

God's promises are given, not to restrain, but to incite to prayer. They show the direction in which we may ask, and the extent to which we may expect an answer. They are the signed cheque, made payable to order, which we must endorse and present for payment.

When your child was a toddling, lisping babe, it asked many things wholly incompatible with your nature and its own welfare; but as the years have passed, increasing experience has molded its requests into shapes suggested by yourself. So, as we know more of God through His promises, we are stayed from asking what He cannot give; and are led to set our hearts on things which lie on His open palm waiting to be taken by the hand of an appropriating faith. This is why all prayer, like Elijah's, should be based on promise. We stand on an adamant foundation, and have an irresistible purchase with God, when we can put our finger on His own promise and say, "Do as Thou hast said."

Explicitness

This is where so many prayers fail. They are like letters which require no answer, because they ask for nothing. This is why they are so wanting in power and interest. We do not pray with any expectation of attaining definite and practical results. Let us amend in this matter. Let us keep a list of petitions, which we shall plead before God. Let us direct our prayer, as David did (Psalm 5:3), and look up for the answer; and we shall find ourselves obtaining new and unwonted blessings. Be definite!

Earnestness

"Elijah prayed earnestly." This is the testimony of the Holy Spirit, through the Apostle James. The prayers of Scripture all glow with the white heat of intensity. Remember how Jacob wrestled, and David panted and poured out his soul;

the importunity of the blind beggar, and the persistency of the distracted mother; the strong crying and tears of our Lord. In each case the whole being seemed gathered up, as a stone into a catapult and hurled forth in vehement entreaty. Prayer is only answered for the glory of Christ; but it is not answered unless it be accompanied with such earnestness as will prove that the blessing sought is really needed.

Humility

"He cast himself down on the ground, and put his face between his knees." A few hours before, he stood erect as an oak of Bashan; now, he is bowed as a bulrush. Then as God's ambassador he pleaded with man; now as man's intercessor he pleads with God. Is it not always so—that the men who stand straightest in the presence of sin bow lowest in the presence of God? Our only plea with God is the merit and blood of our great High Priest. It becomes us to be humble.

Expectation

"Whatsoever things ye desire, when ye pray, believe that ye receive them: and ye shall have them." Faith is the indispensable condition of all true prayer. It is the gift of the Holy Ghost. It thrives by exercise. It grows strong by feeding on the promises: the Word of God is its natural food. It beat strongly in Elijah's heart. He knew that God would keep His word, and so he sent the lad—possibly the widow's son—up to the highest point of Carmel, and bade him look towards the sea; because he was sure that ere long his prayer would be answered, and God's promise would be kept. We have often prayed, and failed to look out for the blessings we have sought. The stately ships of heaven have come up to the quays, laden with the very blessings we asked; but as we have not been there to welcome and unload them, they have put out again to sea.

Perseverance

He said to his servant, "Go up now, look toward the sea" (v.

43). And he went up, and looked, and said, "There is nothing." How often have we sent the lad of eager desire to scan the horizon!—and how often has he returned with the answer, *There is nothing!* When we have just begun to pray, we leave off praying. We do not know that God's answer is upon the way. Not so with Elijah. "And he said, Go again seven times" (v. 43).

Not unfrequently our Father grants our prayer, and labels the answer for us; but He keeps it back, that we may be led on to a point of intensity, which shall bless our spirits for ever, and from which we shall never recede.

Answered Prayer

For weeks and months before, the sun had been gathering up from lake and river, from sea and ocean, the drops of mist; and now the gale was bearing them rapidly towards the thirsty land of Israel. The answer to your prayers may be nearer than you think. On the wings of every moment it is hastening towards you. God shall answer you, and that right early.

Presently the lad, from his tower of observation, beheld on the horizon a tiny cloud, no bigger than a man's hand, scudding across the sky. No more was needed to convince an Oriental that rain was near. The lad was sent with an urgent message to Ahab, to descend from Carmel to his chariot in the plain beneath, lest Kishon, swollen by the rains, should stop him in his homeward course.

Thus by his faith and prayer Elijah brought back the rain to Israel. Why should not we learn and practice his secret? It is certainly within the reach of us all. Then we too might bring from heaven spiritual blessings, which should make the parched places of the church and the world blossom as the rose.

9

How the Mighty Fell!

I Kings 19

Amid the drenching storm with which the memorable day of the convocation closed in, the king and the prophet reached Jezreel. All day long the queen had been wondering how matters were going on Mount Carmel. She cherished the feverish hope that her priests had won the day; and when she saw the rain clouds steal over the sky, she attributed the welcome change to some great interposition of Baal, in answer to their pleadings.

"Then Ahab told Jezebel all that Elijah had done; and withal how he had slain the prophets with the sword" (v. 1).

Jezebel's indignation knew no bounds. Ahab's temperament was sensual and materialistic; if only he had enough to eat and drink, and the horses and mules were cared for, he was content. In his judgment there was not much to choose between God and Baal. Not so Jezebel. To her the crisis was one of gravest moment. If this national reformation were permitted to spread, it would sweep away before it all that she had been laboring at for years. So that very night, amid the violence of the storm, she sent a messenger to Elijah, saying, "So let the gods do to me, and more also, if I make not thy life as the life of one of them, by tomorrow about this time" (v. 2).

Elijah's presence had never been so necessary as now. The tide had turned, and was setting in towards God; and he was needed to direct its flow; to keep the people true to the choice

which they had made; and to complete the work of reformation by a work of construction. From what we have seen of
him, we should have expected that he would receive the
message with unruffled composure; laying it before God in
quiet confidence, assured that He would hide him, in the
secret of His pavilion, from the wrath of man, and shield him
from the strife of tongues. But, instead of this, we are told
(and surely the sacred historian must have heaved a deep
sigh as he wrote the words), "When he saw that, he arose,
and went for his life" (v. 3).

"He went for his life!" Accompanied by his servant, and
under cover of the night, he hurried through the driving
storm, across the hills of Samaria; and directed his course
towards the drear expanse of the Arabian desert. Nor did he
slacken his speed till he had left far behind him the country
over which Jezebel's scepter swayed, and had reached
Beersheba. His spirit seems to have become utterly de-
moralized and panic stricken. He could not even brook the
company of his servant; so, leaving him in Beersheba, he
plunged alone into that wild desert waste that stretched
southwards to Sinai.

Through the weary hours he plodded on beneath the burning sun; his feet blistered by the scorching sands; no ravens,
no Cherith, no Zarephath were there; no human sympathy
lent him its kindly aid; the very presence of God seemed to
have withdrawn itself from his side. At last the fatigue and
anguish overpowered even his sinewy strength, and he cast
himself beneath the slight shadow of a small shrub of
juniper, and asked to die. "It is enough: now, O Lord, take
away my life; for I am no better than my fathers. Let me die
here and now; and bury me with Thine own hand, as Thou
didst Moses in the valley of Bethpeor" (v. 4).

What might have been! If only Elijah had held his
ground—dwelling in the secret place of the Most High, and
hiding under the shadow of the Almighty—he might have
saved his country; and there would have been no necessity
for the captivity and dispersion of his people. The seven

thousand secret disciples would have dared to come forth from their hiding places, and avow themselves; and would have constituted a nucleus of loyal hearts, by whom Baal had been replaced by Jehovah. Yes, and his own character would have escaped a stain which has resisted the obliterating erasure of the ages, and still remains, fraught with shame and sorrow.

What a proof is here of the veracity of the Bible! Had it been merely a human composition, its authors would have shrunk from delineating the failure of one of its chief heroes. Yet if it had not been for this, we should always have thought of Elijah as being too far removed from us to be in any sense a model. But now, as we see him stretched under the shade of the juniper tree asking for death, we feel that he was what he was, only by the grace of God, received through faith. And by a similar faith we may appropriate a similar grace to ennoble our mean lives.

Failure Due to Exhaustion

Consider the tremendous strain which he had undergone since leaving the shelter of the quiet home at Zarephath. He was suffering keenly from reaction, now that the extreme tension was relaxed; and this counted largely in the unutterable depression under which he was suffering.

We are "fearfully and wonderfully made"; and our inner life is very sensitive to our outward conditions. And if any who read these lines are conscious of having lost the sunny gladness and buoyant faith of former days; before they speak of the mysterious hidings of God's face, or lament their own backslidings, it might be well to inquire if there may not be some physical or nervous cause. And if there be, it will attract, not the blame, but the compassionate sympathy of Him who knoweth our frame, and remembereth that we are but dust.

Failure Due to Loneliness

"I only am left" (v. 10). At such a time the human spirit is apt to falter, unless it is sustained by an heroic purpose, and by an unfaltering faith. The shadow of that loneliness fell dark on the spirit of our Divine Master Himself when he said: "Behold, the hour cometh, yea, is now come, that ye shall be scattered, every man to his own, and shall leave Me alone; and yet I am not alone, because the Father is with Me" (John 16:32). If our Lord shrank in the penumbra of that great eclipse, it is not to be wondered at that Elijah cowered in its darksome gloom.

Failure Due to Circumstances

Up to that moment Elijah had been animated by a most splendid faith, because he had never lost sight of God. "He endured as seeing Him who is invisible" (Heb. 11:27). Faith always thrives when God occupies the whole field of vision. But when Jezebel's threats reached him, we are told most significantly, *"when he saw that,* he arose, and went for his life."

Let us refuse to look at circumstances, though they roll before us as a Red Sea, and howl around us like a storm. Circumstances, natural impossibilities, difficulties, are nothing in the estimation of the soul that is occupied with God. They are as the small dust that settles on a scale, and is not considered in the measurement of weight.

It is a great mistake to dictate to God. Elijah wist not what he said, when he told God that he had had enough of life, and asked to die. If God had taken him at his word, he would have died under a cloud; he would never have heard the still small voice; he would never have founded the schools of the prophets; or commissioned Elisha for his work; he would never have swept up to heaven in an equipage of flame.

What a mercy it is that God does not answer all our prayers! How gracious He is in reading their inner meaning, and answering that! This, as we shall see, is what He did for His tired and querulous servant.

10
Lovingkindness Better Than Life

I Kings 19

The Apostle John, whose earliest lessons of the love of God were learned on the bosom of Christ, tells us, in words deep and simple as some transluscent lake, that *"we have known and believed the love that God hath to us"* (I John 4:16). They are wonderful words for mortal to utter. A lifetime would be well spent if, at its close, we could utter them without exaggeration. But alas! many of us have learned some of our deepest lessons of the love of God, in having experienced its gentle kindness amid shortcoming and failure, like that which marred Elijah's course.

If ever it were fitting for a man to reap what he had sown, and to suffer the consequences of his own misdeeds, it would have been so in the case of Elijah. But God's thoughts are not as man's. He knew all the storms of disappointment and broken hope which were sweeping across that noble spirit. His eye followed with tender pity every step of His servant's flight across the hills of Samaria. He did not love him less than when he stood, elate with victory, hard by the burning sacrifice. And His love assumed, if possible, a tenderer, gentler aspect, as He stooped over him, while he slept. As a shepherd tracks the wandering sheep, so did the love of God come upon Elijah, as, worn in body by long fatigue, and in spirit by the fierce war of passion, he lay and slept under the juniper tree.

And God did more than love him. He sought, by tender

helpfulness, to heal and restore His servant's soul to its former health and joy. At His command an angel, twice over, prepared a meal upon the desert sand, and touched him, and bade him eat. No upbraiding speeches; no word of reproach; no threats of dismissal; but only sleep and food, and kindly thoughtfulness of the great journey which he was bent on making to Horeb, the mount of God.

It may be that these words will be read by those who have failed. But remember: though forsaken by man, you are not forgotten of God. He loves you still, and pities you, and yearns over you; and waits beside you, with loving tendance and provender, in order to restore your soul and give you back the years that the cankerworm and caterpillar have eaten.

We have then, in this incident, four thoughts of the love of God which must be a comfort to us all.

God's Constancy

It is not difficult to believe that God loves us when, like Elijah at Cherith and on Carmel, we do His commandments, hearkening unto the voice of His word; but it is not so easy when, like Elijah in the desert, we lie stranded, or, as rudderless vessels, roll in the trough of the waves.

Yet we must learn to know and believe the constancy of the love of God. We may not feel it. We may deem it shut up and gone for ever. We may imagine that we have forfeited all claim to it. But nevertheless, it has not altered; staunch as the affection of a friend; true as the love of a mother, the love of God abides unchangeable as Himself.

God's Special Tenderness

We do not read that an angel ever appeared to Elijah at Cherith or Zarephath, or awakened him with a touch that must have been as thrilling as it was tender. Why these special proofs of tenderness? Certainly it was not because God took any pleasure in His servant's sin, or condoned his grave offense; but because a special manifestation of love was

needed to convince the prophet that he was still dearly loved;
and to soften his spirit; and to lead him to repentance.

Where ordinary methods will not avail, God will employ
extraordinary ones. So eager is He to convince the fallen of
His unaltered love, that He will go out of His way to show it.
He will invent new and unwonted surprises. He will employ
angels with their gentle touch; and bake special cakes on
desert stones.

It may be that you are sleeping the sleep of insensibility or
of despair; but all the while the love of God is inventing
some unique manifestation of its yearning tenderness. All
the while that you are grieving Him, and wandering from
Him, He is encompassing you with blessings. Be conquered!
Yield to Him! Take with you words, and turn again unto the
Lord. He will receive you graciously.

God's Unwearied Care

It is most likely that it was evening when the angel came the
first time and touched him, and bade him arise and eat; for
we are told that he went a day's journey into the wilderness,
before he sat down under the juniper bush. And when the
angel of the Lord came the second time, it would probably be
as morning was breaking over the world. And thus, through
the intervening night, the angels of God kept watch and
ward about the sleeping prophet.

None of us can measure the powers of endurance in the
love of God. It never tires. It fainteth not, neither is weary. It
clings about its object with a Divine tenacity, until the darkness and wandering are succeeded by the blessedness of
former days.

God's Love Anticipating Coming Need

This always stands out as one of the most wonderful passages in the prophet's history. We can understand God giving him, instead of a long discourse, a good meal and sleep,
as the best means of recruiting his spent powers. This is
what we should have expected of One who knows our frame

and remembers that we are dust, and who pities us as a father pitieth his children. But it is very wonderful that God should provision His servant for the long journey that lay before him.

That journey was undertaken at his own whim; it was one long flight from his post of duty; it was destined to meet with a grave remonstrance at its close: "What doest thou here, Elijah?" (v. 9). And yet the Lord graciously gave him food, in the strength of which he could endure the long fatigue. The explanation must be again sought in the tender love of God. Elijah's nature was clearly overwrought. Without doubt he had steadfastly made up his mind for that tedious journey to the Mount of God. Nothing would turn him from his fixed purpose. And therefore, as he would go, God anticipated his needs, though they were the needs of a truant servant.

Surely these thoughts of the love of God will arrest some from pursuing any longer the path of the backslider. You have failed; but do not be afraid of God, or think that He will never look on you again. In thinking thus of Him, you grieve Him more, and aggravate your ill behavior. Rather cast yourself upon His love, as a swimmer flings himself upon the buoyant waves.

And as we close this precious narrative, may we not all receive instruction concerning those meals which Heaven prepares for us, each evening and morning, during our journey across the sands of time? At night the angels bid us partake of the living Bread and Water, on which alone can spirits become strong. And morning by morning their gentle touches awake us from overdue slumbers, as they whisper: "Arise and eat, lest the journey be too great for thee." Their neglect to obey the heavenly summons is the true cause of so much failure in the lives of Christian people.

May we be among the happy number who never need twice calling; but who rise each morning to eat of that flesh, which is meat indeed, and to drink of that blood, which is drink indeed. Then shall we be able to withstand all assaults; to endure all fatigue; and to abide in the realized presence of God.

11

The Still, Small Voice

I Kings 19

Refreshed by sleep and food, Elijah resumed his journey across the desert to Horeb. Perhaps no spot on earth is more associated with the manifested presence of God than that sacred mount. There the bush burned with fire; there the law was given; there Moses spent forty days and nights alone with God. It was a natural instinct that led the prophet thither, and all the world could not have furnished a more appropriate school.

The Voice of God

In some darksome cave, among those rent precipices, Elijah lodged; and, as he waited, in lonely musings, the fire burned in his soul. But he had not long to wait. "Behold, the word of the Lord came unto him."

But though God had often spoken to him before, He had not spoken in the same tone—"What doest thou here, Elijah?"

If the prophet had answered that searching question of God with shame and sorrow; if he had cast himself on the pitifulness and tenderness of his Almighty Friend—there is not the least doubt that he would have been forgiven and restored. But instead of this, he parried the divine question, and evaded it. He did not try to explain how he came there, or what he was doing. He chose rather to dwell upon his own loyalty for the cause of God; and to bring it out into striking relief by contrasting it with the sinful backslidings of his people. All this was well known to God; and I do not think the prophet would ever have alluded to it, unless he had been hard pressed to find an excuse to palliate his own cowardice and neglect of duty.

"What doest thou here, Elijah?" How often is that question put still! When a Christian worker, sorely needed, deserts his post, because of some unforeseen difficulty, or to secure selfish gratification and ease. When a child of God is found in the place of evil companionship; sitting in the seat of scorners, or walking in the way of the ungodly—again must the question come as a thunderbolt out of a clear sky, "What doest thou here?" When one endowed with great faculties digs a hole in the earth, and buries the God-entrusted talent, again must the inquiry ring out, "What doest thou here?"

Life is the time for doing. God Himself worketh as the great Master Builder. There is plenty to do. Evil to put down; good to build up; doubters to be directed; prodigals to be won back; sinners to be sought. "What doest thou here?" Up, Christians, leave your caves, and do! Do not in order to be saved; but being saved, *do!*

A Beautiful Natural Parable

He was bidden to stand at the entrance to the cave; but this he hesitated to do, until afterwards. Did that hesitancy arise from a guilty conscience, reminding him that all was not right between him and God?

Presently there was the sound of the rushing of a mighty wind; and in another moment a violent tornado was sweeping past. It rent the mountains, and broke in pieces the rocks before the Lord; *but the Lord was not in the wind.* And when the wind had died away, there was an earthquake. The mountain swayed to and fro, yawning and cracking; *but the Lord was not in the earthquake.* And when the earthquake was over, there was a fire. The heavens were one blaze of light, each pinnacle and peak glowed in the kindling flame; *but the Lord was not in the fire.*

How strange! Surely these were the appropriate natural symbols of the Divine presence. If we had been asked to describe it, we should have used these first of all. But hark! a still small whisper is in the air—very still, and very small, like the trembling echoes of a flute which is being played among the hills. It touched the listening heart of the prophet. "And it was so, when Elijah heard it, that he wrapped his face in his mantle, and went out, and stood in the entering in of the cave" (v. 13).

What was the meaning of all this? Elijah was most eager that his people should be restored to their allegiance to God; and he thought that it could only be done by some striking and wonderful act. He may have often spoken thus with himself: "Those idols shall never be swept from our land, unless God sends a movement swift and irresistible as the *wind*, which hurries the clouds before it. The land can never be awakened except by a moral *earthquake*. There must be a baptism of *fire*." And when he stood on Carmel, and beheld the panic among the priests and the eagerness among the people, he thought that the time—the set time—had come. But all that died away. That was not God's chosen way of saving Israel. And because He did not go on working thus, Elijah thought that He was not working at all; and abandoned himself to the depths of despondency.

But in this natural parable God seemed to say:—"I am not always to be found in these great visible movements; I love to work gently, softly, and unperceived; and there are in Israel, as the results of My quiet gentle ministry, 'seven thousand, all the knees which have not bowed unto Baal, and every mouth which hath not kissed him.' " Yes, and was not the gentle ministry of Elisha, succeeding the stormy career of his great predecessor, like the still small voice after the wind, the earthquake, and the fire? And is it not probable that more real good was effected by his unobtrusive life and miracles than was even wrought by the splendid deeds of Elijah?

We often fall into similar mistakes. When we wish to promote a revival, we seek to secure large crowds, powerful preachers; influences comparable to the wind, the earthquake, and the fire. When these are present, we account that we are secure of having the presence and power of God. But surely Nature herself rebukes us. At this moment the mightiest forces are in operation around us; but there is nothing to betray their presence. And thus was it with the ministry of the Lord Jesus. He did not strive, nor cry, nor lift up, nor cause His voice to be heard in the streets. While men were expecting Him at the front door, with blare of trumpet, He stepped into His destined home in the disguise of a peasant's child. Let us take heart! God may not be working as we expect; but He is working. If not in the earthquake, yet in the heartbreak. If not in thunder, yet in the still, small voice. If not in crowds, yet in lonely hearts; and in multitudes, who, like the seven thousand of Israel, are unknown as disciples.

It is pleasant to think of those seven thousand disciples, known only to God. We are sometimes sad, as we compare the scanty number of professing Christians with the masses of ungodly. But we may take heart: there are other Christians beside. That harsh-seeming governor is a Joseph in disguise. That wealthy owner of the garden in Arimathea is a lowly follower of Jesus. That member of the Sanhedrin is a disciple; but secretly, for fear of the Jews. For every one entered on our rolls of communicants, there are hundreds—perhaps thousands—whom God shall reckon as His, when He makes up His jewels.

We are all doing more good than we know. Elijah thought that he was doing nothing, except when battling with idolatry and sin. He never thought how often he was helping those seven thousand, by the indirect influence of his example. We, perhaps, accomplish less by our great efforts than we effect by a consistent life, a holy character, a daily shining. Our duty is to shine, not asking questions, not eager for great results; but content to do the will of God, consistently, humbly, and constantly, sure that God is not unrighteous to forget our work of faith and labor of love.

12
Go, Return!

I Kings 19

It is a very solemn thought, that one sin may for ever, so far as this world is concerned, wreck our usefulness. It is not always so. Sometimes—as in the case of the Apostle Peter— the Lord graciously restores, and recommissions for His work, the one who might have been counted unfit ever again to engage in it. "Feed my sheep. Feed my lambs." But against this one case we may put three others, in each of which it would seem as if the sentry angel, who forbade the return of our first parents to Paradise, were stationed with strict injunctions to forbid any return to the former position of noble service.

The first case is that of Moses. No other man has ever been honored as was he, "with whom God spake face to face." Yet, because he spake unadvisedly with his lips, and smote the rock twice, in unbelief and passion, he was compelled to bear the awful sentence: "Because ye believed Me not, to sanctify Me in the eyes of the children of Israel, therefore ye shall not bring this congregation into the land which I have given them" (Num. 20:12).

The second case is that of Saul, the first, ill-fated king of Israel, whose reign opened so auspiciously, as a morning without clouds; but who soon brought upon himself the sentence of deposition. Thus early in his reign, and before his further disobedience in the case of the Amalekites—for that one act of disobedience, revealing a sad state of moral decrepitude—Saul was rejected.

The third case is that of Elijah. He was never reinstated in quite the position which he had occupied before his fatal flight. True, he was bidden to return on his way, and work was indicated for him to do. But that work was the anointing of three men, who were to share among them the ministry which he might have fulfilled if only he had been true to his opportunities, and faithful to his God. Evidently, it was not for him to be the deliverer of his people from the thraldom of Baal. Others were to do his work; another was to be prophet in his room.

The terrible importance of these instances is emphasized by words which ring out with awful force amid the graceful tenderness of the parable of the Vine. "Every branch in me," the Master said, "that beareth not fruit, He taketh away" (John 15:2). It is not a question as to whether we shall be saved or lost; but whether we use the opportunities given to us, and so have them continued, or forfeit them by our inattention and lethargy. If we refuse to let the Vine pour its forces through us, we shall be taken from the position of possible fruitfulness which had been entrusted to us; and the very opportunity of ministry will be withdrawn.

All those who hold prominent positions among us, as public teachers and leaders, may well take warning by these solemn examples standing on the plains of time, as Lot's wife on those of Sodom. We may not all be tempted, as Elijah was, to unbelief and discouragement but there are many other snares prepared for us by our great enemy. There is the adulation given to the successful man, in which so much of the human is mingled with thankfulness for the help or comfort given. There is the desire to be always prominent to the utter neglect of private prayer. There are the insidious attacks of jealousy; depreciation of others; comparison of their standing with our own. And in addition to these, are other modes of failure any one of which may compel God to cast us away from His glorious service; employing us in humbler ministry or to anoint our successors.

As children, He will never cast us away; but as His servants He may. We shall not forfeit heaven; that is guaranteed to us by the precious blood of Christ. We may even be favored by a glorious and triumphant entrance thither in an equipage of flame. But we shall never again ride on the crest of the flowing tide, carrying all before us. Others shall finish our task.

But with the danger there are sufficient safeguards. Let God prune you with the golden pruning knife of His holy Word. Look into the mirror of revealed truth, to see if there is any trace of blemish stealing over the face of the soul. Offer your spirit constantly to the Holy Spirit; that He may detect and reveal to you the beginnings of idolatries and heart-sins. Be very jealous of anything that divides your heart with your Lord. "Watch and pray, lest ye enter into temptation." Trust in Him who is "able to guard you from stumbling, and to set you before the presence of His glory without blemish, in exceeding joy" (Jude 24).

13

Naboth's Vineyard

I Kings 21

In a room of the palace, Ahab, King of Israel, lies upon his couch, his face towards the wall, refusing to eat. What has taken place? Has disaster befallen the royal arms? Have the priests of Baal been again massacred? Is his royal consort dead? No; the soldiers are still flushed with their recent victories over Syria. The worship of Baal has quite recovered the terrible disaster of Carmel; Jezebel—resolute, crafty, cruel, and beautiful—is now standing by his side, anxiously seeking the cause of this sadness; which was, perhaps, assumed to engage her sympathy, and to secure, through her means, ends which he dared not compass for himself.

The story is soon told. Jezreel was the Windsor of Israel; and there stood the favorite residence of the royal house. On a certain occasion, while Ahab was engaged there in superintending his large and beautiful pleasure grounds, his eye lighted on a neighboring vineyard, belonging to Naboth the Jezreelite; which promised to be so valuable an addition to his property, that he resolved to procure it at all hazards. He therefore sent for Naboth, and offered, either a better vineyard in exchange, or the worth of it in money. To his surprise and indignation, Naboth refused both. And Naboth said to Ahab, "The Lord forbid it me, that I should give the inheritance of my fathers unto thee" (v. 3).

Naboth's refusal made Ahab leap into his chariot and drive back to Samaria; and, like a spoiled child, turn his face to the wall, "heavy and displeased." In a few more days the horrid deed of murder was perpetrated; which at one stroke removed Naboth, his sons, and his heirs, and left the unclaimed property to fall naturally into the royal hands. There are many lessons here but we must pass them by, to bend our attention exclusively on the part played by Elijah.

Called Back to Service

How many years had elapsed since last the word of the Lord had come to Elijah, we do not know. Perhaps five or six. All this while he must have waited wistfully for the well-known accents of that voice, longing to hear it once again. And as the weary days, passing slowly by, prolonged his deferred hope into deep and yet deeper regret, he must have been driven to combined soul questionings and searchings of heart; to bitter repentance for the past, and to renewed consecration for whatever service might be imposed upon him.

It may be that these words will be read by some, once prominent in the Christian service, who have been lately cast aside. This may be attributable to the sovereignty of the Great Master—who has a perfect right to do as He will with His own. But we should inquire whether the reason may not lie within our own breasts; in some inconsistency or sin, which needs confession and forgiveness at the hands of our faithful and merciful High Priest, before the word of the Lord can come to us again.

It is also quite possible that we are left unused for our own deeper teaching in the ways of God. Hours, and even years, of silence are full of golden opportunities for the servants of God. Our simple duty, then, is to keep clean, and filled, and ready; sure that we serve if we only stand and wait; and knowing that He will accept, and reward, the willingness for the deed.

Answering the Summons

Once before, when his presence was urgently required, he had arisen to flee for his life. But there was no vacillation, no cowardice now. His spirit had regained its usual posture in the presence of Jehovah, had returned to its equipoise in the will of God. He arose, and went down to the vineyard of Naboth to find the royal criminal. It was nothing to him that there rode behind Ahab's chariot two ruthless captains, Jehu and Bidkar (II Kings 9:25). He did not for a moment consider that the woman who had threatened his life before might now take it. Who does not rejoice that Elijah had such an opportunity of wiping out the dark stain of disgrace, which attached to him from the moment he had forsaken, so faithlessly, the post of duty? His time of waiting had not been lost on him!

An Incarnate Conscience

Naboth was out of the way; and Ahab may have solaced himself, as weak people will do still, with the idea that he was not his murderer. He had simply put his face to the wall and done nothing. He did remember that Jezebel had asked him for his royal seal, to give validity to some letters which she had written in his name; but, then, how was he to know what she had written? With such palliatives he succeeded in stilling the fragment of conscience which alone survived in his heart. And it was then that he was startled by a voice which he had not heard for years, saying "Thus saith the Lord, Hast thou killed, and also taken possession?" No; it was Jezebel that had killed. "Hast thou killed?" The prophet, guided by the Spirit of God, put the burden on the right shoulders.

Hated for the Truth's Sake

"And Ahab said to Elijah, Hast thou found me, O mine enemy?" (v. 20). Though the king knew it not, Elijah was his best friend; Jezebel his direst foe. But sin distorts everything.

When Christian friends remonstrate with evil-doers, and rebuke their sins, and warn them of their doom, they are scouted, hated, and denounced as enemies. The Bible is detested, because it so clearly exposes sin and its consequences. God Himself is viewed with dislike. It cannot be otherwise.

Let us not be surprised if we are hated. Let us even be thankful when men detest us—not for ourselves, but for the truths we speak. Let us "rejoice, and be exceeding glad."

A True Prophet

Each of the woes which Elijah foretold came true. Ahab postponed their fulfilment, by a partial repentance, for some three years; but, at the end of that time, he went back to his evil ways, and every item was fulfilled.

Every word spoken by Elijah was literally fulfilled. Jehovah put His own seal upon His servant's words. The passing years amply vindicated him. And as we close this tragic episode in his career, we rejoice to learn that he was reinstated in the favor of God; and stamped again with the Divine *imprimatur* of trustworthiness and truth.

14

The Old Courage Again

II Kings 1

In order to understand the striking episode before us, we must think ourselves out of this dispensation, the main characteristic of which is gentle mercy; and we must imagine ourselves back in the age that ended at Calvary. It is very important to have a right understanding of our times. We must not judge the past ages by our own high standards of forgiveness and love, learned in the life and death of Jesus Christ, the last and supreme revelation of God. And we must not import into our own age methods of thought and action which were once permissible and necessary, because cognate to the spirit of their times.

Critics—who insensibly have caught their conceptions of infinite love from the Gospels which they affect to despise—find fault with the Old Testament because of its austere tones and severe enactments; they point out many things inconsistent with the gentler spirit of our times. There is nothing surprising here! It could not have been otherwise, in a gradual unfolding of the nature and character of God. The holy men who lived in those days had never heard the gentle voice of the Son of Man speaking the Sermon on the Mount. They had, however, very definite conceptions of the righteousness and holiness of God, and His swift indignation on sin. This inspired many of the Psalms in the hymnal of the Old Testament saints. This stimulated them to do deeds from which our gentler nature shrinks. But for this, Levi had never slain his brethren, or Joshua the Canaanites; Samuel had never hewed Agag in pieces before the Lord; and Elijah had never presumed to slay the priests of Baal, or call down fire from heaven to destroy the captains and their men.

These considerations will help us to understand the narrative that awaits us, and will relieve the character of Elijah from the charge of vindictiveness and passion; so that we can consider, without compunction, the rising up again in his breast of something of his old undaunted courage and heroic bearing.

The story is as follows: Ahaziah, the son of Ahab, had succeeded to his father's throne and his father's sins, leading a self-indulgent life in his palace. But the shafts of death can find us equally in apparent security, as amid threatening dangers. He was leaning on the balustrade that fenced the flat roof of the palace, when suddenly it gave way, and he over-balanced himself, and was flung to the ground. When the first panic was over, the king was seized with intense longings to know how his illness would turn; and, in a strange freak, he sent messengers to one of the ancient shrines of Canaan, dedicated to Baalzebub, the god of flies, the patron saint of medicine, who had some affinity with the Baal of his parents. This was a deliberate rejection of Jehovah; a daring choice of those ways which had brought the wrath of God on his father's house. It could not pass unnoticed; and Elijah was sent to meet his messengers, as they were speeding across the plain of Esdraelon, with the announcement of certain death: "Thus saith Jehovah, thou shalt not come down from that bed on which thou art gone up; but shalt surely die" (v. 4).

The servants did not know the stranger. However, they were so impressed by that commanding figure and authoritative tone, and so awed by that terrible reply, that they determined to return at once to the king. And they told him the reason of their speedy return. Ahaziah must have guessed who he was that had dared to cross their path, and send him such a message. But, to make assurance surer, he asked them to describe the mysterious stranger. They replied that he was "a man of hair." It was enough; the king recognized him at once, and said, "It is Elijah the Tishbite."

Two emotions now filled his heart. He wanted, in exasperation, to get Elijah in his power, to vent on him his wrath; and he, perhaps, cherished a secret hope that the lips which had announced his death might be induced to revoke it. He therefore resolved to capture him: and for that purpose sent a captain and a troop of fifty soldiers; and when they were struck down in death, another captain and his band. These men exceeded their duty; instead of simply acting as the tools and instruments of the royal will, they spoke with an unwarrantable insolence. "Thou man of God, the king hath said, Come down!" (v. 9). Either they did not hold him to be a prophet, or they gloried in putting the power of their master above that of Jehovah. In any case, the insult was less against Elijah than Elijah's God.

There was no personal vindictiveness in the terrible reply of the old prophet. I do not suppose for a moment he considered the indignity done to himself. I believe he was filled with consuming zeal for the glory of God, which had been trodden so rudely under foot; and which he must vindicate in the eyes of Israel. "If I be a man of God, let fire come down from heaven and consume thee and thy fifty." And in a moment the fire leaped from its scabbard, and laid the impious blasphemers low. That there was no malice in Elijah is clear from his willingness to go with the third captain, who spoke with reverence and humility. "And the angel of the Lord said, Go down with him; be not afraid of him. And Elijah went down with him unto the king" (v. 15).

A thought is suggested here of the meekness and gentleness of Christ. How wonderful it is to think that He who, by a single word, could have brought fire from heaven to destroy the bands that came to take Him in Gethsemane, left that word unspoken. He threw them on the ground for a moment, to show them how absolutely they were in His power; but He forbore to hurt one hair of their heads. It was a marvelous spectacle, which the legions of harnessed angels, who in midair waited for a word to bring them to His rescue, must have beheld with speechless amazement. The explanation is of course found in the fact that He was under the compulsion of a higher law—the law of His Father's will; the law of self-sacrificing love; the law of a covenant sealed before the foundation of the world.

There is also suggested here the impossibility of God ever condoning defiant and blasphemous sin. We have fallen on soft and degenerate days when, under false notions of charity and liberality, men are paring down their conceptions of the evil of sin, and of the holy wrath of God, which is revealed from heaven against *all* ungodliness and unrighteousness of men.

It is quite true that God yearns over men with unutterable pleading tenderness. "He is not willing that any should perish; but that all should come to repentance" (II Peter 3:9). As there is not a dying sparrow in the recesses of the deepest woods over whose last agonies the Almighty does not bend with sympathetic interest, and alleviating tenderness; so there is not one waif of humanity excluded from the warm zone of His infinite compassionateness and tender pity.

And yet, side by side with this love to the sinner, there is God's hatred of sin. This longsuffering lasts only so long as there is a possible hope of the transgressor turning from his evil ways. Yet the time of forbearance will end at last, as the waiting did in the days of Noah. And it shall be discovered how bitter a thing it is to encounter the wrath of the Lamb, "when the Lord Jesus shall be revealed from heaven with His mighty angels, in flaming fire, taking vengeance on them that know not God, and obey not the Gospel of our Lord Jesus Christ" (II Thess. 1:7, 8).

We are also assured of Elijah's full restoration to the exercise of a glorious faith. In a former time, the message of Jezebel was enough to make him flee. But in this case he stood his ground, though an armed band came to capture him. And when he was bidden to go down with the third captain to the king, he did not hesitate; though it was to go through the streets of the crowded capital, and into the very palace of his foes. Do you ask the secret, and why he was able to stand so calmly beside the couch of the dying monarch, delivering his message, and retiring unharmed? He was again dwelling in the secret of the Most High.

Is it not beautiful to behold this glorious outburst of the faith of Cherith, Zarephath, and Carmel? The old man, nearing his reward, was as vigorous in this as in his first challenge to Ahab. He bore fruit in old age, like one of God's evergreens, which are full of sap. Glory be to Him who restores the soul of His faltering saints; and brings them up from the grave; and sets them again as stars in His right hand; and deigns to use them once more in His glorious service!

15

Evensong

II Kings 2

There is always something beautiful in the declining years of one who in earlier life has dared nobly and wrought successfully. Memory rescues from the oblivion of the past many priceless records; while hope, standing before the thinning veil, tells of things not perfectly seen as yet, but growing on the gaze of the ripened spirit. The old force still gleams in the eye; but its rays are tempered by that tenderness for human frailty, and that deep self-knowledge, which years alone can yield. Such a life-evening seems to have been Elijah's. He did not reach a great old age. He probably betrayed his age more in the deeds he had done, and the mellowness of his spirit, than in the infirmities of the natural man. Still there is little room for doubt that the noon of his life was well passed when he prepared himself for his final journey. And it must have been very grateful to him, as it was most fruitful of blessing to his country and to the cause of God, that there was granted a time of comparative calm at the close of his tempestuous career.

For those years of retirement were valuable, in the highest degree; both in their immediate results upon hundreds of young lives, and in their far-off results on the coming times.

The Closing Years

His life has been called a "One-man Ministry"; and there is much in it to warrant the description. This one man was, as

Elisha exclaimed, "The chariot of Israel, and the horsemen thereof." He made his age. Towering above all the men of his time, he cleft his way through the crowds of meaner souls; and withstood the onslaughts of evil; as a rock shakes off the waves that break on it into volumes of spray.

But though largely successful in keeping the cause of true religion from dying out, Elijah must often have realized the desirability of carrying on the work more systematically. So, under Divine direction, he carefully fostered, if he did not altogether inaugurate, the Schools of the Prophets. When we use the word Prophet, we think of it as indicating a man who can foretell the future; and thus much confusion is introduced into our reading of Scripture. It includes this idea as a fragment of a larger meaning. The original word means "boiling or bubbling over"; and so a prophet was one whose heart was bubbling over with good matter. He was the mouthpiece and spokesman of God. So these Schools of the Prophets were colleges, in which a number of young men gathered; their hearts open to receive, and their tongues to utter, the messages of God.

These young men were formed into separate companies of fifty, in different towns. They were called sons; the chief among them, like the *abbot* of a monastery, was called "father." Clad in a simple dress, they had their food in common; and dwelt in huts slightly made of the branches of trees. They were well versed in the sacred books, which they probably transcribed for circulation, and read in the hearing of the people. They were frequently sent forth on the errands of God's Spirit—to anoint a king; to upbraid a highhanded sinner; or to take the part of oppressed and injured innocence. It was, therefore, no small work for Elijah to put these schools on so secure a basis that, when he was gone, they might perpetuate his influence and guard the flames which he had kindled.

Anticipating His Translation
The old man clung to those young hearts, and felt that his last

days could not be better spent than in seeing them once more; though he resolved to say nothing of his approaching departure, or of the conspicuous honor that was shortly to be conferred on him. Here is the humility of true greatness! He foresaw that he was to enjoy an exodus, which, in the whole history of the race, there had been but one parallel. Yet he was so reticent about it that, if he had had his way, no mortal eye would have beheld it. Anyone less great would have let the secret out; or have contrived to line the heights of the Jordan with expectant crowds of witnesses. But, instead of this, Elijah kept the secret well locked up within him, and tried to dissuade Elisha from accompanying him a single step. "Tarry thou here." Perhaps that loyal heart feared attracting to himself, either then or afterwards, honor due only to God.

Alas! what a rebuke is here for ourselves! The prophet's evident desire to die alone shames us, when we remember how eager we are to tell men, by every available medium, of what we are doing for the Lord. What wonder that our Father dare not give us much marked success, or many conspicuous spiritual endowments—lest we be tempted further to our ruin!

We are also deeply impressed by the calm tenor of the prophet's course through those closing days. He knew that ere many suns had set he would be standing in the light of eternity, mingling with his peers, understanding all the mysteries that had puzzled his eager spirit, and beholding the face of God; and we might have expected him to fill the preceding hours with ecstatic offices of devotion. But instead, he spent the days, as he had often spent them before, visiting the schools of the prophets, and quietly conversing with his friend, till the chariot swept him from his side. And, as we consider that spectacle, we learn that a good man should so live that he need make no extra preparation when death suddenly summons him; and that our best method of awaiting the great exchange of worlds is to go on doing the duties of daily life.

Greatly Loved

It strongly showed itself in Elisha. And, in spite of many persuasives to the contrary, he went with him down the steep descent to Bethel and Jericho. The sacred historian accentuates the strength of their affection, as he says thrice over, *they two* went on; *they two* stood by Jordan; *they two* went over. And again the strength of that love, which the cold waters of death could not extinguish, approved itself in the repeated asseveration: "As the Lord liveth, and as thy soul liveth, I will not leave thee" (v. 6).

But in all their intercourse, how real and near the Lord seemed! To Elijah it was the Lord who was sending him from place to place: "the Lord hath sent me." To Elisha, it was the living Lord to whom he constantly appealed: "as the Lord thy God liveth"—living on the other side of the great change through which his master was to pass to Him. Surely those who speak thus have reached a position in which they can meet death without a tremor. And what is death but, as we shall see in our next chapter, a translation!

What is the Lord to thee, my reader? Is He a dear and familiar friend, of whom thou canst speak with unwavering confidence? Then thou needest not fear to tread the verge of Jordan. Otherwise, it becomes thee to get to His precious blood, and to wash thy garments white; that thou mayest have right to the tree of life, and mayest enter in through the gates into the city.

16

The Translation

II Kings 2

We have reached at length one of the sublimest scenes of Old Testament story. We should have been glad to learn the most minute particulars concerning it; but the historian contents himself with the simplest statements. Just one or two broad, strong outlines; and all is told that we may know. "They still went on, and talked; and it came to pass that there appeared a chariot of fire, and horses of fire, and parted them both asunder; and Elijah went up by a whirlwind into heaven" (v. 11).

But there was one symptom, at least, of the coming wonder, which was clearly witnessed by more than the solitary companion who had so faithfully and tenaciously kept Elijah's side. The two friends halted for a moment before the broad waters of the Jordan, which threatened to bar their onward steps; and then Elijah's spirit was thrilled with the old omnipotent faith; such as had so often enabled him to overcome the working of natural laws, by the introduction of the laws of that higher sphere which only answer the summons of a mighty faith.

He knew that the Lord had sent him thither, and that his road lay further into the country on the other side. He was sure that, since his way led through the waters, God was prepared to make it possible and easy for him to tread it. And, therefore, he dared to strike the waters, believing that Divine power was working in every stroke; and the waters parted hither and thither, leaving a clear passage, through which they went.

Child of God, your path seems sometimes to lie right through a flowing Jordan. There is no alternative but that you should go straight on. Forward moves the cloud. Forward points the signpost of circumstance. Forward bids the inward prompting. But how, when Jordan rolls in front? Now is the time for faith! Where God's finger points, there God's hand will make the way. Believe that it shall be so! Advance in unfaltering faith! Step down the shelving bank, and the waters of difficulty shall part before you; and you shall find a pathway where to human vision there was none. So through parting Jordans you shall march to your reward.

A Fitting Translation

There was fitness *in the place.* Amid the scenery familiar to his early life; in view of localities for ever associated with the most memorable events of his nation's history; surrounded by the lonely grandeur of some rocky gorge—*there* God chose to send His chariot to fetch him home.

There was fitness *in the method.* And nothing could be more appropriate than that the stormy energy of his career should be set forth in the rush of the whirlwind; and the intensity of his spirit by the fire that flashed in the harnessed seraphim. What a contrast to the gentle motion of the ascending Saviour!

There was fitness *in the exclamation* with which Elisha bade him farewell. He cried, "My father, my father! the chariot of Israel and the horsemen thereof!" That man, whom he had come to love as a father, had indeed been as an armed chariot of defense to Israel. By his faith, and prayers, and deeds, he had often warded off evil and danger with more certain success than could have been effected by an armed troop.

A Meaningful Translation

One of the chief reasons was, no doubt, as a witness to his times. The men of his day were plunged in sensuality, and had little thought of the hereafter. But here a convincing evidence was given that there was a spiritual world into which the righteous entered; and that, when the body sank in death, the spirit did not share its fate, but entered into a state of being in which its noblest instincts found their befitting environment and home—fire to fire; spirit to spirit; the man of God to God.

Another reason was evidently the desire on the part of God to give a striking sanction to His servant's words. How easy was it for the men of that time to evade the force of Elijah's ministry, by asserting that he was an enthusiast, an alarmist, a firebrand! But the mouths of blasphemers and gainsayers were stopped, when God put such a conspicuous seal upon His servant's ministry. It was as if Jehovah had stepped out of the unseen to vindicate him; and to affirm that He was His chosen ambassador; and that the word in his lips was true. The translation was to the lifework of Elijah what the resurrection was to that of Jesus—God's testimony to the world.

The Translation Applied
Let us take care not to dictate to God. This was the man who lay down upon the ground, and asked to die. If he had had his will, he would have had the desert sands for his shroud, and the desert winds for his requiem. How good it was of God to refuse him the answer he craved!

Let us learn what death is. It is simply a translation: not a state, but an act; not a condition, but a passage. There is no interval of unconsciousness, no parenthesis of suspended animation. "Absent from the body," we are instantly "present with the Lord." Oh, do not think of death as the jailer of a prisonhouse, in which he is collecting the saints against some final order for their liberty. As by the single act of birth we entered into this lower life, so by the single act—which men call death, but which angels call birth (for Christ is the Firstborn from among the dead)—we pass into the real life. The fact that Elijah appeared on the Transfiguration Mount in holy converse with Moses and with Christ proves that the blessed dead are really the living ones, sentient, active, intensely in earnest; and they entered that life in a single moment, the moment of death. Would it not be truer to speak of them not as the dead, but as those who have died, and are alive for ever.

Let us see here a type of the rapture of the saints. We do not know what change passed over the mortal body of the ascending prophet. This is all we know, that "mortality was swallowed up of life." Corruption put on incorruption. The mortal put on immortality. The body of humiliation was exchanged for the body of glory.

Such a change, unless Christ tarry longer than the term of our natural life, shall be the portion of many who read these lines—"caught up to meet the Lord in the air." It becomes us then to walk as Elijah did, with alert and watchful spirit; talking only on themes that would not be inconsistent with an instantaneous flash into the presence of God.

Was it not some reference to this august event that was in the mind of the Welsh preacher, Christmas Evans, who, when dying, majestically waved his hand to the bystanders, and looked upward with a smile, and uttered these last words, *"Drive on!"* "The chariots of God are twenty thousands." May we not suppose that one awaits each departing spirit, standing ready at hand to convey it into the presence of the King, to whom be glory for ever and ever!

17

A Double Portion of Elijah's Spirit

II Kings 2

There is one incident for ever associated with the translation of Elijah; which, though it largely concerns his friends and successor, is so characteristic of the great prophet himself that we must not pass it over without some notice. It is deeply significant. We are told that, after they had passed the Jordan, the two friends *went on and talked*. What sublime themes must have engaged them, standing as they did on the very confines of heaven, and in the vestibule of eternity!

It was in the course of the conversation that "Elijah said unto Elisha, Ask what I shall do for thee, before I be taken away from thee" (v. 9). It was a very wide door flung open by the elder to his younger friend. And, at first, we are surprised to think that Elijah could offer to supply anything for which Elisha asked. Is not this rather the prerogative of God? Surely God alone can do whatsoever we desire when we pray; and even He is limited by the fulfilment, on our part, of certain essential conditions. But we must remember that Elijah was intimately familiar with the mind and heart of his brother. It was not in vain that they had spent those years of ministry together. It was with the object of testing the spirit of his friend that the departing seer had urged him again and again to leave him. And it was only when Elisha had stood the test with such unwavering resolution that Elijah was able

to give him this *carte blanche*. He knew that that faithful soul
would ask nothing for which he could not exercise his
mighty faith, or which God could not, and would not bestow. He was only "a man of like passions with ourselves";
cast in the ordinary mold of human nature: but, by close and
intimate communion with God, he had reached such a pitch
of holy boldness that the very keys of spiritual blessing
seemed put into his hand, so that he might dispense to
kindred spirits the priceless gifts of God. Why should not we
strive after and attain "like precious faith"?

Elijah's confidence was not misplaced. Elisha sought
neither wealth, nor position, nor worldly power; nor a share
in those advantages on which he had turned his back for ever
when he said farewell to home, and friends, and worldly
prospects. "And Elisha said, I pray thee, let a double portion
of thy spirit be upon me" (v. 9).

What did Elisha mean by this request? I do not interpret
his request to mean that he should have twice as much of the
faith and spiritual force as characterized his master. What he
intended was to ask that he might be considered as Elijah's
eldest son; the heir to his spirit; the successor to his work.
There is a passage in the law of Moses which clearly proves
that "the double portion" was the right of the first born and
heir (Deut. 21:17). This the prophet sought; and this he certainly obtained.

It was a noble request! He was evidently called to succeed
to Elijah's work; but he felt that he dare not undertake its
responsibilities, or face its inevitable perils unless he were
specially equipped with spiritual power. Oh for this spiritual
hunger, insatiable for the best gifts! Men of the world hunger
for name, and rank, and wealth; and they get what they seek
because they will not take no. Blessed should we be if we
were as eager after the Spirit of God; and if, instead of giving
up opportunities of usefulness because we did not feel qualified to fill them, we rather sought and received a new baptism of power, a fresh endowment of the Holy Spirit.

There is no work to which God calls you for which He is

not prepared to qualify you. Elijah himself did what he did, not by inherent qualities, but because through faith he had received such copious bestowments of the Spirit of God.

Tenacity of Purpose

Elijah tested it severely at every step of that farewell journey. Repeatedly he said, "Tarry here." But he might as well have tried to uproot a cedar of Lebanon, or to stir Carmel from its base. And though their course lay through the Jordan-flood of death, it sufficed not to deter that eager spirit. Elisha knew what he sought; he read the meaning of the discipline to which he was being exposed; and his heroic resolution grew.

How often we persuade ourselves that we can acquire the greatest spiritual blessings without paying the equivalent price! We must pass through the Jordan; the Divine will must be lovingly accepted, though it cost tears of blood and bitter sorrow. Then, having evinced the steadfastness of our purpose, we shall approve ourselves worthy to be recipients of God's supreme gift.

Spiritual Insight

"If thou see me when I am taken from thee, it shall be so unto thee; but if not, it shall not be so" (v. 10). There was nothing arbitrary in this demand. And it would have been hardly possible to have devised a more complete criterion of the spiritual conditions of this eager aspirant. To see the transactions of the spirit world requires a spirit of no ordinary purity, and of no ordinary faith. But since Elisha saw it all, it is clear that his passions were under control; his temper refined; his spiritual life in healthy exercise; and his whole being of such an order, as to admit him into the foremost rank of the spiritual world, without risk. Such must we be, by the grace of God, ere we can aspire to possess or wield similar powers.

The Answer

"He took up also the mantle of Elijah that fell from him" (v.

13). Ah, that falling mantle! How much it meant! It is said that the bestowal of the mantle has always been considered by Eastern people an indispensable part of consecration to a sacred office. When, therefore, Elijah's mantle fluttered to Elisha's feet, he knew at once that Heaven itself had ratified his request. He knew that he had Elijah's post. He believed that he was anointed with Elijah's power.

Directly we receive some great spiritual endowment, we may expect to have it tested. It was so with Elisha. "He went back, and stood by the bank of Jordan" (v. 13). He had seen Elijah go; and he believed, though probably he did not feel, that therefore the double portion of his spirit had fallen to his lot. He, therefore, acted upon the assurance of his faith. "He took the mantle of Elijah that fell from him, and smote the waters, and said, Where is the Lord God of Elijah? and when he also had smitten the waters, they parted hither and thither: and Elisha went over. And when the sons of the prophets which were to view at Jericho saw him, they said, The Spirit of Elijah doth rest on Elisha" (vv. 14, 15).

"Where is the Lord God of Elijah?" That cry has often been raised where the Church, bereft of its leaders, has stood face to face with some great and apparently insuperable difficulty. And sometimes there has been more of despair than hope in the cry. But though Elijah goes, Elijah's God remains. He takes His weary workers home; but He is careful to supply their place, and to anoint others to carry on their work. It is His work, not ours. On Him is the responsibility, as to Him shall be the glory. If you ask where He is, an answer close behind you whispers, "I am here." Catch up the mantle of the departed. Emulate their lives. Seek their spirit. Smite the bitter waves of difficulty in unwavering faith: and you shall find that the Lord God of Elijah will do as much for you as for the saints who have been swept to their reward, and are now mingling with the great cloud of witnesses that are watching your conflicts, your triumphs, and your joys.

18

"Filled With the Holy Ghost"

Luke 1:15, 17

What may not one man do in one brief life, if he is willing to be simply a living conduit pipe through which the power of God may descend to men? There, on the one hand, is the oceanic fullness of God; here, on the other, are the awful need and desolation of man. All that is required is a channel of communication between the two; and when the channel is made and opened, and kept free from the silting sand, there will ensue one great, plenteous, and equable flow of power carrying the fullness of God to the weary emptiness of man.

If I may venture so to put it, God is in extremity for men who, thoughtless for themselves, will desire only to be receivers and channels of His power. He will take young men and women, old men and children, servants and handmaidens, in the waning days of this era, and will fill them with the selfsame Spirit whose power was once reserved for a favored few. Besides all this, the positive command has never been repealed which bids us be "filled with the Spirit" (Eph. 5:18). Moreover, what God commands, He is prepared to do all that is needful on His side to effect.

Blessings on Blessings

The presence of the Holy Ghost in the heart, in all His glorious fullness, cannot be hid. It will surely betray itself. There will be no effort; no striving after great effect; no ostentatious show. He distills as the dew upon the tender herb; and de-